D1400469

Accounting
TWENTY-FIRST EDITION

CARL S. WARREN • JAMES M. REEVE • PHILIP E. FESS

Prepared by

Carl S. Warren
Professor Emeritus of Accounting
University of Georgia, Athens

James M. Reeve
Professor of Accounting
University of Tennessee, Knoxville

THOMSON
™
SOUTH-WESTERN

Australia · Canada · Mexico · Singapore · Spain · United Kingdom · United States

THOMSON
™
SOUTH-WESTERN

Study Guide to accompany Accounting, 21e, Chapters 12-25

Carl S. Warren, James M. Reeve, Philip E. Fess

VP/Editorial Director:
Jack W. Calhoun

VP/Editor-in-Chief:
George Werthman

Publisher:
Rob Dewey

Executive Editor:
Sharon Oblinger

Developmental Editor:
Erin Joyner

Marketing Manager:
Keith Chassé

Production Editor:
Heather Mann

Manufacturing Coordinator:
Doug Wilke

Technology Project Editor:
Sally Neiman

Media Editor:
Robin Browning

Design Project Manager:
Michelle Kunkler

Production Services:
Mary Hartkemeyer

Illustrator:
Matsu

Cover Designer:
Michael H. Stratton

Printer:
Thomson West
Eagan, MN

CONTENTS

		Problems	Solutions

12 Corporations: Organization, Capital Stock Transactions, and Dividends

QUIZ AND TEST HINTS

The following hints may be helpful to you in preparing for a quiz or a test over the material covered in Chapter 12.

1. Many new terms related to the corporate form of organization are introduced in this chapter that may be tested using true/false or multiple-choice questions. Do the Matching exercises included in this Study Guide.

2. You should be able to compute the amount of dividends allocated between nonparticipating cumulative preferred stock and common stock.

3. You should be able to prepare journal entries for the issuance of par and no-par stock, treasury stock transactions, and cash and stock dividends. Expect at least one problem requiring such entries.

4. It is unlikely that you will be required to prepare a journal entry for organization expenses. However, you may be asked a multiple-choice question related to organization expenses.

MATCHING

Instructions: Match each of the statements below with its proper term. Some terms may not be used.

A.	cash dividend	**J.**	premium
B.	common stock	**K.**	stated value
C.	cumulative preferred stock	**L.**	statement of stockholders' equity
D.	discount	**M.**	stock
E.	dividend yield	**N.**	stock dividend
F.	nonparticipating preferred stock	**O.**	stock split
G.	outstanding stock	**P.**	stockholders
H.	par	**Q.**	treasury stock
I.	preferred stock		

_____ **1.** Shares of ownership of a corporation.

_____ **2.** The owners of a corporation.

_____ **3.** The stock in the hands of stockholders.

_____ **4.** A value, similar to par value, approved by the board of directors of a corporation for no-par stock.

_____ **5.** The stock outstanding when a corporation has issued only one class of stock.

_____ **6.** A class of stock with preferential rights over common stock.

_____ **7.** A class of preferred stock whose dividend rights are usually limited to a certain amount.

_____ **8.** A class of preferred stock that has a right to receive regular dividends that have been passed (not declared) before any common stock dividends are paid.

_____ **9.** The excess of the issue price of a stock over its par value.

_____ **10.** The excess of the par value of a stock over its issue price.

_____ **11.** Stock that a corporation has once issued and then reacquires.

_____ **12.** A reduction in the par or stated value of a common stock and the issuance of a proportionate number of additional shares.

_____ **13.** A cash distribution of earnings by a corporation to its shareholders.

_____ **14.** A distribution of shares of stock to its stockholders.

_____ **15.** A ratio, computed by dividing the annual dividends paid per share of common stock by the market price per share at a specific date, that indicates the rate of return to stockholders in terms of cash dividend distributions.

_____ **16.** The monetary amount printed on a stock certificate.

_____ **17.** A statement summarizing significant changes in stockholders' equity that have occurred during a period.

FILL IN THE BLANK—PART A

Instructions: Answer the following questions or complete the statements by writing the appropriate words or amounts in the answer blanks.

1. Shares of ownership of a corporation are called _____.

2. The owners' equity in a corporation is reported on the balance sheet under the caption _____ _____.

3. Net income retained in a corporation is reported on the balance sheet as _____ _____.

4. The stockholders' equity section of a balance sheet is composed of preferred $7 stock, $250,000; discount on preferred stock, $25,000; common stock, $750,000; premium on common stock, $100,000; retained earnings, $190,000; treasury stock, $80,000. The total paid-in capital is _____.

5. Stock in the hands of stockholders is called _____ stock.

6. When a corporation has issued only one class of stock, it is called _____ stock.

7. A class of preferred stock whose dividend rights are usually limited to a certain amount is referred to as _____ preferred stock.

8. A company has outstanding stock that is composed of 10,000 shares of $5 cumulative, nonparticipating, $50 par preferred stock and 150,000 shares of $10 par common stock. Preferred dividends were passed last year, and no dividends have been paid thus far in the current year. A total of $280,000 in dividends is to be distributed. The total amount of dividends to be paid on the preferred stock is _____.

9. When the issuance price of a stock exceeds its par value, the stock is said to have been issued at a(n) _____.

10. Land is acquired by issuing 5,000 shares of $20 par common stock with a current market price of $32 per share. The land should be recorded at a cost of _____.

11. If a corporation issues stock and then reacquires the stock, the stock reacquired is referred to as _____ stock.

12. A company purchases 500 shares of its $50 par common stock for $32,500 cash. The effect (increase, decrease, or none) of this purchase on the company's retained earnings is _____ (indicate amount and effect).

13. A(n) _____ is a cash distribution of earnings by a corporation to its shareholders.

14. A balance sheet indicated 20,000 shares of common stock authorized, 8,000 shares issued, and 1,500 shares of treasury stock. If a cash dividend of $5 per share is declared on the common stock, the total amount of the dividend is _____.

15. The effect of a stock dividend on the stockholders' equity of a corporation's balance sheet is to increase paid-in capital and decrease _____ _____.

FILL IN THE BLANK—PART B

Instructions: Answer the following questions or complete the statements by writing the appropriate words or amounts in the answer blanks.

1. The owners of a corporation are the _____.

2. Capital contributed to a corporation by the stockholders and others is reported on the balance sheet as _____-_____ capital.

3. A debit balance in the retained earnings account is called a(n) _____.

4. A value, similar to par value, approved by the board of directors of a corporation for no-par stock is called _____ value.

5. A class of stock with preferential rights over common stock is called _____ stock.

6. _____ preferred stock has a right to receive regular dividends that have been passed (not declared) before any common stock dividends are paid.

7. A company has outstanding stock that is composed of 25,000 shares of $3 cumulative, nonparticipating, $100 par preferred stock and 150,000 shares of $10 par common stock. Preferred dividends were passed last year, and no dividends have been paid thus far in the current year. A total of $140,000 in dividends is to be distributed. The total amount of dividends to be paid on the preferred stock is _____.

8. When the par value of a stock exceeds its issuance price, the stock is said to have been issued at a(n) _____.

9. A company purchases 500 shares of its $50 par common stock for $32,500 cash. The effect (increase, decrease, or none) of this purchase on the company's paid-in capital is _____ (indicate amount and effect).

10. The stockholders' equity section of a balance sheet is composed of preferred $7 stock, $250,000; discount on preferred stock, $25,000; common stock, $750,000; premium on common stock, $100,000; retained earnings, $100,000 deficit; treasury stock, $80,000. The total stockholder's equity is _____.

11. A(n) _____ _____ is the reduction in the par or stated value of common stock and the issuance of a proportionate number of additional shares.

12. A corporation announced a 5-for-1 stock split of its $100 par value stock, which is currently trading for $180. The estimated market value of the stock after the split is _____.

13. A(n) _____ _____ is a distribution of shares of stock to its stockholders.

14. The _____ value is the monetary amount printed on a stock certificate.

15. The _____ _____ is a ratio computed by dividing the annual dividends paid per share of common stock by the market price per share at a specific date, and it indicates the rate of return to stockholders in terms of cash dividend distributions.

MULTIPLE CHOICE

Instructions: Circle the best answer for each of the following questions.

1. Which of the following is not a characteristic of the corporate form of organization?

   a. ownership represented by shares of stock

   b. separate legal existence

   c. unlimited liability of stockholders

   d. earnings subject to the federal income tax

2. The amount printed on a stock certificate is known as:

   a. stated value

   b. premium

   c. discount

   d. par value

3. Assume that a corporation has outstanding 5,000 shares of $6 cumulative preferred stock of $100 par and dividends have been passed for the preceding four years. What is the amount of preferred dividends that must be declared in the current year before a dividend can be declared on common stock?

   a. $90,000

   b. $120,000

   c. $150,000

   d. $180,000

4. When a corporation purchases its own stock, what account is debited for the cost of the stock?

   a. Common Stock Subscribed

   b. Treasury Stock

   c. Preferred Stock

   d. Common Stock Receivable

5. The excess of the proceeds from selling treasury stock over its cost should be credited to:

   a. Retained Earnings

   b. Premium on Capital Stock

   c. Gain from Sale of Treasury Stock

   d. Paid-In Capital from Sale of Treasury Stock

6. The claims of the _____ must first be satisfied upon liquidation of a corporation.

   a. preferred stockholders

   b. cumulative preferred stockholders

   c. common stockholders

   d. creditors

7. A company with 20,000 authorized shares of $20 par common stock issued 12,000 shares at $50. Subsequently, the company declared a 5% stock dividend on a date when the market price was $60 per share. What is the amount transferred from the retained earnings account to paid-in capital accounts as a result of the stock dividend?

   a. $36,000

   b. $30,000

   c. $12,000

   d. $6,000

8. The charter of a corporation provides for the issuance of 100,000 shares of common stock. Assume that 60,000 shares were originally issued and 5,000 were subsequently reacquired. What is the number of shares outstanding?

   a. 5,000

   b. 55,000

   c. 60,000

   d. 100,000

9. The entry to record the issuance of common stock at a price above par would include a credit to:

   a. Donated Capital

   b. Retained Earnings

   c. Treasury Stock

   d. Paid-In Capital in Excess of Par—Common Stock

10. A corporation purchases 10,000 shares of its own $20 par common stock for $35 per share, recording it at cost. What will be the effect on total stockholders' equity?

   a. increase, $200,000

   b. increase, $350,000

   c. decrease, $200,000

   d. decrease, $350,000

TRUE/FALSE

Instructions: Indicate whether each of the following statements is true or false by placing a check mark in the appropriate column.

	True	False
1. A partnership is similar to a proprietorship except that it has more than one owner.	____	____
2. A corporation may acquire, own, and dispose of property in its corporate name.	____	____
3. The two main sources of stockholders' equity are paid-in capital and long-term debt.	____	____
4. The common stockholders have a greater chance of receiving regular dividends than do preferred stockholders.	____	____
5. The board of directors has the sole authority to distribute earnings to the stockholders in the form of dividends.	____	____
6. The specified minimum stockholders' contribution that a corporation is required by law to retain for protection of its creditors is called legal capital.	____	____
7. Preferred stock for which dividend rights are limited to a certain amount is said to be noncumulative.	____	____
8. When par stock is issued for more than par, the excess of the contract price over par is termed a premium.	____	____
9. Sales of treasury stock result in a net decrease in paid-in capital.	____	____
10. Expenditures incurred in organizing a corporation, such as legal fees, taxes, fees paid to the state, and promotional costs, are charged to an intangible asset account entitled Goodwill.	____	____
11. A commonly used method for accounting for the purchase and resale of treasury stock is the derivative method.	____	____

	True	False

12. A major objective of a stock split is to increase stock-holders' equity. ....   _____   _____

13. Paid-in capital and retained earnings are two major sub-divisions of stockholders' equity. ....   _____   _____

14. A liability for a dividend is normally recorded in the accounting records on the date of record. ....   _____   _____

15. An accounting entry is required to record a stock dividend.   _____   _____

EXERCISE 12-1

Prepare the entries in general journal form to record each of the following unrelated transactions. (Omit explanations.)

(1) Cannuck Corp. issued 20,000 shares of no-par common stock for cash at $35 per share.

JOURNAL   PAGE

	DATE	DESCRIPTION	POST. REF.	DEBIT	CREDIT	
1						1
2						2
3						3
4						4
5						5
6						6
7						7

(2) Dunlo Corp. issued 20,000 shares of $25 par common stock for cash at $25 per share.

JOURNAL   PAGE

	DATE	DESCRIPTION	POST. REF.	DEBIT	CREDIT	
1						1
2						2
3						3
4						4
5						5
6						6
7						7

(3) Erickson Corp. issued 20,000 shares of $50 par common stock for cash at $60 per share.

JOURNAL PAGE

	DATE	DESCRIPTION	POST. REF.	DEBIT	CREDIT	
1						1
2						2
3						3
4						4
5						5
6						6
7						7

(4) Felix Corp. issued 10,000 shares of $10 par common stock in exchange for new manufacturing equipment with a fair market value of $145,000.

JOURNAL PAGE

	DATE	DESCRIPTION	POST. REF.	DEBIT	CREDIT	
1						1
2						2
3						3
4						4
5						5
6						6
7						7

(5) Huddley Corp. issued 10,000 shares of $25 par preferred stock for cash at $30 per share.

JOURNAL PAGE

	DATE	DESCRIPTION	POST. REF.	DEBIT	CREDIT	
1						1
2						2
3						3
4						4
5						5
6						6
7						7

Exercise 12-2

Prepare the entries in general journal form to record each of the following treasury stock transactions of Pinell Corp. using the cost basis method. (Omit explanations.)

(1) On October 1, Pinell purchased 2,000 shares of treasury stock at $75.

(2) On October 31, Pinell sold 800 shares of the treasury stock it purchased on October 1 at $82.

(3) On November 20, Pinell sold 100 shares of the treasury stock it purchased on October 1 at $70.

JOURNAL
PAGE

	DATE		DESCRIPTION	POST. REF.	DEBIT	CREDIT	
1							1
2							2
3							3
4							4
5							5
6							6
7							7
8							8
9							9
10							10
11							11
12							12
13							13
14							14
15							15
16							16
17							17
18							18
19							19
20							20
21							21
22							22
23							23
24							24
25							25
26							26
27							27

EXERCISE 12-3

Journalize the following transactions of Copper Corp. (Omit explanations.)

(1) On February 20, Copper declared a $60,000 cash dividend.

(2) On March 22, Copper paid the cash dividend declared on February 20.

(3) On December 15, Copper declared a 5% stock dividend on 160,000 shares of $20 par value common stock with a market value of $25 per share.

(4) On January 14, Copper issued the stock certificates for the stock dividend declared on December 15.

(5) On February 20, Copper declared a 2 for 1 stock split, exchanging 380,000 shares of $10 par common stock for 190,000 shares of $20 par common stock.

JOURNAL

PAGE _____

	DATE		DESCRIPTION	POST. REF.	DEBIT	CREDIT	
1							1
2							2
3							3
4							4
5							5
6							6
7							7
8							8
9							9
10							10
11							11
12							12
13							13
14							14
15							15
16							16
17							17
18							18
19							19
20							20
21							21
22							22
23							23
24							24
25							25

PROBLEM 12-1

Pattering Corp. has 4,000 shares of $10 par common stock outstanding and 1,000 shares of $100 par 8% preferred stock outstanding. Pattering expects to pay annual dividends of $7,000, $9,000, $28,000, and $48,000 respectively for the next four years.

Instructions: By completing the following forms, indicate how the dividends should be distributed in each case if the preferred stock is given the rights or the restrictions indicated.

(1) The preferred stock is cumulative and nonparticipating.

Year	Total Dividends	Preferred Dividends		Common Dividends	
		Total	Per Share	Total	Per Share
1	$ 7,000				
2	9,000				
3	28,000				
4	48,000				

(2) The preferred stock is noncumulative and nonparticipating.

Year	Total Dividends	Preferred Dividends		Common Dividends	
		Total	Per Share	Total	Per Share
1	$ 7,000				
2	9,000				
3	28,000				
4	48,000				

PROBLEM 12-2

The stockholders' equity of Southland Corp. consists of 100,000 shares of $25 par stock, additional paid-in capital of $1,500,000, and retained earnings of $6,440,000. Theodore Rafael owns 1,000 of the outstanding shares.

Instructions:

(1) In Column A below, fill in the blanks with the appropriate figures based on the data given.

(2) In Column B, fill in the blanks with the appropriate figures based on the data given, but after a $1.50 per share cash dividend has been declared and paid.

(3) In Column C, fill in the blanks with the appropriate figures based on the data given, but after a 5% stock dividend has been declared and distributed. The market value of Southland Corp.'s stock is $30. (Ignore the instructions in (2) when making these calculations.)

	A	B	C
	Before Any Dividend	After Cash Dividend	After Stock Dividend
a. Total number of shares outstanding...................................			
b. Total par value of shares outstanding...................................			
c. Total additional paid-in capital.........			
d. Total retained earnings....................			
e. Total stockholders' equity................			
f. Amount required to pay a $1.50 per share cash dividend next year. (Assume no further changes in the capital structure.)....................			
g. Percentage of total stock owned by Rafael			
h. Total number of shares owned by Rafael			
i. Total par value of Rafael's shares...			
j. Total equity of Rafael's shares........			

Problem 12-3

The following accounts and their balances appear in the ledger of Charleston Corporation on December 31, the end of the current fiscal year.

Common Stock, $25 par	$2,500,000
Paid-In Capital in Excess of Par—Common Stock	500,000
Paid-In Capital in Excess of Par—Preferred Stock	375,000
Paid-In Capital in Excess of Par—Treasury Stock	4,000
Preferred $10 Stock, $100 par	750,000
Retained Earnings	1,000,000
Treasury Stock—Common	50,000

Instructions: Prepare the stockholders' equity section of the balance sheet as of December 31, the end of the current year. Ten thousand shares of preferred and 150,000 shares of common stock are authorized. One thousand shares of common stock are held as treasury stock.

13 Accounting for Partnerships and Limited Liability Corporations

QUIZ AND TEST HINTS

The following hints may be helpful to you in preparing for a quiz or a test over the material covered in Chapter 13.

1. Note the similarity between a partnership and a limited liability corporation (LLC). LLCs use slightly different terms, such as members' equity, but employ similar accounting approaches.

2. You should be able to prepare journal entries for the formation and the dissolution of a partnership or LLC. Pay particular attention to the payment of a bonus on the admission of a new partner.

3. Expect at least one question involving distribution of partnership net income among the partners (or LLC members). This question may involve salary allowances and interest allowances on partners' capital balances. Remember, if the partnership agreement does not indicate how income is shared among the partners, it is shared equally. Also, be able to prepare the journal entries distributing a partnership net income or loss. The entry for distributing net income debits Income Summary and credits the partners' capital accounts.

4. If your instructor assigned a homework problem involving partnership liquidation or covered it in class, you may see a question in a quiz or test related to liquidating a partnership. You should understand how to account for gains, losses, and satisfying partner deficiencies in the liquidating process. The final distribution must be according to the final capital balances of the partners, not according to the income-sharing ratio. Review the chapter illustrations and the Illustrative Problem at the end of the chapter.

MATCHING

Instructions: Match each of the statements below with its proper term. Some terms may not be used.

A.   deficiency
B.   initial public offering (IPO)
C.   limited liability corporation
D.   liquidation
E.   partnership
F.   partnership agreement
G.   realization

H.   statement of members' equity
I.   statement of partnership capital
J.   statement of stockholders' equity
K.   underwriting firms
L.   venture capitalist

_____ 1. A summary of the changes in each partner's capital of a partnership that have occurred during a specific period of time.

_____ 2. A business form consisting of one or more persons or entities filing an operating agreement with a state to conduct business with limited liability to the owners, yet treated as a partnership for tax purposes.

_____ 3. The formal written contract creating a partnership.

_____ 4. The debit balance in the owner's equity account of a partner.

_____ 5. The sale of assets when a partnership is being liquidated.

_____ 6. A summary of the changes in each member's equity of a limited liability corporation that have occurred during a specific period of time.

_____ 7. The winding-up process when a partnership goes out of business.

_____ 8. A summary of the changes in the stockholders' equity of a corporation that have occurred during a specific period of time.

_____ 9. An individual or firm that provides equity financing to new firms with the intent of selling their interest for a profit after the firm has matured.

_____ 10. The first offering of common stock to the investing public.

_____ 11. An unincorporated business form consisting of two or more persons conducting business as co-owners for profit.

FILL IN THE BLANK—PART A

Instructions: Answer the following questions or complete the statements by writing the appropriate words or amounts in the answer blanks.

1. A(n) _____ is a business owned by a single individual.

2. Limited liability is a feature of _____ _____ _____ and _____ forms of business organization.

3. The characteristic of _____ _____ means the acts of any partner can bind, or obligate, the entire partnership.

4. The _____ form of organization has an unlimited life.

5. The _____ _____ _____ _____ discloses changes in paid-in capital, retained earnings, and treasury stock accounts.

6. If the partnership agreement is silent, partnership income is divided _____ among the partners.

7. A method for recognizing differences in partner ability or effort in dividing partnership income is a(n) _____ _____.

8. If Dunn and Street share income at the ratio of 2:3, Dunn would be credited with income of _____ out of total partnership income of $150,000.

9. A partnership's assets should be stated at _____ _____ _____ when a new partner is admitted.

10. If Hastings, with a $60,000 capital account, admits Cortez to a 20% interest in a partnership for a $20,000 investment, then the bonus paid to Hastings is _____.

11. If Mann, with a $20,000 capital account, admits Owens to a 40% interest in a partnership for a $10,000 investment, then a bonus is paid to _____.

12. In liquidation, cash is distributed to partners according to their _____ _____.

13. If Burns and Kraft sell $42,000 book value of noncash assets for $30,000 in liquidating a partnership, then Burn's capital account will decline by _____ if the income-sharing ratio is 3:1.

14. If cash is not collected from a deficient partner upon liquidation, then the deficiency becomes a(n) _____ to the partnership and is divided among the remaining partners' capital accounts according to their _____-_____ _____.

15. A(n) _____ _____ is an individual or firm that provides equity financing for new companies.

FILL IN THE BLANK—PART B

Instructions: Answer the following questions or complete the statements by writing the appropriate words or amounts in the answer blanks.

1. A(n) _____, _____ _____ _____, and _____ are nontaxable (flow-through) business entities.

2. A partnership is created by contract, known as the _____ _____.

3. A major disadvantage of a partnership is the feature of _____ _____.

4. A corporation is a preferred organizational form if there is a need for _____ in raising capital.

5. The _____ _____ _____ _____ discloses changes in member's equity for a limited liability corporation.

6. The method for dividing income between partners should be explained in the _____ _____.

7. A method for recognizing differences in partner investments is by awarding _____ on partner capital balances when dividing income between partners.

8. If Todd and Mellon shared partnership income in the ratio of 1:3, Mellon would be credited with income of _____ out of a total partnership income of $200,000.

9. Upon admitting a new partner, the _____ or _____ in adjusting assets to current values should be divided among the capital accounts of the existing partners according to their income-sharing ratio.

10. If Collins, with a $30,000 capital account, admits McCain to a 40% interest in a partnership for a $50,000 investment, then the bonus paid to Collins is _____.

11. If Long, with a $80,000 capital account, admits Bradley to a 50% interest in a partnership for a $100,000 investment, then a bonus is paid to _____.

12. Prior to liquidating a partnership, cash must be _____ from the sale of assets.

13. A debit balance in a partner's capital account upon liquidation is termed a(n) _____.

14. If Howe and Martin sell $75,000 book value of noncash assets for $120,000 in liquidating a partnership, then Martin's capital account will increase by _____ if the income-sharing ratio is 1:2.

15. A(n) _____ _____ specializes in helping companies price and sell their initial public offerings.

MULTIPLE CHOICE

Instructions: Circle the best answer for each of the following questions.

1. If a partnership agreement is silent on dividing net income or net losses, the partners divide income/losses:

    a. according to their original capital investments

    b. equally

    c. according to skills possessed by each partner

    d. on the basis of individual time devoted to the business

2. Which of the following is not an advantage of a partnership?

    a. It is possible to bring together more capital than in a sole proprietorship.

    b. Partners' income taxes may be less than the income taxes would be on a corporation.

    c. It is possible to bring together more managerial skills than in a sole proprietorship.

    d. Each partner has limited liability.

3. Which features of a limited liability corporation provide it advantages over a partnership or a corporation?

    a. unlimited liability, taxed as a separate entity

    b. limited life, nontaxable (flow-through) entity

    c. limited liability, nontaxable (flow-through) entity

    d. limited liability, taxed as a separate entity

4. When a new partner is admitted to a partnership by a contribution of assets to the partnership:

    a. neither the total assets nor the total owner's equity of the business is affected

    b. only the total assets are affected

    c. only the owner's equity is affected

    d. both the total assets and the total owner's equity are increased

5. Boxer and Campbell have capital accounts of $25,000 and $35,000, respectively. Hansen contributes $40,000 for a 30% interest. What is the total bonus to Boxer and Campbell?

    a. $0

    b. $10,000

    c. $20,000

    d. $40,000

6. Columbo, Dexter, and Flamingo share income and losses in the ratio of 1:2:2 according to their partnership agreement. The partnership income is $80,000. How much income is allocated to Dexter's capital account?

    a. $16,000

    b. $26,666

    c. $32,000

    d. $40,000

7. Haley and Zeff share income and losses in the ratio of 2:3 according to their partnership agreement. Prior to admitting Brown, $90,000 of inventory is revalued to a current market value of $75,000. What is the impact of the revaluation on Zeff's capital account?

    a. There is no impact because the revaluation is not realized.

    b. a $6,000 debit

    c. a $9,000 debit

    d. a $22,500 debit

8. Ford, Hill, and Patterson share income and losses at the ratio of 1:2:3. At the final stages of liquidating the partnership, it is determined that Patterson has a capital deficiency of $60,000, and thus, there is insufficient cash to pay the remaining partners equal to their capital accounts. What share of the deficiency will be allocated to Ford, assuming no additional cash is collected from Patterson?

    a. $10,000

    b. $20,000

    c. $30,000

    d. $40,000

9. If there is a loss on the sale of noncash assets when a partnership goes out of business, the loss should be divided among the partners:

    a. according to their original capital investments

    b. according to their current capital balances

    c. according to their income-sharing ratio

    d. equally

10. An individual or firm that provides private equity financing for new businesses is termed a(n):

    a. underwriting firm

    b. founding stockholder

    c. member

    d. venture capitalist

TRUE/FALSE

Instructions: Indicate whether each of the following statements is true or false by placing a check mark in the appropriate column.

		True	False
1.	Partners are legally employees of the partnership, and their capital contributions are considered a loan.	____	____
2.	Each partner is individually liable to creditors for debts incurred by the partnership.	____	____
3.	Salary allowances are treated as divisions of partnership net income and are credited to the partners' capital accounts.	____	____
4.	The property invested in a partnership by a partner remains identified as that partner's property.	____	____
5.	A partner's claim against the assets of the partnership in the event of dissolution is measured by the amount of the partner's initial investment.	____	____
6.	At the time a partnership is formed, the market values of the assets should be considered in determining each partner's investment.	____	____
7.	In the absence of an agreement for income or loss distributions among the partners, the partners should share income equally, even if there are differences in their capital contributions.	____	____
8.	Regardless of whether partners' salaries and interest are treated as expenses of the partnership or as a division of net income, the total amount allocated to each partner will not be affected.	____	____
9.	A partnership is required to pay federal income taxes.	____	____
10.	Any change in the personnel of the ownership results in a dissolution of a partnership.	____	____
11.	A new partner may be admitted to a partnership without the consent of the current partners.	____	____
12.	A partner's interest may be disposed of without the consent of the remaining partners.	____	____
13.	When a new partner is admitted by purchasing an interest from one or more of the existing partners, the purchase price is recorded in the accounts of the partnership.	____	____

	True	False

14. It is appropriate to adjust the old partnership assets to current market values at the time a new partner is admitted. ....   ____   ____

15. At the time a new partner is admitted, a bonus may be paid to the incoming partner. ....   ____   ____

16. A person may be admitted to a partnership by purchasing an interest from one or more of the existing partners. The only entry required by the partnership is to transfer owner's equity amounts from the capital accounts of the selling partner(s) to the capital account of the new partner. ....   ____   ____

17. As cash is realized from the sale of assets during the liquidation of a partnership, the cash is applied first to the payment of the claims of the limited partners. ....   ____   ____

18. If the distribution of the loss on the sale of noncash assets when a partnership goes out of business causes a partner's account to have a debit balance, this balance represents a claim of the partnership against the partner. ....   ____   ____

19. If a deficiency of a partner is uncollectible, this represents a loss that is written off against the capital balances of the remaining partners. ....   ____   ____

EXERCISE 13-1

Ruth Cutco and Darrell Robbs formed a partnership. Cutco invested $100,000 cash and merchandise valued at $80,000. Robbs invested $10,000 cash, land valued at $115,000, equipment valued at $45,000, and merchandise valued at $5,000.

Instructions: Prepare the entries to record the investments of Cutco and Robbs on the partnership books. Use the current date.

JOURNAL

PAGE

	DATE		DESCRIPTION	POST. REF.	DEBIT	CREDIT	
1							1
2							2
3							3
4							4
5							5
6							6
7							7
8							8
9							9
10							10
11							11
12							12
13							13
14							14
15							15
16							16
17							17
18							18
19							19
20							20
21							21
22							22
23							23
24							24
25							25
26							26
27							27
28							28

EXERCISE 13-2

Ann Hartly, Barry Smetz, and Lynette Grasso are partners, having capitals of $100,000, $55,000, and $35,000, respectively. They share net income equally.

Instructions: Prepare the entries to record each of the following situations. (Omit explanations.)

(1) On June 30, John Schafer is admitted to the partnership by purchasing one-fifth of the respective capital interests of the three partners. He pays $30,000 to Hartly, $15,000 to Smetz, and $10,000 to Grasso.

JOURNAL   PAGE

	DATE	DESCRIPTION	POST. REF.	DEBIT	CREDIT	
1						1
2						2
3						3
4						4
5						5
6						6
7						7
8						8
9						9
10						10

(2) On July 1, Laura Masko is admitted to the partnership for an investment of $50,000, and the parties agree to pay a bonus of $21,000 to Masko.

JOURNAL   PAGE

	DATE	DESCRIPTION	POST. REF.	DEBIT	CREDIT	
1						1
2						2
3						3
4						4
5						5
6						6
7						7
8						8
9						9
10						10

EXERCISE 13-3

Arway, Batts, and Carlone are partners, having capital balances of $65,000, $55,000, and $40,000, respectively. The partners share net income equally. Carlone has decided to leave the partnership.

Instructions: Prepare the entries to record each of the following situations. (Omit explanations.)

(1)   The partners agree that the inventory of the partnership should be increased by $12,750 to recognize its fair market value. Arway buys Carlone's interest in the partnership for $53,000.

JOURNAL   PAGE

	DATE	DESCRIPTION	POST. REF.	DEBIT	CREDIT	
1						1
2						2
3						3
4						4
5						5
6						6
7						7
8						8
9						9

(2)   The partners agree that the inventory of the partnership should be increased by $6,000 to recognize its fair market value. The partnership pays Carlone cash for her interest, as reflected by the balance in her capital account.

JOURNAL   PAGE

	DATE	DESCRIPTION	POST. REF.	DEBIT	CREDIT	
1						1
2						2
3						3
4						4
5						5
6						6
7						7
8						8
9						9

PROBLEM 13-1

On January 2 of the current year, Bulley and Scram formed a partnership in which Bulley invested $300,000 and Scram invested $700,000. During the year, the partnership had a net income of $200,000.

Instructions: Show how this net income would be distributed under each of the following conditions.

(1) The partnership agreement says nothing about the distribution of net income.

Bulley's share.. $ _____

Scram's share .... _____

Total .... $ _____

(2) The partnership agreement provides that Bulley and Scram are to share net income in a 2:3 ratio, respectively.

Bulley's share.. $ _____

Scram's share .... _____

Total .... $ _____

(3) The partnership agreement provides that Bulley and Scram are to share net income in accordance with the ratio of their original capital investments.

Bulley's share.. $ _____

Scram's share .... _____

Total .... $ _____

(4) The partnership agreement provides that Bulley is to be allowed a salary of $30,000 and Scram a salary of $50,000, with the balance of net income distributed equally.

Division of Net Income	Bulley	Scram	Total
Salary allowance..............................	$ _____	$ _____	$ _____
Remaining income..........................	_____	_____	_____
Net income.......................................	$ _____	$ _____	$ 200,000

(5) The partnership agreement provides that interest at 5% is to be allowed on the beginning capital and that the balance is to be distributed equally.

Division of Net Income	Bulley	Scram	Total
Interest allowance	$	$	$
Remaining income............................			
Net income	$	$	$ 200,000

(6) The partnership agreement provides that Bulley is to be allowed a salary of $15,000 and Scram a salary of $25,000; that interest at 5% is to be allowed on beginning capital; and that the balance is to be distributed equally.

Division of Net Income	Bulley	Scram	Total
Salary allowance	$	$	$
Interest allowance			
Remaining income............................			
Net income	$	$	$ 200,000

(7) The partnership agreement provides that Bulley is to be allowed a salary of $80,000 and Scram a salary of $78,000; that interest at 5% is to be allowed on beginning capital; and that the balance is to be distributed equally.

Division of Net Income	Bulley	Scram	Total
Salary allowance	$	$	$
Interest allowance			
Total...	$	$	$
Excess of allowances over income			
Net income	$	$	$ 200,000

PROBLEM 13-2

Tropical Products, LLC consists of two members, Baskin and Robbins, who share in all income and losses according to a 3:1 income-sharing ratio. Dreyer has been asked to join the LLC. Prior to admitting Dreyer, the assets of Tropical Products were revalued to reflect their current market values. The revaluation resulted in the value of processing equipment being increased by $20,000. Prior to the revaluation, the member equity balances for Baskin and Robbins were $385,000 and $195,000, respectively.

Instructions:

(1) Provide the journal entry for the asset revaluation.

JOURNAL   PAGE

	DATE	DESCRIPTION	POST. REF.	DEBIT	CREDIT	
1						1
2						2
3						3
4						4
5						5
6						6
7						7
8						8
9						9

(2) Provide the journal entry and supporting calculations for the bonus under the following independent assumptions.

(a) Dreyer purchased a 20% interest in Tropical Products, LLC for $100,000.

JOURNAL   PAGE

	DATE	DESCRIPTION	POST. REF.	DEBIT	CREDIT	
1						1
2						2
3						3
4						4
5						5
6						6

(Provide supporting calculations on the following page.)

Supporting calculations:

(b) Dreyer purchased a 15% interest in Tropical Products, LLC for $180,000.

JOURNAL

PAGE

	DATE	DESCRIPTION	POST. REF.	DEBIT	CREDIT	
1						1
2						2
3						3
4						4
5						5
6						6

Supporting calculations:

PROBLEM 13-3

Prior to the liquidation of the partnership of Triste, Sandpipe, and Hinkle, the ledger contained the following accounts and balances:

Cash	$100,000
Noncash Assets	$300,000
Liabilities	$120,000
Triste, Capital	$90,000
Sandpipe, Capital	$60,000
Hinkle, Capital	$130,000

Assume that the noncash assets are sold for $400,000. Triste, Sandpipe, and Hinkle share profits in a 30:50:20 ratio.

Instructions:

(1) Complete the following schedule showing the sale of assets, payment of liabilities, and distribution of the remaining cash to the partners.

	Cash	+	Noncash Assets	=	Liabilities	+	Triste (30%)	+	Sandpipe (50%)	+	Hinkle (20%)
Balances before realization	$100,000		$300,000		$120,000		$90,000		$60,000		$130,000
Sale of noncash assets and division of gain											
Balances after realization											
Payment of liabilities											
Balances after payment of liabilities											
Distribution of cash to partners											
Final balances											

(2) Assume that the noncash assets are sold for $130,000 and that the partner with a debit balance pays the entire deficiency. Complete the following schedule showing the sale of assets, payment of liabilities, and distribution of the remaining cash to the partners.

	Cash	+	Noncash Assets	=	Liabilities	+	Capital Triste (30%)	+	Sandpipe (50%)	+	Hinkle (20%)
Balances before realization...............	$100,000		$300,000		$120,000		$90,000		$60,000		$130,000
Sale of noncash assets and division of loss......................											
Balances after realization...............											
Payment of liabilities....................											
Balances after payment of liabilities........											
Receipt of deficiency..................											
Balances...................											
Distribution of cash to partners											
Final balances...........											

(3) Prepare the journal entries to record the liquidation of the partnership based on the facts in (2). Use the current date. (Omit explanations.)

JOURNAL

	DATE	DESCRIPTION	POST. REF.	DEBIT	CREDIT	
1						1
2						2
3						3
4						4
5						5
6						6
7						7
8						8
9						9
10						10
11						11
12						12
13						13
14						14
15						15
16						16
17						17
18						18
19						19
20						20
21						21
22						22
23						23
24						24
25						25
26						26
27						27
28						28
29						29
30						30
31						31
32						32
33						33

14 Income Taxes, Unusual Income Items, and Investments in Stocks

QUIZ AND TEST HINTS

The following hints may be helpful to you in preparing for a quiz or a test over the material covered in Chapter 14.

1. Many new terms are introduced in this chapter. Oftentimes terms are tested using true/false or multiple-choice questions.

2. You should be able to prepare journal entries for deferred taxes. The most common examples involve (1) the difference between depreciation used for financial reporting and tax purposes and (2) the revenue recognition differences between book and tax.

3. The discussion of the reporting of unusual items in the financial statements is an important part of this chapter. You should be able to describe each of the types of unusual items and how they are reported in the financial statements. Be especially careful in studying how discontinued operations, extraordinary items, and changes in accounting principles are reported on the income statement, including the reporting of earnings per common share. Note that these three unusual items are reported *below* the income from continuing operations. Asset impairments and restructuring charges are unusual items that are reported *above* the income from continuing operations. The Illustrative Problem in the text is a good review of the reporting of unusual items. You might also look for several multiple-choice questions related to this topic.

4. You should be able to prepare journal entries for investments in stocks. The accounting for investments depends upon whether the investment is treated as an available-for-sale security or is accounted for under the equity method. The former uses lower-of-cost-or-market valuation with unrealized gains and losses becoming part of other comprehensive income. The equity method is a method used for long-term investments in which there is significant control of the investee.

Name:

MATCHING

Instructions: Match each of the statements below with its proper term. Some terms may not be used.

A.	accumulated other comprehensive income	**L.**	investments
B.	available-for-sale securities	**M.**	merger
C.	comprehensive income	**N.**	minority interest
D.	consolidated financial statements	**O.**	other comprehensive income
E.	consolidation	**P.**	parent company
F.	discontinued operations	**Q.**	price-earnings ratio
G.	earnings per common share (EPS)	**R.**	purchase method
H.	equity method	**S.**	restructuring charge
I.	equity securities	**T.**	subsidiary company
J.	extraordinary items	**U.**	taxable income
K.	fixed asset impairments	**V.**	temporary differences
		W.	temporary investments
		X.	trading securities
		Y.	unrealized holding gain or loss

_____ 1. The income according to the tax laws that is used as a base for determining the amount of taxes owed.

_____ 2. Differences between taxable income and income before income taxes, created because items are recognized in one period for tax purposes and in another period for income statement purposes. Such differences reverse or turn around in later years.

_____ 3. Operations of a major line of business for a company, such as a division, a department, or a certain class of customer, that have been disposed of.

_____ 4. Events and transactions that (1) are significantly different (unusual) from the typical or the normal operating activities of a business and (2) occur infrequently.

_____ 5. Net income per share of common stock outstanding during a period.

_____ 6. The cumulative effects of other comprehensive income items reported separately in the stockholders' equity section of the balance sheet.

_____ 7. The costs associated with involuntarily terminating employees, terminating contracts, consolidating facilities, or relocating employees.

_____ 8. All changes in stockholders' equity during a period except those resulting from dividends and stockholders' investments.

_____ 9. The preferred and common stock of a firm.

_____ 10. Securities that management intends to actively trade for profit.

____ **11.** Securities that management expects to sell in the future but which are not actively traded for profit.

____ **12.** The balance sheet caption used to report investments in income-yielding securities that can be quickly sold and converted to cash as needed.

____ **13.** The difference between the fair market values of the securities and their cost.

____ **14.** The balance sheet caption used to report long-term investments in stocks not intended as a source of cash in the normal operations of the business.

____ **15.** A condition when the fair value of a fixed asset falls below its book value and is not expected to recover.

____ **16.** A method of accounting for an investment in common stock by which the investment account is adjusted for the investor's share of periodic net income and cash dividends of the investee.

____ **17.** The joining of two corporations in which one company acquires all the assets and liabilities of another corporation, which is then dissolved.

____ **18.** The creation of a new corporation by the transfer of assets and liabilities of two or more existing corporations, which are then dissolved.

____ **19.** The corporation owning all or a majority of the voting stock of the other corporation.

____ **20.** The corporation that is controlled by a parent company.

____ **21.** The accounting method used when a corporation acquires the controlling share of the voting common stock of another corporation by paying cash, exchanging other assets, issuing debt, or some combination of these methods.

____ **22.** Specified items that are reported separately from net income, including foreign currency items, pension liability adjustments, and unrealized gains and losses on investments.

____ **23.** Financial statements resulting from combining parent and subsidiary statements.

____ **24.** The portion of a subsidiary corporation's stock owned by outsiders.

____ **25.** The ratio computed by dividing a corporation's stock market price per share at a specific date by the company's annual earnings per share.

FILL IN THE BLANK—PART A

Instructions: Answer the following questions or complete the statements by writing the appropriate words or amounts in the answer blanks.

1. The _____ income is used as a base for determining the amount of taxes owed.

2. Income before income tax reported on the income statement for the first year of operations is $300,000. Because of timing differences in accounting and tax methods, the taxable income for the same year is $250,000. If the income tax rate is 50%, the amount of income tax expense reported on the income statement should be _____.

3. _____ _____ are associated with involuntarily terminating employees, terminating contracts, consolidating facilities, or relocating employees.

4. When a company disposes of operations of a major line of business for a company (such as a division, a department, or a certain class of customer), the gain or loss is reported on the income statement as a gain or loss from _____ operations.

5. Events and transactions that (1) are significantly different (unusual) from the typical or the normal operating activities of a business and (2) occur infrequently are reported in the income statement as _____ _____.

6. A company which recently decided to stop producing and selling its products in foreign markets would report the resulting loss on its income statement as a(n) _____ _____ _____ _____.

7. Net income per share of common stock outstanding during a period is called _____ _____ _____.

8. If a company has preferred stock, the earnings per share reported on the income statement should subtract the _____ _____ from the net income in the numerator.

9. All changes in stockholders' equity during a period except those resulting from investments by stockholders and dividends should be reported as part of _____ income.

10. Securities that management intends to actively trade for profit are referred to as _____ securities.

11. The balance sheet caption _____ _____ is used to report investments in income-yielding securities that can be quickly sold and converted to cash as needed.

12. The _____ method is used in accounting for an investment in common stock, by which the investment account is adjusted for the investor's share of periodic net income and property dividends of the investee.

13. A(n) _____ is the creation of a new corporation by the transfer of assets and liabilities of two or more existing corporations that are then dissolved.

14. The corporation that is controlled by a parent company is referred to as the _____ company.

15. The portion of a subsidiary corporation's stock owned by outsiders is called _____ _____.

FILL IN THE BLANK—PART B

Instructions: Answer the following questions or complete the statements by writing the appropriate words or amounts in the answer blanks.

1. Differences between taxable income and income before income tax that reverse or turn around in later years are called _____ differences.

2. Income before income tax reported on the income statement for the first year of operations is $300,000. Because of timing differences in accounting and tax methods, the taxable income for the same year is $250,000. If the income tax rate is 50%, the amount of deferred income tax payable is _____.

3. A company must record a(n) _____ _____ _____ on the income statement if the carrying amount of an asset exceeds its fair value.

4. A company that has never experienced a loss from a hurricane would report an uninsured hurricane loss on its income statement as a(n) _____ _____.

5. A statement of _____ _____ summarizes significant changes in stockholders' equity that have occurred during a period.

6. Preferred or common stock are referred to as _____ securities.

7. Securities that management expects to sell in the future, but which are not actively traded for profit, are referred to as _____-_____-_____ securities.

8. The difference between the fair market values of the securities and their cost is a(n) _____ gain or loss.

9. The _____ method is used in accounting for an investment in common stock, by which the investor recognizes as income its share of cash dividends of the investee.

10. A(n) _____ is the joining of two corporations in which the acquiring company acquires all the assets and liabilities of another corporation that is then dissolved.

11. The balance sheet caption _____ is used to report long-term investments in stocks not intended as a source of cash in the normal operations of the business.

12. The corporation owning all or a majority of the voting stock of another corporation is referred to as the _____ company.

13. Other comprehensive income is closed to _____ _____ _____ _____ on the balance sheet.

14. The combining of parent and subsidiary financial statements for reporting purposes results in _____ financial statements.

15. The _____-_____ ratio is computed by dividing a corporation's stock market price per share at a specific date by the company's annual earnings per share.

MULTIPLE CHOICE

Instructions: Circle the best answer for each of the following questions.

1. During its first year of operations, a corporation elected to use the straight-line method of depreciation for financial reporting purposes and the sum-of-the-years-digits method for reporting taxable income. If the income tax is 40% and the amount of depreciation expense is $200,000 under the straight-line method and $300,000 under the sum-of-the-years-digits method, what is the amount of income tax deferred to future years?

   a. $40,000

   b. $80,000

   c. $100,000

   d. $120,000

2. All except which of the following are examples of items that create temporary differences?

   a. A method of recognizing revenue when the sale is made is used for financial statements, and a method of recognizing revenue at the time the cash is collected is used for tax reporting.

   b. Warranty expense is recognized in the year of sale for financial statements and when paid for tax reporting.

   c. An accelerated depreciation method is used for tax reporting, and the straight-line method is used for financial statements.

   d. Interest income on municipal bonds is recognized for financial statements and not for tax reporting.

3. Which of the following would appear as an extraordinary item on the income statement?

   a. correction of an error in the prior year's financial statements

   b. gain resulting from the sale of fixed assets

   c. loss on sale of temporary investments

   d. loss on condemnation of land

4. Earnings per share is required to be presented on the face of the income statement for:

   a. extraordinary items

   b. discontinued operations

   c. income from continuing operations and net income

   d. all of the above

5. All changes in stockholders' equity during a period except those resulting from investments by stockholders and dividends is the definition of:

   a. income from continuing operations

   b. comprehensive income

   c. net income

   d. retained earnings

6. The receipt of cash dividends on a long-term investment in common stock is accounted for as a debit to Cash and a credit to Dividend Revenue. Which of the following methods is being used to account for the investment?

   a. equity method

   b. market method

   c. cost method

   d. revenue method

7. The receipt of cash dividends on a long-term investment in common stock is accounted for as a debit to Cash and a credit to Investment in Spacek Inc. Which of the following methods is being used to account for the investment?

   a. equity method

   b. market method

   c. cost method

   d. revenue method

8. During the year in which Parent Company owned 75% of the outstanding common stock of Subsidiary Company, Subsidiary reported net income of $200,000 and dividends declared and paid of $50,000. What is the amount of net increase in the Investment in Subsidiary account for the year?

   a. $37,500

   b. $112,500

   c. $200,000

   d. $250,000

9. An investor purchased 800 shares of common stock, $50 par, for $96,000. Subsequently, 200 shares were sold for $115 per share. What is the amount of gain or loss on the sale?

   a. $1,000 loss

   b. $1,000 gain

   c. $4,000 loss

   d. $4,000 gain

10. In what section of the parent company's balance sheet would the balance of the account Investment in Subsidiary appear?

   a. current assets

   b. temporary investments

   c. investments

   d. stockholders' equity

11. If the other comprehensive loss is $5,000, what would be the balance of the accumulated other comprehensive income at the end of the period if the beginning balance were $12,000?

   a. $5,000

   b. $7,000

   c. $12,000

   d. $17,000

TRUE/FALSE

Instructions: Indicate whether each of the following statements is true or false by placing a check mark in the appropriate column.

	True	False
1. Income that is exempt from federal taxes, such as interest income on municipal bonds, is an example of a temporary tax difference...	____	____
2. Restructuring charges should have a separate earnings per share disclosure..	____	____
3. The amount reported as a gain or loss from discontinued operations on the income statement should be reported net of related income tax...	____	____
4. Income tax should be allocated to the fiscal year in which the related income is reported and earned.	____	____
5. To be classified as an extraordinary item, an item must be unusual in nature and infrequent in occurrence..................	____	____

	True	False

6. Over the life of a business, temporary differences reduce the total amount of tax paid. .... _____ _____

7. All changes in stockholders' equity during a period except those resulting from investments by stockholders and dividends should be reported as part of comprehensive income. .... _____ _____

8. The accumulated other comprehensive income should be disclosed in the income statement, in a separate statement of comprehensive income, or in the statement of stockholders' equity. .... _____ _____

9. Under the cost method of accounting for investments in stocks, the investor records its share of cash dividends as a decrease in the investment account and an increase in the cash account... _____ _____

10. A corporation that is controlled by another corporation is known as a subsidiary. .... _____ _____

11. The two methods of accounting for investments in stock are the cost method and the equity method. .... _____ _____

12. When two or more corporations transfer their assets and liabilities to a corporation that has been created for the purpose of the takeover, the combination is called a merger.. _____ _____

13. Mergers and consolidations should be accounted for by the purchase method. .... _____ _____

14. Subsequent to acquisition of a subsidiary, a parent company's investment account should be increased periodically for its share of the subsidiary's income. .... _____ _____

15. A note representing a loan by a parent corporation to its subsidiary would appear as a note receivable in the parent's balance sheet and a note payable in the subsidiary's balance sheet. .... _____ _____

EXERCISE 14-1

(1) Jabbs Corp. reported $550,000 income before tax on its income statement for the year. Because of temporary differences in accounting and tax methods, taxable income for the year is $320,000. Assuming an income tax rate of 40%, prepare the journal entry to record the income tax expense, liability, and deferred liability of Jabbs Corp.

JOURNAL   PAGE

	DATE	DESCRIPTION	POST. REF.	DEBIT	CREDIT	
1						1
2						2
3						3
4						4
5						5
6						6
7						7
8						8
9						9
10						10

(2) In the following year, Jabbs Corp. reported $500,000 income before income tax. Because of temporary differences in accounting and tax methods, taxable income for this year is $600,000. Assuming an income tax rate of 40%, prepare the journal entry to record the income tax expense, liability, and reduction of the deferred liability of Jabbs Corp.

JOURNAL   PAGE

	DATE	DESCRIPTION	POST. REF.	DEBIT	CREDIT	
1						1
2						2
3						3
4						4
5						5
6						6
7						7
8						8
9						9
10						10

EXERCISE 14-2

Mills Corp. estimates its income tax expense for the year to be $250,000. At the end of the year, Mills Corp. determines that its actual income tax for the year is $280,000.

(1) Prepare the entry to record one of the four estimated income tax payments.

JOURNAL
PAGE

	DATE	DESCRIPTION	POST. REF.	DEBIT	CREDIT	
1						1
2						2
3						3
4						4
5						5
6						6
7						7
8						8
9						9
10						10
11						11
12						12

(2) Prepare the entry to record the additional income tax liability for the year.

JOURNAL
PAGE

	DATE	DESCRIPTION	POST. REF.	DEBIT	CREDIT	
1						1
2						2
3						3
4						4
5						5
6						6
7						7
8						8
9						9
10						10
11						11
12						12

PROBLEM 14-1

During a recent year of operations, the Emory Corporation purchased the following securities as temporary investments:

Security	Shares Purchased	Cost	Market Value, End of Period
X-Tex	2,000	$15,000	$14,000
Dylan Company	500	25,000	32,000

Emory's net income for the year was $124,000, while the accumulated other comprehensive income balance at the beginning of the period was $3,000. The retained earnings had a balance of $521,000 at the beginning of the period. The tax rate on capital gains was 15%. These were the only securities held by Emory during the year, and there were no other comprehensive income items during the year.

Instructions:

(1) Prepare the balance sheet presentation for the temporary investments at the end of the period.

(2) Prepare the balance sheet presentation for retained earnings and accumulated other comprehensive income at the end of the period.

(3) Prepare a statement of comprehensive income for the period.

PROBLEM 14-2

(1) Record the following transactions for Richards Inc.

(a) As a long-term investment, Richards Inc. acquires 40,000 shares of Norris Inc. common stock at a cost of $600,000. Richards Inc. uses the equity method of accounting for this investment because it represents 25% of the voting stock of Norris Inc.

(b) On May 18, a cash dividend of $.75 per share is paid by Norris Inc.

(c) Norris Inc. reports net income of $900,000 for the year.

JOURNAL   PAGE

	DATE	DESCRIPTION	POST. REF.	DEBIT	CREDIT	
1						1
2						2
3						3
4						4
5						5
6						6
7						7
8						8
9						9

(2) Record the following transactions for Smith Inc.

(a) As a long-term investment, Smith Inc. acquires 10,000 shares of Kline Inc. common stock at a cost of $150,000. Smith uses the cost method of accounting for this investment, because it represents 5% of the voting stock of Kline Inc.

(b) On September 3, a cash dividend of $.50 per share is paid by Kline Inc.

(c) Kline Inc. reports a net income of $350,000 for the year.

JOURNAL   PAGE

	DATE	DESCRIPTION	POST. REF.	DEBIT	CREDIT	
1						1
2						2
3						3
4						4
5						5
6						6
7						7
8						8

PROBLEM 14-3

Summary data for Wess Corp. for the current fiscal year ended March 31 are as follows:

Cost of merchandise sold...	$1,800,000
Restructuring charge...	200,000
Cumulative effect on prior years of changing to a different depreciation method...	80,000
Loss on disposal of a segment of the business	70,000
Income taxes:	
Applicable to a change in depreciation method.........................	18,000
Reduction applicable to loss on disposal of segment	20,000
Applicable to ordinary income	176,000
Reduction applicable to loss from earthquake	48,000
Loss from earthquake...	240,000
Operating expenses	100,000
Sales	2,700,000

Instructions: Use the form on the following page to prepare an income statement for Wess Corp., including a section for earnings per share as illustrated in this chapter. There were 50,000 shares of common stock outstanding throughout the year, and the effect of the change in depreciation method was to increase income.

15

Bonds Payable and Investment in Bonds

QUIZ AND TEST HINTS

The following hints may be helpful to you in preparing for a quiz or a test over the material covered in Chapter 15.

1. Study the new terminology introduced in this chapter for possible use in fill-in-the-blank, multiple-choice, or true/false questions. As a review of the key terms, do the Matching exercises included in this Study Guide.

2. It is unlikely that you will see a problem related to the Financing Corporations section of the chapter. Instead, you should focus primarily on being able to prepare the various journal entries illustrated throughout the chapter. The Illustrative Problem is a good study aid for reviewing the various journal entries.

3. If your instructor discussed the computation of present value of bonds payable, you should expect one or more questions on this topic.

4. Be ready to prepare entries for the issuance of bonds at face value, at a discount, and at a premium; for discount and premium amortization; and for bond redemption.

5. Be able to prepare journal entries for bond investments. You will more likely see a question requiring journal entries for the issuance of bonds payable, but occasionally instructors will include short problems on bond investments. You can assess the likelihood of such a problem by the amount of time your instructor spent lecturing on bond investments and whether you were assigned a homework problem on bond investments.

MATCHING

Instructions: Match each of the statements below with its proper term. Some terms may not be used.

A. annuity
B. available-for-sale securities
C. bond
D. bond fund
E. bond indenture
F. carrying amount
G. contract rate
H. discount
I. dividend yield
J. effective interest rate method

K. effective rate of interest
L. future value
M. held-to-maturity securities
N. number of times interest charges earned
O. premium
P. present value
Q. present value of an annuity
R. sinking fund

_____ 1. A form of an interest-bearing note used by corporations to borrow on a long-term basis.

_____ 2. The contract between a corporation issuing bonds and the bond-holders.

_____ 3. The periodic interest to be paid on the bonds that is identified in the bond indenture; expressed as a percentage of the face amount of the bond.

_____ 4. A series of equal cash flows at fixed intervals.

_____ 5. The sum of the present values of a series of equal cash flows to be received at fixed intervals.

_____ 6. The estimated worth today of an amount of cash to be received (or paid) in the future.

_____ 7. The estimated worth in the future of an amount of cash on hand today invested at a fixed rate of interest.

_____ 8. The excess of the face amount of bonds over their issue price.

_____ 9. The excess of the issue price of bonds over their face amount.

_____ 10. A fund in which cash or assets are set aside for the purpose of paying the face amount of the bonds at maturity.

_____ 11. The balance of the bonds payable account (face amount of the bonds) less any unamortized discount or plus any unamortized premium.

_____ 12. Investments in bonds or other debt securities that management intends to hold to their maturity.

_____ 13. A ratio that measures the risk that interest payments to debtholders will continue to be made if earnings decrease.

_____ 14. The market rate of interest at the time bonds are issued.

FILL IN THE BLANK—PART A

Instructions: Answer the following questions or complete the statements by writing the appropriate words or amounts in the answer blanks.

1. A corporation issuing bonds enters into a contract with the bondholders. This contract is known as a(n) _____ _____.

2. A corporation reserves the right to redeem _____ bonds before they mature.

3. Bonds issued on the general credit of the issuing corporation are called _____ _____.

4. The _____ rate determines the periodic interest paid on a bond.

5. When the market rate of interest on bonds is lower than the contract rate, the bonds will sell at a(n) _____.

6. Assuming an interest rate of 10%, $110 to be received a year from today is called the _____ _____ of $100 today.

7. The present value of $1,000 to be paid one year later, using an interest rate of 10% is _____.

8. If the market rate of interest is 11%, the present value of $10,000 to be received in each of the next 2 years is _____ (round to the nearest dollar).

9–10. The two methods for amortizing a bond discount are the _____-_____ method and the _____ _____ _____ method.

11. The amount set aside for the payment of bonds at maturity is called a(n) _____ _____.

12. The balance of the bonds payable account (face amount of the bonds) less any unamortized discount or plus any unamortized premium is called the _____ _____.

13. If the balances of Bonds Payable and Discount on Bonds Payable are $400,000 and $12,000, respectively, the carrying amount of the bonds is _____.

14. If $2,000,000 of bonds are sold at 101½, the amount of cash received is _____.

15. Bonds with a face amount of $100,000 were purchased through a broker at 103 plus accrued interest of $2,000 and brokerage commissions of $650. The amount to be debited to the investment account is _____.

16–17. A corporation purchased bonds at a premium several years ago. When this year ends, the company makes an entry to record the amortization of the premium.

16. The account to be debited is _____ _____.

17. The account to be credited is _____ ___ _____.

18. Jones Company has redeemed bonds at 102. The bonds have a face value of $600,000 and an unamortized premium of $10,000. Jones Company will record a gain (or loss) on redemption of _____ (indicate amount and gain or loss).

19. Smith Company intends to hold 10-year bonds until they mature. This asset is called a(n) _____-____-_____ _____.

20. River Company had interest expenses of $2,500,000 and income before tax of $29,000,000. The number of times interest charges are earned is _____.

FILL IN THE BLANK—PART B

Instructions: Answer the following questions or complete the statements by writing the appropriate words or amounts in the answer blanks.

1. All of Sand Company's bonds mature at the same time. These are known as _____ bonds.

2. Bonds that may be exchanged for other securities are called _____ bonds.

3. When the contract rate of interest on bonds is lower than the market rate of interest, the bonds sell at a(n) _____.

4. The present value of the face amount of a $1,000, 5-year bond, using an interest rate of 7% is _____.

5. Oliver Company issues 10-year, 12% bonds with a face value of $100,000. The present value of the bonds' interest payments using an effective rate of interest of 12% is _____ (round to the nearest dollar).

6. A series of equal cash payments at fixed intervals is called a(n) _____.

7. A firm redeemed bonds at 95. The bonds have a face value of $500,000 and an unamortized discount of $15,000. The firm will record a gain (or loss) on redemption of _____ (indicate amount and gain or loss).

8–11. Under which caption (current assets, investments, fixed assets, current liabilities, long-term liabilities, stockholders' equity) would each of the following appear on the balance sheet?

    8. Investment in X Co. Bonds (management intends to hold to maturity in 5 years) would appear in the _____ section of the balance sheet.

    9. Premium on Bonds Payable would appear in the _____ _____ section of the balance sheet.

  10. Bonds Payable due in ten years would appear in the _____ _____ section of the balance sheet.

  11. Bond sinking fund investments would appear in the _____ section of the balance sheet.

  12. Bonds with a face value of $75,000 were purchased through a broker at 98 plus accrued interest of $1,000 and brokerage commissions of $350. The amount to be debited to the investment account is _____.

  13. If Bonds Payable has a balance of $5,000,000 and Premium on Bonds Payable has a balance of $45,000, the carrying amount of the bonds is _____.

14–16. On April 1, Avery Company issued $4,000,000, 5-year, 12% bonds for $4,280,000 with semiannual interest payable on March 31 and September 30. If the effective rate of interest is 10%, determine the following:

  14. The interest paid on September 30 is _____.

  15. The amount of premium amortized on September 30, using the straight-line method is _____.

  16. The accrued interest payable on December 31 is _____.

  17. In No. 14, the total amount of annual interest expense _____ (increases, decreases, or remains the same) over the life of the bonds as the premium on bonds payable is amortized.

  18. A ratio that indicates the likelihood a company will be able to continue paying interest to its debtholders if the company's earnings decrease is called the _____ _____ _____ _____ _____ _____.

  19. Canary Company had interest expenses of $8,250,000 and income before tax of $60,500,000. The number of times interest charges are earned is _____.

  20. The estimated worth today of an amount of cash to be received (or paid) in the future is called the _____ _____.

MULTIPLE CHOICE

Instructions: Circle the best answer for each of the following questions.

1. A bond that gives the bondholder a right to exchange the bond for other securities under certain conditions is called a:

    a. convertible bond

    b. sinking fund bond

    c. term bond

    d. debenture bond

2. What is the present value of $2,000 to be paid in one year if the current interest rate is 6%?

    a. $1,880

    b. $1,887

    c. $2,000

    d. $2,120

3. The entry to record the amortization of a discount on bonds payable is:

    a. debit Bonds Payable; credit Interest Expense

    b. debit Interest Expense; credit Discount on Bonds Payable

    c. debit Discount on Bonds Payable; credit Interest Expense

    d. debit Discount on Bonds Payable; credit Bonds Payable

4. Under the straight-line method of bond discount amortization, as a bond payable approaches maturity, the total yearly amount of interest expense will:

    a. increase

    b. decrease

    c. remain the same

    d. increase or decrease, depending on the size of the original discount

5. On May 1, a $1,000 bond was purchased as a long-term investment at 104, and $8 was paid as the brokerage commission. If the bond bears interest at 6%, which is paid semiannually on January 1 and July 1, what is the total cost to be debited to the investment account?

    a. $1,000

    b. $1,040

    c. $1,048

    d. $1,068

6. What method of amortizing bond discount or premium is required by generally accepted accounting principles?

    a. declining balance method

    b. future value method

    c. principal method

    d. interest method

7. Bonds that do not provide for any interest payments are called:

    a. interest-free bonds

    b. held-to-maturity securities

    c. sinking-fund bonds

    d. zero-coupon bonds

8. The principal of each bond is also called the:

    a. present value

    b. future value

    c. face value

    d. contract value

9. A special fund accumulated over the life of a bond issue and kept separate from other assets in order to provide for payment of bonds at maturity is called a(n):

    a. sinking fund

    b. investment fund

    c. retirement fund

    d. redemption fund

10. Held-to-maturity securities are classified on the balance sheet as:

    a. current assets

    b. investments

    c. long-term liabilities

    d. sinking-fund assets

TRUE/FALSE

Instructions: Indicate whether each of the following statements is true or false by placing a check mark in the appropriate column.

		True	**False**
1.	The interest rate specified on the bond indenture is called the contract rate or effective rate.	____	____
2.	If the market rate is lower than the contract rate, the bonds will sell at a discount.	____	____
3.	When zero-coupon bonds are issued, the discount is amortized as interest expense over the life of the bonds.	____	____
4.	The straight-line method of allocating bond discount provides for a constant amount of interest expense each period.	____	____
5.	Bonds that may be exchanged for other securities under certain conditions are called callable bonds.	____	____
6.	When cash is transferred to the sinking fund, it is recorded in an account called Sinking Fund Investments.	____	____
7.	A corporation's earnings per share can be affected by whether it finances its operations with common stock, preferred stock, or bonds.	____	____
8.	If the price paid to redeem bonds is below the bond carrying value, the difference is recorded as a gain.	____	____
9.	The balance in a discount on bonds payable account is reported in the balance sheet as a deduction from the related bonds payable.	____	____
10.	The present value of a future amount becomes less as the interest rate used to compute the present value increases.	____	____

EXERCISE 15-1

(1) Star Corp. issued $500,000 of 10-year, 12% bonds on June 1 of the current year with interest payable on June 1 and December 1. Journalize the entries to record the following selected transactions for the current year:

June 1. Issued the bonds for cash at face amount.
Dec. 1. Paid the interest on the bonds.

JOURNAL

PAGE

	DATE	DESCRIPTION	POST. REF.	DEBIT	CREDIT	
1						1
2						2
3						3
4						4
5						5
6						6
7						7
8						8

(2) On April 1, Turner Inc. issued $1,000,000 of 10-year, 11% bonds, with interest payable semiannually on April 1 and October 1 at an effective interest rate of 12%, receiving cash of $942,645. Journalize the entries to record the following selected transactions for the current year:

Apr. 1. Sold the bonds.
Oct. 1. Made first interest payment and amortized discount for six months using the straight-line method.

JOURNAL

PAGE

	DATE	DESCRIPTION	POST. REF.	DEBIT	CREDIT	
1						1
2						2
3						3
4						4
5						5
6						6
7						7
8						8
9						9
10						10
11						11

(3) On March 1, Sullivan Inc. issued $700,000 of 10-year, 11% bonds at an effective interest rate of 10%. Interest is payable semiannually on March 1 and September 1. Journalize the entries to record the following selected transactions for the current year. (Hint: To complete this portion of the exercise, you must compute the present value of the bonds at the issue date.)

Mar. 1. Sold the bonds.

Sept. 1. Made first interest payment and amortized premium for six months using the straight-line method.

JOURNAL PAGE

	DATE	DESCRIPTION	POST. REF.	DEBIT	CREDIT	
1						1
2						2
3						3
4						4
5						5
6						6
7						7
8						8
9						9
10						10
11						11
12						12

EXERCISE 15-2

Grimes Co. issued $5,000,000 of 10-year bonds at face value on January 1 of the current year.

Instructions:

(1) Assume the bonds are called at 101. Prepare the entry to record the redemption of the bonds.

JOURNAL PAGE

	DATE	DESCRIPTION	POST. REF.	DEBIT	CREDIT	
1						1
2						2
3						3
4						4
5						5

(2) Assume the bonds are purchased on the open market at 98. Prepare the entry to record the redemption of the bonds.

JOURNAL   PAGE

	DATE		DESCRIPTION	POST. REF.	DEBIT	CREDIT	
1							1
2							2
3							3
4							4
5							5

EXERCISE 15-3

Record the following transactions. (Omit explanations.)

(1) On October 1, 20XA, purchased for cash, as a long-term investment, $400,000 of Elgin Inc. 10% bonds at 99 plus accrued interest of $10,000.

(2) On December 31, 20XA received first semiannual interest.

(3) On December 31, 20XA amortized $120 discount on the bond investment.

(4) On December 1, 20XC, sold the bonds at 102 plus accrued interest of $16,667. The carrying amount of the bonds was $397,040 at the time of sale.

JOURNAL   PAGE

	DATE		DESCRIPTION	POST. REF.	DEBIT	CREDIT	
1							1
2							2
3							3
4							4
5							5
6							6
7							7
8							8
9							9
10							10
11							11
12							12
13							13
14							14
15							15

PROBLEM 15-1

Jackson Inc. issued $2,000,000 of 10-year, 11% bonds with interest payable semiannually.

Instructions:

(1) Compute (a) the cash proceeds and (b) the amount of premium or discount from the sale of the bonds if the effective interest rate is 11%.

(2) Compute (a) the cash proceeds and (b) the amount of premium or discount from the sale of the bonds if the effective interest rate is 12%.

(3) Compute (a) the cash proceeds and (b) the amount of premium or discount from the sale of the bonds if the effective interest rate is 10%.

PROBLEM 15-2

On December 31 of the current fiscal year, Palus Inc. issued $500,000 of 10-year, 11% bonds. The bonds were dated December 31 of the same year. Interest on the bonds is payable on June 30 and December 31 of each year.

Instructions:

Record the following transactions. (Omit explanations and round to the nearest dollar.)

(1) The bonds were sold for $531,161 on December 31 of the current year. The market rate of interest on this date was 10%.

(2) Interest was paid on June 30, and the related amount of bond premium was amortized, based on the straight-line method.

(3) Interest was paid on December 31, and the related amount of bond premium was amortized, based on the straight-line method.

(4) On December 31 (bonds are one year old), one-half of the bonds were redeemed at 103.

JOURNAL

PAGE

	DATE		DESCRIPTION	POST. REF.	DEBIT	CREDIT	
1							1
2							2
3							3
4							4
5							5
6							6
7							7
8							8
9							9
10							10
11							11
12							12
13							13
14							14
15							15
16							16
17							17
18							18
19							19
20							20
21							21
22							22

PROBLEM 15-3

On January 1 of the current fiscal year, Block Co. issued $1,000,000 of 10-year, 10% bonds. The bonds were dated January 1 of the same year. Interest on the bonds is payable on June 30 and December 31 of each year.

Instructions:

Record the following transactions. (Omit explanations and round to the nearest dollar.)

(1) The bonds were sold for $885,295 on January 1 of the current year. The market rate of interest on that date was 12%.

(2) Interest was paid on June 30, and the related amount of bond discount was amortized, based on the straight-line method.

(3) Interest was paid on December 31, and the related amount of bond discount was amortized, based on the straight-line method.

(4) On December 31 (bonds are one year old), one-half of the bonds were redeemed at 98.

JOURNAL   PAGE

	DATE	DESCRIPTION	POST. REF.	DEBIT	CREDIT	
1						1
2						2
3						3
4						4
5						5
6						6
7						7
8						8
9						9
10						10
11						11
12						12
13						13
14						14
15						15
16						16
17						17
18						18
19						19
20						20
21						21

16 Statement of Cash Flows

QUIZ AND TEST HINTS

The following hints may be helpful to you in preparing for a quiz or a test over the material covered in Chapter 16.

1. Study the new terminology introduced in this chapter for possible use in fill-in-the-blank, multiple-choice, or true/false questions.

2. You should be able to classify different types of cash flows as operating, investing, or financing activities. Test questions on this material often appear in a true/false or multiple-choice format.

3. Instructors may emphasize the indirect method, the direct method, or both methods of preparing the statement of cash flows. Adjust your studying to the method or methods that your instructor emphasized during class lectures and in homework assignments. You should be able to prepare a statement of cash flows using one or both methods. Often, instructors will include a partially completed statement of cash flows on an examination and require students to complete it. The Illustrative Problem is a good study aid for both the indirect and direct methods.

4. The work sheets for preparing the statement of cash flows appear in the Appendix to the chapter. Study the Appendix if your instructor has expressed a preference for use of the work sheet in preparing the statement of cash flows.

5. The statement of cash flows can be prepared by evaluating the changes in the noncash balance sheet accounts. Changes in the noncash current accounts are adjustments to net income in determining cash flows from operating activities under the indirect method. While changes in long-term assets are usually investing activities, changes in long-term liabilities and stockholders' equity paid in capital accounts are usually financing activities. The cash dividends are also financing activities.

MATCHING

Instructions: Match each of the statements below with its proper term. Some terms may not be used.

A. cash flows from financing activities
B. cash flows from investing activities
C. cash flows from operating activities
D. direct method

E. free cash flow
F. indirect method
G. statement of cash flows

_____ 1. The section of the statement of cash flows that reports cash flows from transactions affecting the equity and debt of the business.

_____ 2. The section of the statement of cash flows that reports cash flows from transactions affecting investments in noncurrent assets.

_____ 3. A summary of the major cash receipts and cash payments for a period.

_____ 4. A method of reporting the cash flows from operating activities as the difference between the operating cash receipts and the operating cash payments.

_____ 5. The section of the statement of cash flows that reports the cash transactions affecting the determination of net income.

_____ 6. A method of reporting the cash flows from operating activities as the net income from operations adjusted for all deferrals of past cash receipts and payments and all accruals of expected future cash receipts and payments.

_____ 7. The amount of operating cash flow remaining after replacing current productive capacity and maintaining current dividends.

FILL IN THE BLANK—PART A

Instructions: Answer the following questions or complete the statements by writing the appropriate words or amounts in the answer blanks.

1. The financial statement that reports a firm's major cash inflows and outflows for a period is the _____ _____ _____ _____.

2. The two alternative methods of reporting operating activities in the statement of cash flows are the _____ and _____ methods.

3–7. Indicate the section of the statement of cash flows in which each of the following would appear (answer operating activities, investing activities, or financing activities):

   3. Depreciation expense on equipment would appear under _____ activities.

   4. Sale of long-term investments would appear under _____ activities.

   5. Sale of equipment would appear under _____ activities.

   6. Issuance of bonds would appear under _____ activities.

   7. Sale of patents would appear under _____ activities.

8–10. This year, Young Company issued 500,000 shares of common stock, inventory increased by $20,000, and a new asset was purchased for $1,000,000. For each of these events, indicate whether net cash flows increased or decreased:

   8. Common stock issued. Net cash flows _____.

   9. Inventory increased. Net cash flows _____.

   10. New asset purchased. Net cash flows _____.

   11. Cash dividends of $35,000 were declared during the year. Cash dividends payable were $8,000 and $8,750 at the beginning and end of the year, respectively. The amount of cash flows for payment of dividends during the year is _____.

   12. The net income from operations was $75,000, and the only revenue or expense item not affecting cash was depreciation expense of $27,000. The amount of net cash flows from operating activities that would appear on the statement of cash flows is _____.

   13. A corporation purchased and retired 3,000 shares of its $50 par common stock, originally issued at par, for $65. Cash flows amounted to _____.

   14. If a fixed asset having a book value of $54,000 is sold (for cash) at a gain of $6,000, the total amount reported as a cash flow is _____.

   15. The $47,000 net income for the year included a loss of $2,500 on the sale of land. Exclusive of the effect of other adjustments, the amount of net cash flows from operating activities is _____.

   16. A corporation issued $1,000,000 of bonds payable at 104. Cash flow from this transaction was _____.

   17. If 15,000 shares of $20 par common stock were issued at 22, the amount to be reported in the cash flows from financing activities section of the statement of cash flows would be _____.

18. Cash flows resulting from the redemption of debt securities are classified in the statement of cash flows as related to _____ activities.

19. Jones Company had cash flow from operations of $75,000. This year, dividends paid amounted to $6,000, and the company purchased $9,000 in spare parts for machines used on the factory floor. Jones Company's free cash flow is _____.

20. A cash flow term for which an amount should not be reported in the financial statements because it could mislead readers is _____ _____ _____ _____.

FILL IN THE BLANK—PART B

Instructions: Answer the following questions or complete the statements by writing the appropriate words or amounts in the answer blanks.

1. The _____ method of analyzing operating cash flows begins with net income and adjusts it for revenues and expenses that do not involve the receipt or payment of cash.

2. The statement of cash flows groups cash flow activities as financing, investing, or _____.

3. When the _____ method of reporting cash flows is used, a supplemental schedule reconciling net income and net cash flow from operating activities must also be prepared.

4–8. Indicate the section of the statement of cash flows in which each of the following would appear (answer operating activities, investing activities, or financing activities):

4. Retirement of long-term debt would appear under _____ activities.

5. Sale of common stock would appear under _____ activities.

6. Net income would appear under _____ activities.

7. Payment of cash dividends would appear under _____ activities.

8. Purchase of equipment would appear under _____ activities.

9. _____ investing and financing activities that will affect future cash flows are reported in a separate schedule to the statement of cash flows.

10–11. Indicate whether each of the following items would be added to or deducted from net income on the schedule reconciling net income with cash flows from operating activities:

10. Increase in inventories would be _____ _____ net income.

11. Increase in accounts payable would be _____ _____ net income.

12. If a loss of $15,000 is incurred in selling (for cash) store equipment having a book value of $345,000, the total amount reported as a cash flow is _____.

13. A corporation issued $750,000 of 20-year bonds at 99½. Cash flows were _____.

14. A corporation purchased 25,000 shares of its $100 par common stock, originally issued at par, as treasury stock for $125. Cash flows were _____.

15. Cash dividends of $50,000 were declared during the year. Cash dividends payable were $8,500 and $12,500 at the beginning and end of the year, respectively. The amount of cash flows for the payment of dividends during the year is _____.

16. The net loss from operations was $15,000, and the only revenue or expense item not affecting cash was depreciation expense of $35,000. The amount to be reported as net cash flow from operating activities on the statement of cash flows is _____.

17. In preparing a statement of cash flows under the indirect method, it is efficient to analyze the _____ _____ account first.

18. The $55,000 net income for the year included a gain of $4,000 on the sale of equipment. Exclusive of the effect of other adjustments, the amount of net cash flows from operating activities is _____.

19. Cash flow for interest expense is included on the statement of cash flows as an _____ activity.

20. A measure of cash available for corporate purposes, after productive assets are maintained and the business owners are paid dividends, is called _____ _____ _____.

MULTIPLE CHOICE

Instructions: Circle the best answer for each of the following questions.

1. Which of the following is not one of the major sections of the statement of cash flows?

   a. cash flows from financing activities

   b. cash flows from selling activities

   c. cash flows from operating activities

   d. cash flows from investing activities

2. Noncash investing and financing activities which may have a significant effect on future cash flows are reported:

   a. in the statement of cash flows

   b. in a separate schedule to accompany the statement of cash flows

   c. in the retained earnings statement

   d. in a footnote accompanying the balance sheet

3. Under the indirect method, which of the following items must be deducted from reported net income to determine net cash flow from operating activities?

   a. depreciation of fixed assets

   b. decreases in current assets

   c. decreases in current liabilities

   d. loss on sale of equipment

4. During the past year, Lockhart Inc. declared $40,000 in cash dividends. If the beginning and ending balance of the dividends payable account was $12,000 and $10,000, respectively, what amount of cash paid for dividends will appear in the cash flow from financing activities section of the statement of cash flows?

   a. $30,000

   b. $38,000

   c. $40,000

   d. $42,000

5. Under the direct method, which of the following items must be added to operating expenses reported on the income statement to determine cash payments for operating expenses?

   a. increase in accrued expenses

   b. decrease in prepaid expenses

   c. increase in income taxes payable

   d. increase in prepaid expenses

6. An example of a cash flow from a financing activity is:
   a. receipt of cash from sale of land
   b. receipt of cash from collection of accounts receivable
   c. payment of cash for acquisition of treasury stock
   d. payment of cash for new machinery

7. Which of the following items appears first on the statement of cash flows prepared using the direct method?
   a. retained earnings
   b. cash received from customers
   c. net income
   d. depreciation

8. Which of the following would not be considered a noncash investing and financing activity in preparing a statement of cash flows?
   a. withdrawal of cash by the owner of a business
   b. issuance of common stock to retire long-term debt
   c. acquisition of a manufacturing plant by issuing bonds
   d. issuance of common stock in exchange for convertible preferred stock

9. To convert the cost of merchandise sold as reported on the income statement to cash payments for merchandise, the cost of merchandise sold is increased for the:
   a. increase in inventories
   b. increase in accounts payable
   c. decrease in inventories
   d. decrease in accounts receivable

10. Cash payments for income taxes are included on the statement of cash flows as:
    a. financing activities
    b. investing activities
    c. operating activities
    d. nonoperating activities

11. A loss on the sale of land is reflected on the statement of cash flows by:
    a. adding the loss to the book value of the land to determine the cash flow from investing activities.
    b. deducting the loss from net income to determine the cash flow from operating activities.
    c. deducting the loss from the book value of the land to determine the cash flow from investing activities.
    d. both b and c

12. Caldwell Company had cash flows from operating activities of $290,000. Depreciation expense for the year was $25,000. Cash flows for dividends totaled $32,000. Cash flows used for purchasing property, plant, and equipment were $60,000. It is determined that of this amount, $20,000 was used for expansion, while the remainder was used for replacing existing fixed assets. What is the free cash flow?

   a. $193,000

   b. $218,000

   c. $238,000

   d. $250,000

TRUE/FALSE

Instructions: Indicate whether each of the following statements is true or false by placing a check mark in the appropriate column.

	True	False
1. The statement of cash flows is required as part of the basic set of financial statements.		
2. Cash outflows from the payment of cash dividends is a type of financing activity.		
3. Cash receipts from the sale of fixed assets would be classified as a cash flow from investing activities.		
4. Under the direct method, depreciation is the first noncash account balance analyzed.		
5. Under the indirect method, increases in current liabilities are deducted from net income reported on the income statement in determining cash flows from operating activities.		
6. Noncash investing and financing activities that may have a significant effect on future cash flows should be included in a separate schedule to the statement of cash flows.		
7. The correct amount to include in cash flows from financing activities is cash dividends paid, not cash dividends declared.		
8. The analysis of retained earnings provides the starting point for determining cash flows from operating activities under the indirect method only.		
9. The direct method provides a more accurate figure of cash flows from operating activities than does the indirect method.		
10. Under the direct method, the increase in the trade receivables account is deducted from sales to determine the cash received from customers.		

EXERCISE 16-1

Instructions: Listed in the first column below are selected transactions and account balance changes of Mason Inc. for the current year. Indicate by placing a check mark in the appropriate column(s) how each of the items would be reported in the statement of cash flows.

Item	Cash Flows From			Schedule of Noncash Investing and Financing Activities
	Operating Activities	Investing Activities	Financing Activities	
1. Decrease in prepaid expenses...........				
2. Retirement of bonds				
3. Proceeds from sale of investments				
4. Increase in inventories				
5. Issuance of common stock.................				
6. Purchase of equipment				
7. Cash dividends paid				
8. Acquisition of building in exchange for bonds...				
9. Amortization of patents......................				
10. Amortization of discount on bonds payable				

EXERCISE 16-2

The net income reported on the income statement of Hunter Inc. for the current year was $150,000. Depreciation recorded on equipment and building amounted to $45,000 for the year. Balances of the current asset and current liability accounts at the beginning and end of the year are as follows:

	End of Year	Beginning of Year
Cash	$ 42,875	$ 36,250
Trade receivables (net)	147,500	137,500
Inventories	109,375	93,750
Prepaid expenses	9,250	11,875
Accounts payable (merchandise creditors)	57,000	40,000
Salaries payable	7,625	10,625

Instructions: Prepare the cash flows from operating activities section of the statement of cash flows using the indirect method.

EXERCISE 16-3

The income statement of Hunter Inc. for the current year is as follows:

Sales	$530,000
Cost of merchandise sold	130,000
Gross profit	$400,000
Operating expenses:	
Depreciation expense .... $ 45,000	
Other operating expenses 160,000	
Total operating expenses	205,000
Income before income tax	$195,000
Income tax	45,000
Net income	$150,000

Instructions: Using the income statement presented above and the account balances provided in Exercise 16-2, prepare the cash flows from operating activities section of the statement of cash flows using the direct method.

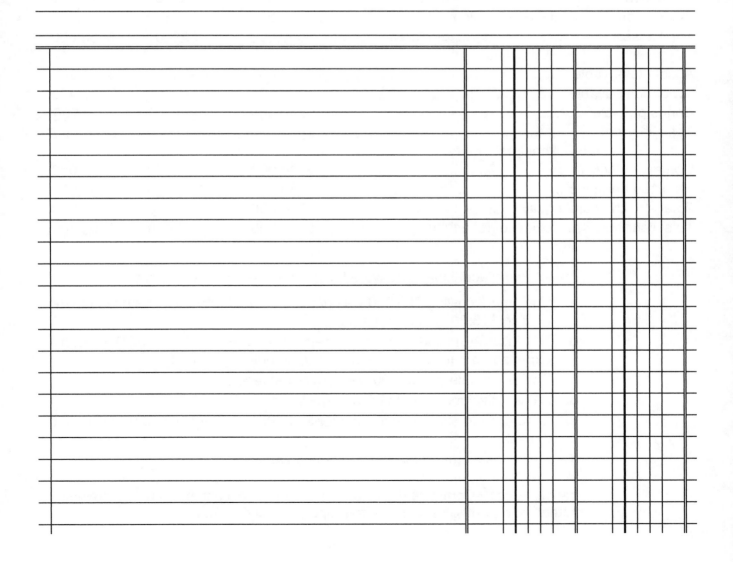

PROBLEM 16-1

The comparative balance sheet of Stellar Inc. at December 31, 2006, appears below.

Stellar Inc.
Comparative Balance Sheet
December 31, 2006 and 2005

	2006	2005	Increase Decrease*
Assets			
Cash	$ 84,000	$ 66,000	$ 18,000
Trade receivables (net)	156,000	144,000	12,000
Inventories	300,000	306,000	6,000*
Prepaid expenses	12,000	14,400	2,400*
Land	80,000	96,000	16,000*
Building	360,000	360,000	0
Accumulated depreciation—building	(120,000)	(91,200)	(28,800)
Equipment	180,000	102,000	78,000
Accumulated depreciation—equipment	(72,000)	(70,800)	(1,200)
Total assets	$980,000	$926,400	$ 53,600
Liabilities			
Accounts payable	$216,000	$208,800	$ 7,200
Dividends payable	24,000	21,600	2,400
Bonds payable	240,000	300,000	60,000*
Total liabilities	$480,000	$530,400	$ 50,400*
Stockholders' Equity			
Common stock	$140,000	$120,000	$ 20,000
Retained earnings	360,000	276,000	84,000
Total stockholders' equity	$500,000	$396,000	$104,000
Total liabilities and stockholders' equity	$980,000	$926,400	$ 53,600

The following additional data were taken from the records of Stellar Inc.:

a. Equipment costing $96,000 was purchased, and fully depreciated equipment costing $18,000 was discarded.

b. Net income, including gain on sale of land, was $114,000. Depreciation expense on equipment was $19,200; on building, $28,800.

c. Bonds payable of $60,000 were retired at face value.

d. A cash dividend of $30,000 was declared.

e. Land costing $36,000 was sold for $54,000, resulting in an $18,000 gain on the sale.

f. Land was acquired by issuing common stock, $20,000.

Instructions: Complete the following statement of cash flows using the indirect method of reporting cash flows from operating activities.

Stellar Inc.
Statement of Cash Flows
For Year Ended December 31, 2006

Cash flows from operating activities:

    Net income, per income statement .... $ _____

    Add: Depreciation .... $ _____

        Decrease in inventories ....   _____

        Decrease in prepaid expenses ....   _____

        Increase in accounts payable ....   _____   _____

                                   $ _____

    Deduct: Increase in trade receivables .... $ _____

          Gain on sale of land ....   _____   _____

    Net cash flow from operating activities .... $ _____

Cash flows from investing activities:

    Cash received from land sold .... $ _____

    Less cash paid for purchase of equipment ....   _____

    Net cash flow used for investing activities .....   _____

Cash flows from financing activities:

    Cash used to retire bonds payable .... $ _____

    Cash paid for dividends ....   _____

    Net cash flow used for financing activities .....   _____

Increase in cash .... $ _____

Cash, January 1, 2006 ....   _____

Cash, December 31, 2006 .... $ _____

Schedule of Noncash Investing and Financing Activities:

Acquisition of land by issuance of common stock .... $ _____

PROBLEM 16-2

The income statement of Stellar Inc. is provided below. Stellar's comparative balance sheet data were provided in Problem 16-1.

Instructions: Complete the statement of cash flows for Stellar Inc. using the direct method of reporting cash flows from operating activities.

Stellar Inc.
Income Statement
For Year Ended December 31, 2006

Sales		$575,000
Cost of merchandise sold		225,000
Gross profit		$350,000
Operating expenses:		
Depreciation expense	$ 48,000	
Other operating expenses	172,000	
Total operating expenses		220,000
Income from operations		$130,000
Other income:		
Gain on sale of land		18,000
Income before income tax		$148,000
Income tax		34,000
Net income		$114,000

Stellar Inc.
Statement of Cash Flows
For Year Ended December 31, 2006

Cash flows from operating activities:

Cash received from customers .... $ _____

Deduct: Cash payments for merchandise ...... $ _____

Cash payments for operating
expenses ....   _____

Cash payments for income tax ....   _____   _____

Net cash flow from operating activities .... $ _____

Cash flows from investing activities:

Cash received from land sold .... $ _____

Less cash paid for purchase of equipment ....   _____

Net cash flow used for investing activities .....   _____

Cash flows from financing activities:

Cash used to retire bonds payable .... $ _____

Cash paid for dividends ....   _____

Net cash flow used for financing activities .....   _____

Increase in cash .... $ _____

Cash, January 1, 2006 ....   _____

Cash, December 31, 2006 .... $ _____

Schedule of Noncash Investing and Financing Activities:

Acquisition of land by issuance of common stock .... $ _____

Schedule Reconciling Net Income with Cash Flows from Operating Activities:

Net income, per income statement .... $ _____

Add: Depreciation .... $ _____

Decrease in inventories ....   _____

Decrease in prepaid expenses ....   _____

Increase in accounts payable ....   _____   _____

   $ _____

Deduct: Increase in trade receivables .... $ _____

Gain on sale of land ....   _____   _____

Net cash flow provided by operating activities .... $ _____

Supporting calculations:

17 Financial Statement Analysis

QUIZ AND TEST HINTS

The following hints may be helpful to you in preparing for a quiz or a test over the material covered in Chapter 17.

1. When studying this chapter, you should focus primarily on the various analytical measures described and illustrated. These measures are also summarized in Exhibit 10 of the chapter. Pay special attention to each measure's computation, its use, and its classification as either a solvency or profitability measure. A good study aid for the computation of the measures is the Illustrative Problem at the end of the chapter.

2. Instructors will often include exam problems asking you to provide either a horizontal or vertical analysis. Be familiar with both of these.

3. Instructors often use true/false and multiple-choice questions to test this chapter. Such questions may require the computation of ratios or test your understanding of various terms introduced in the chapter.

MATCHING

Instructions: Match each of the statements below with its proper term. Some terms may not be used.

A.   accounts receivable turnover
B.   asset turnover
C.   common-size statement
D.   current ratio
E.   dividend yield
F.   dividends per share
G.   earnings per share (EPS) on common stock
H.   horizontal analysis
I.   inventory turnover
J.   leverage
K.   Management Discussion and Analysis
L.   number of days' sales in inventory
M.   number of days' sales in receivables

N.   number of times interest charges earned
O.   price-earnings (P/E) ratio
P.   profitability
Q.   quick assets
R.   quick ratio
S.   rate earned on common stockholders' equity
T.   rate earned on stockholders' equity
U.   rate earned on total assets
V.   ratio of fixed assets to long-term liabilities
W.   ratio of liabilities to stockholders' equity
X.   solvency
Y.   vertical analysis

_____   1.   The percentage of increases and decreases in corresponding items in comparative financial statements.

_____   2.   The sum of cash, receivables, and marketable securities.

_____   3.   The relationship between the volume of sales and inventory, computed by dividing the inventory at the end of the year by the average daily cost of goods sold.

_____   4.   The ability of a firm to pay its debts as they come due.

_____   5.   The relationship between credit sales and accounts receivable, computed by dividing the net accounts receivable at the end of the year by the average daily sales on account.

_____   6.   The relationship between credit sales and accounts receivable, computed by dividing net sales on account by the average net accounts receivable.

_____   7.   The tendency of the rate earned on stockholders' equity to vary from the rate earned on total assets because the amount earned on assets acquired through the use of funds provided by creditors varies from the interest paid to these creditors.

_____   8.   A financial statement in which all items are expressed only in relative terms.

_____   **9.**   A measure of profitability computed by dividing net income by total stockholders' equity.

_____   **10.**   The ratio of the market price per share of common stock, at a specific date, to the annual earnings per share.

_____   **11.**   A measure of the profitability of assets, without regard to the equity of creditors and stockholders in the assets.

_____   **12.**   The profitability ratio of net income available to common shareholders to the number of common shares outstanding.

_____   **13.**   The number of sales dollars earned for each dollar of total assets calculated as the ratio of sales to total assets.

_____   **14.**   The percentage analysis of component parts in relation to the total of the parts in a single financial statement.

_____   **15.**   A measure of profitability computed by dividing net income, reduced by preferred dividend requirements, by common stockholders' equity.

_____   **16.**   The ratio of current assets to current liabilities.

_____   **17.**   The relationship between the volume of goods sold and inventory, computed by dividing the cost of goods sold by the average inventory.

_____   **18.**   The ability of a firm to earn income.

_____   **19.**   An annual report disclosure that provides an analysis of the results of operations and financial condition.

FILL IN THE BLANK—PART A

Instructions: Answer the following questions or complete the statements by writing the appropriate words or amounts in the answer blanks.

1. Percentage analysis used to show the relationship of the component parts to the total in a single statement is called _____ _____.

2. _____ _____ focuses primarily on the relationship between operating results as reported in the income statement and resources available to the business as reported in the balance sheet.

3. The use of ratios showing the ability of an enterprise to pay its current liabilities is known as _____ _____ _____.

4. _____ is the ability of a business to meet its financial obligations as they come due.

5. _____-_____ statements are prepared in order to compare percentages of the current period with past periods, to compare individual businesses, or to compare one business with industry percentages published by trade associations or financial information services.

6. The ratio of current assets to current liabilities is called the _____ ratio.

7. The ratio of _____ _____ _____ _____ is a profitability measure that shows how effectively a firm utilizes its assets.

8. The ratio of the sum of cash, receivables, and marketable securities to current liabilities is called the _____ ratio.

9. _____ _____ _____ _____ _____ _____ is the ratio of net income available to common shareholders to the number of common shares outstanding.

10. The excess of the current assets of a business over its current liabilities is called _____ _____.

11. _____ _____ _____ is computed by dividing net sales by the average net accounts receivable.

12. _____ _____ is computed by dividing the cost of goods sold by the average inventory.

13. The ratio of _____ _____ _____ _____ is a solvency measure that indicates the margin of safety for creditors.

14. The number of times _____ _____ _____ _____ is a measure of the risk that dividends to preferred stockholders may not be paid.

15. If significant amounts of nonoperating income and expense are reported on the income statement, it may be desirable to compute the ratio of _____ _____ _____ to total assets as a profitability measure.

16. The rate earned on _____ _____ focuses only on the rate of profits earned on the amount invested by common stockholders.

17. Earnings per share and _____ per share on common stock are commonly used by investors in assessing alternative stock investments.

18. All publicly held corporations are required to have a(n) _____ _____ of their financial statements.

19. The ratio of _____ _____ _____ _____-_____ _____ is a solvency measure that indicates the margin of safety of the noteholders or bondholders.

20. In a vertical analysis of the income statement, each item is stated as a percent of _____ _____.

FILL IN THE BLANK—PART B

Instructions: Answer the following questions or complete the statements by writing the appropriate words or amounts in the answer blanks.

1. The percentage analysis of increases and decreases in corresponding items in comparative financial statements is called _____ _____.

2. The _____ _____ is a profitability measure that shows the rate of return to common stockholders in terms of cash dividend distributions.

3. The _____ _____ report describes the results of an independent examination of the financial statements.

4. The _____ _____ _____ _____ _____ _____ is computed by dividing the net accounts receivable at the end of the year by the average daily net sales.

5. The _____ _____ _____ _____ _____ _____ is computed by dividing the inventory at the end of the year by the average daily cost of goods sold.

6. The number of times _____ _____ _____ is a measure of the risk that interest payments will not be made if earnings decrease.

7. The _____ _____ _____ _____ _____ measures the profitability of total assets, without considering how the assets are financed.

8. The _____ _____ _____ _____ _____ is computed by dividing net income by average total stockholders' equity.

9. The difference between the rate earned by a business on the equity of its stockholders and the rate earned on total assets is called _____.

10. The _____-_____ ratio is computed by dividing the market price per share of common stock at a specific date by the annual earnings per share.

11. The _____ _____ _____ _____ section of a corporate annual report includes management's analysis of the results of operations, financial condition, and significant risks.

12. _____ _____ are cash and other current assets that can be quickly converted to cash.

13. In a(n) _____-_____ statement, all items are expressed as percentages.

14. _____ _____ focuses on the ability of a business to pay or otherwise satisfy its current and noncurrent liabilities.

15. The current ratio is sometimes called the working capital ratio or the _____ ratio.

16. Two measures that are useful for evaluating the management of inventory are the inventory turnover and the _____ _____ _____ _____ _____ _____.

17. A profitability measure often quoted in the financial press and normally reported in the income statement in corporate annual reports is _____ _____ _____.

18. All items in _____-_____ statements are expressed only in relative terms.

19. Quick assets normally include cash, marketable securities, and _____.

20. Beginning in 2004, the Sarbanes-Oxley Act will require independent auditors to attest to management's assessment of _____ _____.

MULTIPLE CHOICE

Instructions: Circle the best answer for each of the following questions.

1. Statements in which all items are expressed only in relative terms (percentages of a common base) are:

    a. relative statements

    b. horizontal statements

    c. vertical statements

    d. common-size statements

2. Which one of the following measures is a solvency measure?

    a. rate earned on total assets

    b. price-earnings ratio

    c. accounts receivable turnover

    d. ratio of net sales to assets

3. Based on the following data for the current year, what is the inventory turnover?

Net sales	$6,500,000
Cost of goods sold	$4,000,000
Inventory, beginning of year	$250,000
Inventory, end of year	$345,000
Accounts receivable, beginning of year	$175,000
Accounts receivable, end of year	$297,000

    a. 26.7

    b. 16

    c. 13.4

    d. 11.6

4. Based on the following data for the current year, what is the accounts receivable turnover?

Net sales	$6,500,000
Cost of goods sold	$4,000,000
Inventory, beginning of year	$250,000
Inventory, end of year	$345,000
Accounts receivable, beginning of year	$175,000
Accounts receivable, end of year	$297,000

    a. 37.1

    b. 27.5

    c. 21.8

    d. 17

5. Which of the following sections of corporate annual reports normally includes a statement concerning future prospects and risks?

   a. independent auditor's report

   b. footnotes to the financial statements

   c. management's internal control assertion

   d. management discussion and analysis

6. A measure used in evaluating the efficiency in collecting receivables is:

   a. working capital ratio

   b. quick ratio

   c. receivables/inventory ratio

   d. number of days' sales in receivables

7. Based on the following data for the current year, compute the number of times interest charges are earned.

Income before income tax.........	$510,000
Interest expense.......................	$30,000
Total assets.............................	$4,080,000

   a. 8

   b. 17

   c. 18

   d. 136

8. Based on the following data for the current year, what is the quick ratio?

Cash...	$27,000
Marketable securities................	$23,000
Receivables...............................	$90,000
Inventory	$105,000
Current liabilities.......................	$70,000

   a. 2.0

   b. 3.5

   c. 0.7

   d. 1.5

9. In vertical analysis of the balance sheet, each asset item is stated as a percent of total:

   a. current assets

   b. assets

   c. current liabilities

   d. liabilities

10. Based on the following data for the current year, what is the earnings per share on common stock?

Net income..	$460,000
Preferred dividends..................................	$50,000
Interest expense	$24,000
Shares of common stock outstanding	50,000

    a. $9.20

    b. $8.68

    c. $8.20

    d. $7.72

11. Companies with high P/E ratios are usually associated with:

    a. a high-dividend yield

    b. high-profit growth

    c. low long-term debt to total assets

    d. strong current position

12. Based on the following data, what is the rate earned on total assets?

Net income..	$240,000
Preferred dividends..................................	$60,000
Interest expense	$120,000
Interest income	$40,000
Average total assets	$1,000,000

    a. 18%

    b. 28%

    c. 30%

    d. 36%

TRUE/FALSE

Instructions: Indicate whether each of the following statements is true or false by placing a check mark in the appropriate column.

		True	False

1. In horizontal analysis of the income statement, each item is stated as a percentage of total sales............................... _____ _____

2. Solvency is the ability of a business to meet its financial obligations as they come due. .... _____ _____

3. The ratio of net sales to assets provides a solvency measure that shows the margin of safety of the debtholders. .... _____ _____

4. The quick ratio or acid-test ratio is the ratio of the sum of cash, receivables, and marketable securities to current liabilities.. _____ _____

5. Net sales divided by the year-end net accounts receivable gives the accounts receivable turnover............................... _____ _____

6. Net income minus the amount required for preferred dividends divided by the average common stockholders' equity gives the rate earned on common stockholders' equity.. _____ _____

7. The rate earned on total assets is calculated by subtracting interest expense from net income and dividing this sum by the average total assets. .... _____ _____

8. The tendency on the rate earned on stockholders' equity to vary disproportionately from the rate earned on total assets is referred to as financial leverage. .... _____ _____

9. A profitability measure that shows the rate of return to common stockholders in terms of cash dividends is known as the dividend yield on common stock. .... _____ _____

10. The excess of the current assets of an enterprise over its current liabilities and stockholders' equity is called working capital.. _____ _____

EXERCISE 17-1

Instructions: Using the condensed income statement information presented below, perform a vertical analysis for Delta Corp. for the years ending December 31, 2007 and 2006, stating each item as a percent of revenues.

	2007	Percent	2006	Percent
Revenues	$450,000		$389,000	
Costs and expenses:				
Cost of sales	$200,000		$176,000	
Selling and administrative expenses	100,000		73,000	
Total costs and expenses	$300,000		$249,000	
Earnings before income taxes	$150,000		$140,000	
Income taxes	34,500		32,200	
Net earnings	$115,500		$107,800	

EXERCISE 17-2

Instructions: Using the condensed balance sheet data presented below, perform a horizontal analysis for Carson Inc. on December 31, 2007. Indicate the amount and percent increase (decrease) in the columns provided.

			Increase (Decrease)	
	2007	2006	Amount	Percent
Current assets	$250,000	$219,500		
Fixed assets	435,000	401,600		
Intangible assets	43,700	46,000		
Current liabilities	88,000	80,000		
Long-term liabilities	225,000	250,000		
Common stock	214,000	167,600		
Retained earnings	200,000	170,000		

PROBLEM 17-1

Instructions: Using the information below and on the following page, perform a horizontal analysis for Nordic Inc. by filling in the Amount and Percent columns that are provided. (Round all percents to one decimal place.)

Nordic Inc.
Comparative Income Statement
For the Years Ended December 31, 2007 and 2006

			Increase (Decrease)	
	2007	2006	Amount	Percent
Sales	$690,500	$585,000		
Sales returns and allowances	25,500	23,000		
Net sales	$665,000	$562,000		
Cost of goods sold	420,000	330,000		
Gross profit	$245,000	$232,000		
Selling expenses	$ 43,000	$ 47,700		
Administrative expenses	31,000	31,000		
Total operating expenses	$ 74,000	$ 78,700		
Operating income	$171,000	$153,300		
Other income	13,000	16,400		
	$184,000	$169,700		
Other expense	58,000	53,500		
Income before income taxes	$126,000	$116,200		
Income taxes	34,000	32,400		
Net income	$ 92,000	$ 83,800		

Nordic Inc.
Comparative Balance Sheet
December 31, 2007 and 2006

Assets	2007	2006	Increase (Decrease) Amount	Percent
Cash	$ 76,000	$ 69,000		
Marketable securities	98,900	130,000		
Accounts receivable (net)	199,000	195,000		
Inventory	450,000	375,000		
Prepaid expenses	28,000	26,300		
Long-term investments	35,000	35,000		
Fixed assets (net)	871,000	835,000		
Intangible assets	18,000	22,800		
Total assets	$1,775,900	$1,688,100		
Liabilities				
Current liabilities	$ 129,000	$ 107,000		
Long-term liabilities	420,000	440,000		
Total liabilities	$ 549,000	$ 547,000		
Stockholders' Equity				
Preferred 3% stock, $100 par	$ 102,000	$ 93,000		
Common stock, $50 par	549,900	530,100		
Retained earnings	575,000	518,000		
Total stockholders' equity	$1,226,900	$1,141,100		
Total liabilities and stockholders' equity	$1,775,900	$1,688,100		

PROBLEM 17-2

Instructions: Using the information below and on the following page, perform a vertical analysis for Voyageur Inc. by filling in the Percent columns on the statements provided. (Round all percents to one decimal place.)

Voyageur Inc.
Comparative Balance Sheet
December 31, 2006 and 2005

	2006		2005	
Assets	Amount	Percent	Amount	Percent
Cash	$ 500,000		$ 425,000	
Marketable securities	200,000		185,000	
Accounts receivable (net)	680,000		575,000	
Inventory	860,000		740,000	
Prepaid expenses	104,000		95,000	
Long-term investments	450,000		410,000	
Fixed assets	6,556,000		5,420,000	
Total assets	$9,350,000	100%	$7,850,000	100%
Liabilities				
Current liabilities	$1,090,000		$1,050,000	
Long-term liabilities	2,150,000		2,050,000	
Total liabilities	$3,240,000		$3,100,000	
Stockholders' Equity				
Preferred 5% stock, $100 par	$ 350,000		$ 350,000	
Common stock, $10 par	2,550,000		2,550,000	
Retained earnings	3,210,000		1,850,000	
Total stockholders' equity	$6,110,000		$4,750,000	
Total liabilities and stockholders' equity	$9,350,000	100%	$7,850,000	100%

Voyageur Inc.
Income Statement
For the Year Ended December 31, 2006

	Amount	Percent
Sales	$12,800,000	
Sales returns and allowances	300,000	
Net sales	$12,500,000	100%
Cost of goods sold	7,550,000	
Gross profit	$ 4,950,000	
Selling expenses	$ 1,550,000	
Administrative expenses	825,000	
Total operating expenses	$ 2,375,000	
Operating income	$ 2,575,000	
Other income	125,000	
	$ 2,700,000	
Other expense (interest)	150,000	
Income before income taxes	$ 2,550,000	
Income taxes	937,000	
Net income	$ 1,613,000	

PROBLEM 17-3

Voyageur Inc. declared $250,000 of common stock dividends during 2006. The price of Voyageur's common stock on December 31, 2006 is $29.75.

Instructions: Using the data for Voyageur Inc. from Problem 17-2, determine the following amounts and ratios for 2006. (Round all ratios to one decimal point.)

	Calculation	Final Result
a. Working capital		
b. Current ratio		
c. Quick ratio		
d. Accounts receivable turnover		
e. Number of days' sales in receivables		
f. Inventory turnover		
g. Number of days' sales in inventory		
h. Ratio of fixed assets to long-term liabilities		
i. Ratio of liabilities to stockholders' equity		

	Calculation	Final Result
j. Number of times interest charges earned		
k. Number of times preferred dividends earned		
l. Ratio of net sales to assets		
m. Rate earned on total assets		
n. Rate earned on stockholders' equity		
o. Rate earned on common stockholders' equity		
p. Earnings per share on common stock		
q. Price-earnings ratio		
r. Dividends per share of common stock		
s. Dividend yield		

18 Introduction to Managerial Accounting and Job Order Cost Systems

QUIZ AND TEST HINTS

The following hints may be helpful to you in preparing for a quiz or a test over the material covered in Chapter 18.

1. This chapter introduces managerial accounting concepts and terminology. Instructors normally test this material using true/false and multiple-choice questions. Review the key terms on the next page using the Matching exercises.

2. It is important to be able to distinguish between direct and indirect materials, labor, and overhead; and between product and period costs.

3. You should be able to prepare journal entries for the recording of transactions using a job order cost system. Carefully review the chapter illustration of the job order cost system. Also, the Illustrative Problem provided in the text chapter is a useful study aid.

4. You should be able to calculate factory overhead application rates using activity bases.

MATCHING

Instructions: Match each of the statements below with its proper term. Some terms may not be used.

A. activity base
B. activity-based costing
C. controller
D. conversion costs
E. cost
F. cost accounting system
G. cost allocation
H. cost of goods sold
I. direct labor cost
J. direct materials cost
K. factory overhead cost
L. financial accounting
M. finished goods inventory
N. finished goods ledger
O. job cost sheet

P. job order cost system
Q. managerial accounting
R. materials inventory
S. materials ledger
T. materials requisitions
U. overapplied factory overhead
V. period costs
W. predetermined factory overhead rate
X. process cost system
Y. product costs
Z. receiving report
AA. time tickets
BB. work in process inventory

_____ 1. The chief management accountant of a division or other segment of a business.

_____ 2. The branch of accounting that is concerned with the recording of transactions using generally accepted accounting principles (GAAP) for a business or other economic unit and with a periodic preparation of various statements from such records.

_____ 3. The branch of accounting that uses both historical and estimated data in providing information that management uses in conducting daily operations, in planning future operations, and in developing overall business strategies.

_____ 4. A payment of cash (or a commitment to pay cash in the future) for the purpose of generating revenues.

_____ 5. A system used to accumulate manufacturing costs for decision-making and financial reporting purposes.

_____ 6. A type of cost accounting system that provides for a separate record of the cost of each particular quantity of product that passes through the factory.

_____ 7. All of the costs of operating the factory except for direct materials and direct labor.

_____ 8. The cost of materials that are an integral part of the finished product.

_____ 9. Wages of factory workers who are directly involved in converting materials into a finished product.

____ **10.** The combination of direct labor and factory overhead costs.

____ **11.** The three components of manufacturing cost: direct materials, direct labor, and factory overhead costs.

____ **12.** The direct materials costs, the direct labor costs, and the factory overhead costs that have entered into the manufacturing process but are associated with products that have not been finished.

____ **13.** An account in the work in process subsidiary ledger in which the costs charged to a particular job order are recorded.

____ **14.** The form or electronic transmission used by a manufacturing department to authorize the issuance of materials from the storeroom.

____ **15.** The cost of materials that have not yet entered into the manufacturing process.

____ **16.** The cost of the manufactured product sold.

____ **17.** The subsidiary ledger containing the individual accounts for each type of material.

____ **18.** The form or electronic transmission used by the receiving personnel to indicate that materials have been received and inspected.

____ **19.** The form on which the amount of time spent by each employee and the labor cost incurred for each individual job, or for factory overhead, are recorded.

____ **20.** The process of assigning indirect costs to a cost object, such as a job.

____ **21.** A measure of activity that is related to changes in cost and is used in the denominator in calculating the predetermined factory overhead rate to assign factory overhead costs to cost objects.

____ **22.** The rate used to apply factory overhead costs to the goods manufactured. The rate is determined from budgeted overhead cost and estimated activity usage data at the beginning of the fiscal period.

____ **23.** The amount of factory overhead applied in excess of the actual factory overhead costs incurred for production during a period.

____ **24.** An accounting framework based on determining the cost of activities.

____ **25.** The subsidiary ledger that contains the individual accounts for each kind of commodity or product produced.

____ **26.** The cost of finished products on hand that have not been sold.

____ **27.** Those costs that are used up in generating revenue during the current period and that are not involved in the manufacturing process.

____ **28.** A type of cost accounting system in which costs are accumulated by department or process within a factory.

FILL IN THE BLANK—PART A

Instructions: Answer the following questions or complete the statements by writing the appropriate words or amounts in the answer blanks.

1. _____ accounting information is prepared in accordance to generally accepted accounting principles for the use of government agencies, creditors, and public investors.

2. A(n) _____ department is one that provides services and assistance to other departments.

3. A(n) _____ is a payment of cash or its equivalent or the commitment to pay cash in the future for the purpose of generating revenues.

4. If a technician is directly involved in converting materials into finished products, his or her salary should be classified as a(n) _____ _____ cost.

5. Shark Company owns dozens of machines used on its product assembly line. Depreciation expenses for these assets should be classified as _____ _____ costs.

6. A company uses an electric furnace to melt iron ore. Costs of running the furnace, a necessary step in converting iron ore into steel, are known as factory burden or _____ costs.

7. Beta Company manufactures customized fiber-optic systems for NASA's space missions. If separate records are kept for the cost of each individual product that the company produces, Beta's accountants are using a(n) _____ _____ cost system.

8. If 1,000 springs are moved out of the storeroom and into the assembly line, the company's accounting system will reflect this flow of materials by _____ the materials account and _____ the work in process account.

9. With a job order cost system, factory workers record the hours they spend working on specific jobs using forms known as _____ _____.

10. Cost _____ is the process of assigning factory overhead costs to a cost object, such as a job.

11. Amber Company estimates that its total factory overhead costs will amount to $75,000 this year. If the company operated its only machine for 1,800 hours this year, the predetermined factory overhead rate per hour of machine time is _____ (round your answer to the nearest whole dollar).

12. A new method of allocating factory overhead costs using different rates corresponding to different activities is known as _____-_____ costing.

13. If the factory overhead account has a credit balance at the end of the period, the credit is described as _____ overhead.

14. During one month, Smith Company had a beginning debit balance of $13,200 in its factory overhead account. By the end of the month, the account had increased 75%, ending with a debit balance of $23,100. The company's accountant should investigate the overhead _____ to determine whether it needs revision.

15. One approach for disposing of the balance of factory overhead at the end of the year is to transfer the entire balance to the _____ _____ _____ _____ account.

16. Direct materials costs are debited to Work in Process based on data obtained from a summary of _____ _____.

17. The finished goods account is a controlling account with a subsidiary ledger called a finished goods ledger or _____ _____.

18. Expenses that are not incurred to support the manufacturing process, and which are incurred during the current period of time, are called _____ costs.

19. _____ expenses are incurred in the administration of the business and are not related to the manufacturing or selling functions.

20. A job order cost system is useful for both manufacturing and _____ businesses.

FILL IN THE BLANK—PART B

Instructions: Answer the following questions or complete the statements by writing the appropriate words or amounts in the answer blanks.

1. _____ accounting information includes both historical and estimated data used by a company to conduct daily operations, plan future operations, and develop an overall business strategy.

2. If a department is directly involved in manufacturing activities, it is known as a(n) _____ department.

3. Another title for a firm's chief management accountant is the firm's _____.

4. Woods Company, a manufacturer of air compressors, regularly buys flow regulators from an outside vendor. If they are an integral component for the final product, flow regulators should be classified as _____ _____ costs.

5. Labor costs that do not enter directly into the manufacture of a product are classified as _____ _____ and are recorded as factory overhead.

6. Managerial accountants gather information related to product costs. Managers frequently use this information to establish _____ _____, control operations, and develop financial statements.

7. Each inventory account, including Raw Materials Inventory, Work in Process Inventory, and Finished Goods Inventory, is _____ for all additions and _____ for all deductions.

8. Materials are released from the storeroom to the factory in response to materials _____ received from the production department.

9. Under the job order cost system, a(n) _____ _____ sheet is used to keep track of the resources consumed during the production of a specific customer order.

10. A summary of the _____ _____ at the end of each month is the basis for recording the direct and indirect labor costs incurred in production.

11. The measure used to allocate factory overhead is frequently called an activity base, allocation base, or _____ _____.

12. Green Company has a predetermined factory overhead rate of $3.75 per direct labor hour. If Green Company uses 1,500 hours as the activity cost driver for direct labor, the estimated total factory overhead cost is _____.

13. Gold Company uses $4.00 per hour as a cost driver for allocating direct labor costs as factory overhead. If Job A requires a total of 16½ hours of direct labor, the amount of factory overhead to be applied to Job A is _____.

14. Factory overhead costs applied to production are periodically debited to the _____ _____ _____ account and credited to the factory overhead account.

15. If the factory overhead account has a debit balance at the end of the period, the debit is described as _____ overhead.

16. Direct labor and factory overhead costs are debited to Work in Process based on data obtained from a summary of _____ _____.

17. Each account in the _____ _____ ledger contains cost data including the units manufactured, units sold, and the units on hand for each of the individual product types which the company manufactures.

18. Randolph Company completed 20,000 units at a cost of $175,000. The beginning finished goods inventory was 3,500 units, costing a total of $26,600. The cost of goods sold for 12,000 units, assuming a fifo cost flow, is _____.

19. _____ expenses are incurred in marketing the product and delivering the sold product to customers.

20. The Silver Agency sells advertising services. When the agency completes a job and a client is billed, the accountant will transfer the job's costs from a work in process account to a(n) _____ _____ _____ account.

MULTIPLE CHOICE

Instructions: Circle the best answer for each of the following questions.

1. For which of the following businesses would the process cost system be most appropriate?
   a. building contractor
   b. cookie processor
   c. plumber
   d. textbook publisher

2. The production department requests that materials be released from the storeroom to the factory based on which of the following forms?
   a. receiving report
   b. purchase order
   c. purchase requisition
   d. materials requisition

3. The amount of time spent by each employee on an individual job is recorded on a(n):
   a. clock card
   b. time ticket
   c. in-and-out card
   d. labor requisition

4. For which of the following businesses would the job order cost system be most appropriate?
   a. oil refinery
   b. meat processor
   c. a hotel
   d. textbook publisher

5. The subsidiary ledger that contains the individual accounts for each product produced is called the:
   a. work in process ledger
   b. finished goods ledger
   c. factory overhead ledger
   d. materials ledger

6. Which of the following would not be considered part of factory overhead costs?
   a. property taxes on factory building
   b. insurance on factory building
   c. sales salaries
   d. depreciation on factory plant and equipment

7. A characteristic of managerial accounting is:
   a. strict adherence to GAAP
   b. a focus on external decision maker needs
   c. a focus on management decision needs
   d. all of the above

8. The amount of actual factory overhead in excess of the factory overhead applied to production during a period is called:
   a. underapplied factory overhead
   b. excess factory overhead
   c. overapplied factory overhead
   d. excess capacity

9. A method of accumulating and allocating factory overhead costs to products using many overhead rates is:
   a. variable costing
   b. flexible costing
   c. activity-based costing
   d. service function allocation

10. Which of the following would be considered a staff position in a business organization?
    a. controller
    b. plant manager
    c. regional sales manager
    d. all of the above

11. Total budgeted factory overhead is $360,000, while the budgeted direct labor hours are 15,000 hours. Job 115 took 16 direct labor hours at a direct labor rate of $12 per hour. What is the amount of factory overhead applied to this job?
    a. $24
    b. $192
    c. $384
    d. $576

TRUE/FALSE

Instructions: Indicate whether each of the following statements is true or false by placing a check mark in the appropriate column.

		True	False
1.	A cost accounting system uses perpetual inventory procedures in accounting for manufacturing costs.	_____	_____
2.	A process cost system provides for a separate record of cost of each particular quantity of product that passes through the factory.	_____	_____
3.	A publishing company which produces a variety of different publication titles would normally use a process cost accounting system.	_____	_____
4.	The two principal types of cost systems for manufacturing operations are job order cost accounting and process cost accounting systems...	_____	_____
5.	Materials are transferred from the storeroom to the factory in response to purchase requisitions.	_____	_____
6.	As a practical matter, unless the total amount of the underapplied or overapplied overhead balance is large, it is transferred to Cost of Goods Sold.	_____	_____
7.	If the factory overhead account has a debit balance, the factory overhead is said to be overapplied.	_____	_____
8.	The subsidiary ledger that contains the individual accounts for each kind of product is the finished goods ledger.	_____	_____
9.	A manufacturer that uses a job order cost system for one product must use that system for all products.	_____	_____
10.	The predetermined factory overhead rate is calculated by relating the estimated amount of factory overhead for the period to an activity base.	_____	_____

EXERCISE 18-1

Instructions: Indicate the flow of costs through the perpetual inventory accounts and into the cost of goods sold account for a cost accounting system by connecting with arrows the letters that should be paired together in the following diagram.

Materials		Work in Process		Finished Goods	
Purchased	Dir. used a	e	Finished k	l	Sold m
	Indir. used b	f			
		g			

Wages Payable		Factory Overhead		Cost of Goods Sold	
Paid	Dir. used c	h	Applied j	n	
	Indir. used d	i			
		Other costs			

EXERCISE 18-2

Instructions: Indicate the flow of costs through a service business using a job order cost accounting system by connecting with arrows the letters that should be paired together in the following diagram.

Wages Payable		Work in Process		Cost of Services	
Paid	Dir. labor a	d	Completed	j	
	Indir. labor b	g	jobs i		

Supplies		Overhead		
Purchased	Used c	e	Applied h	
		f		
		Other costs		

EXERCISE 18-3

Foley Company operates two factories. It applies factory overhead to jobs on the basis of machine hours in Factory 1 and on the basis of direct labor costs in Factory 2. Estimated factory overhead costs, direct labor costs, and machine hours for the year and actual amounts for January are as follows:

	Factory 1	Factory 2
Estimated factory overhead cost for year	$65,000	$243,600
Estimated direct labor costs for year		$580,000
Estimated machine hours for year	20,000	
Actual factory overhead costs for January	$6,050	$20,100
Actual direct labor costs for January		$48,500
Actual machine hours for January	1,800	

Instructions:

(1) Determine the factory overhead rate for Factory 1. _____

(2) Determine the factory overhead rate for Factory 2. _____

(3) Journalize the entries to apply factory overhead to production in each factory for January.

JOURNAL   PAGE

	DATE	DESCRIPTION	POST. REF.	DEBIT	CREDIT	
1						1
2						2
3						3
4						4
5						5
6						6
7						7
8						8
9						9
10						10

(4) Determine the balance of the factory overhead account in each factory as of January 31, and indicate whether the amounts represent overapplied or underapplied factory overhead.

EXERCISE 18-4

D'Amato CPAs use a job order cost system to determine the cost of serving clients. The following client information is available for work completed in February of the current year:

Client	Service	Job Costs	Billable Hours	Job Cost per Billable Hour
Astor Co.	Audit	$11,040	240	
Brown, Inc.	Audit	11,750	250	
Singhal Co.	Audit	14,880	310	
Martinez Co.	Compilation	1,875	75	
Ng, Inc.	Compilation	2,040	85	
Wrigley Co.	Compilation	2,185	95	
Zane, Inc.	Compilation	4,950	110	
Howard Co.	Tax	10,395	165	
McNelly Co.	Tax	9,000	150	

Audit services relate to annual financial statement audits for the client businesses; compilation refers to bookkeeping services; and tax services relate to preparing and advising clients on tax returns.

Instructions:

(1) Determine the job cost per billable hour for each of the completed jobs in February and complete the table above.

(2) What can you determine from this information?

(3) Prepare the summary journal entry to close out the completed jobs for February.

JOURNAL   PAGE

	DATE	DESCRIPTION	POST. REF.	DEBIT	CREDIT	
1						1
2						2

PROBLEM 18-1

Instructions: Below are listed some transactions of Zintor Inc., which uses a job order cost accounting system. Prepare the entries to record the transactions. (Omit dates and explanations.)

(1) Purchased materials costing $60,000 and incurred prepaid expenses amounting to $5,300, all on account.

(2) Requisitioned $23,200 worth of materials to be used directly in production ($15,400 on Job 101 and $7,800 on Job 102) and $1,200 worth of materials to be used indirectly for repairs and maintenance.

(3) Factory labor used as follows: direct labor, $35,900; indirect labor, $2,700.

(4) Other costs incurred on account as follows: factory overhead, $12,200; selling expenses, $21,950; administrative expenses, $15,300. (Credit Accounts Payable.)

(5) Prepaid expenses expired as follows: factory overhead, $5,000; selling expenses, $800; administrative expenses, $600.

(6) The predetermined rate for the application of factory overhead to jobs (work in process) was 70% of direct labor cost. (See transaction 3.)

(7) The cost of jobs completed was $53,000.

(8) The sales on account for the period amounted to $160,000. The cost of goods sold was $110,000.

JOURNAL

PAGE

	DATE	DESCRIPTION	POST. REF.	DEBIT	CREDIT	
1						1
2						2
3						3
4						4
5						5
6						6
7						7
8						8
9						9
10						10
11						11
12						12
13						13
14						14
15						15
16						16

JOURNAL

PAGE

	DATE		DESCRIPTION	POST. REF.	DEBIT	CREDIT	
1							1
2							2
3							3
4							4
5							5
6							6
7							7
8							8
9							9
10							10
11							11
12							12
13							13
14							14
15							15
16							16
17							17
18							18
19							19
20							20
21							21
22							22
23							23
24							24
25							25
26							26
27							27
28							28
29							29
30							30
31							31
32							32
33							33
34							34
35							35
36							36

PROBLEM 18-2

Instructions: Post the following transactions to the proper T accounts below. Identify the postings with the transactions by using the number preceding each transaction.

(1) Purchased materials for $78,000 cash.

(2) Requisitioned $56,000 worth of direct materials and $2,400 worth of indirect materials from the storeroom.

(3) The factory labor cost for the period amounted to $75,000. (Credit Wages Payable.) The labor cost is determined to be $70,000 direct labor, $5,000 indirect labor.

(4) Paid $12,500 for factory overhead costs.

(5) Applied $24,000 of factory overhead to work in process.

(6) The cost of jobs completed amounted to $164,000.

	Cash	
Bal.	135,400	

	Finished Goods	
Bal.	50,800	

	Work in Process	
Bal.	33,800	

	Materials	
Bal.	18,000	

	Factory Overhead	
Bal.	3,000	

	Wages Payable	

19 Process Cost Systems

QUIZ AND TEST HINTS

The following hints may be helpful to you in preparing for a quiz or a test over the material covered in Chapter 19.

1. The focus of this chapter is accounting for manufacturing operations using a process cost system. You can expect to see at least one problem requiring you to prepare journal entries for process costing or a cost of production report. The illustration of process costing in the chapter and the Illustrative Problem are good study aids.

2. You have to be able to compute equivalent units of production and cost per equivalent unit. In addition to a problem requiring the preparation of a cost of production report, expect to see some multiple-choice questions requiring equivalent unit computations.

3. Terminology is important. Study the highlighted terms in the chapter for possible true/false or multiple-choice questions. As a review of the key terms, do the Matching exercises included in this Study Guide.

MATCHING

Instructions: Match each of the statements below with its proper term. Some terms may not be used.

A.   cost of production report
B.   cost per equivalent unit
C.   equivalent units of production
D.   first-in, first-out (FIFO) cost method
E.   just-in-time processing

F.   manufacturing cells
G.   oil refinery
H.   process cost system
I.   process manufacturers
J.   transferred-out costs
K.   yield

_____   **1.**   A type of cost system that accumulates costs for each of the various departments within a manufacturing facility.

_____   **2.**   Manufacturers that use large machines to process a continuous flow of raw materials through various stages of completion into a finished state.

_____   **3.**   The number of production units that could have been completed within a given accounting period, given the resources consumed.

_____   **4.**   A method of inventory costing that assumes the unit product costs should be determined separately for each period in the order in which the costs were incurred.

_____   **5.**   The rate used to allocate costs between completed and partially completed production.

_____   **6.**   A report prepared periodically by a processing department, summarizing the costs incurred by the department and the allocation of those costs between completed and incomplete production.

_____   **7.**   A measure of materials usage efficiency.

_____   **8.**   A grouping of processes where employees are cross-trained to perform more than one function.

_____   **9.**   A processing approach that focuses on eliminating time, cost, and poor quality within manufacturing and nonmanufacturing processes.

FILL IN THE BLANK—PART A

Instructions: Answer the following questions or complete the statements by writing the appropriate words or amounts in the answer blanks.

1. A _____ (specify process or job order) cost system would be more appropriate for a shipbuilding company.

2. A _____ (specify process or job order) cost system would be more appropriate for an oil refining company.

3. Direct materials, direct labor, and _____ _____ are the three elements of product costs.

4. In a process cost system, the amount of work in process inventory is determined by _____ costs between completed and partially completed units within a department.

5. In a process cost system, product cost flows should reflect the _____ flow of materials passing through the manufacturing process.

6. Smith Company refines oil. If the company sells 5,000 gallons of oil, should the finished goods account be debited or credited?

    _____

7. The first step in determining the cost of goods completed and the ending inventory valuation is to determine the _____ _____ _____ _____ _____.

8. Omega Department had a beginning in-process inventory of 24,000 pounds. During the month, 58,500 pounds were completed and transferred to another department. The ending in-process inventory was 16,000 pounds. During the period, _____ pounds were started and completed.

9. The number of units that could have been completed during a given accounting period is called the _____ units of production.

10–13. Department G had 8,000 units in work in process that were 40% converted at the beginning of the period at a cost of $19,450. During the period, 18,000 units of direct materials were added at a cost of $54,000, 18,500 units were completed, and 7,500 units were 40% completed. Direct labor was $32,500, and factory overhead was $66,320 during the period.

10. The number of conversion equivalent units was _____.

11. The total conversion costs were _____.

12. The conversion costs of the units started and completed during the period were _____.

13. The conversion costs of the 7,500 units in process at the end of the period were _____.

14. The _____ _____ _____ _____ is determined by dividing the direct materials and conversion costs by the respective total equivalent units for direct materials and conversion costs.

15. The oxidation department had $68,000 of direct materials cost and 128 direct materials equivalent units. The cost per equivalent unit of direct materials is _____.

16. Department Z had $99,510 of conversion costs and $5.35 of cost per equivalent unit of conversion. The number of conversion equivalent units is _____.

17. The _____ _____ _____ report summarizes (1) the units for which the department is accountable and their disposition, and (2) the costs charged to the department and their allocation.

18. The ratio of the materials output quantity to the materials input quantity is known as the _____.

19. A production philosophy focused on reducing production time and costs and eliminating poor quality is known as _____-_____-_____ processing.

20. Separate process functions combined into "work centers" are sometimes called _____ _____.

FILL IN THE BLANK—PART B

Instructions: Answer the following questions or complete the statements by writing the appropriate words or amounts in the answer blanks.

1. A _____ (specify process or job order) cost system would be more appropriate for a company that continually produces a homogenous product.

2. A _____ (specify process or job order) cost system would be more appropriate for a company that builds specialized products according to individual contracts with its customers.

3. In a process cost system, product costs are accumulated by _____.

4. The two elements of conversion costs are _____ _____ and _____ _____.

5. Costs transferred from one department to another normally include direct materials and _____ costs.

6. When the first units entering a production process are the first to be completed, the flow of production would be described as a(n) _____ flow.

7. The last step in determining the cost of goods completed and the ending inventory valuation is "to allocate costs to transferred and _____ _____ units."

8. The three categories of units to be assigned costs for an accounting period are (1) units in beginning in-process inventory, (2) units started and completed during the period, and (3) units in _____ ___- _____ _____.

9. This month, Alpha Department had 100 units in beginning in-process inventory that were completed during the month, 300 units started and completed, and 200 units in ending in-process inventory. In order to reflect this month's activity, _____ total units should be assigned costs.

10. The number of units in production during a period, regardless of whether they are completed or not, is called the _____ units of production.

11. On April 1, Department X had a beginning in-process inventory of 300 gallons of a special chemical. The 300 gallons should be counted as equivalent units of direct materials for the month of _____.

12. Conversion costs are usually incurred _____ throughout a process.

13. Department B had a beginning work in process inventory of 200 half-finished assemblies. This month the department completed 550 assemblies, leaving 120 half-finished assemblies in ending work in process inventory. The equivalent units for conversion costs are _____.

14. Echo Department had $25,000 in conversion costs and 1,000 conversion equivalent units. The cost per equivalent unit of conversion is _____.

15. Department 2 had $55,000 of conversion costs and $6.25 of cost per equivalent unit of conversion. The number of conversion equivalent units is _____.

16. The cost of transferred and partially completed units is calculated by _____ equivalent unit rates by the number of equivalent units.

17–19. A department calculated that it had 600 equivalent units for direct materials and 300 equivalent units for conversion in this month's ending inventory. Equivalent cost per unit of direct materials was $17.25, and equivalent cost per unit of conversion was $5.30.

17. The cost of direct materials in ending inventory is _____.

18. The cost of conversion in ending inventory is _____.

19. The total cost of ending inventory is _____.

20. In a JIT system, each work center may be connected to the other work centers through information contained on _____, which is a Japanese term for cards.

MULTIPLE CHOICE

Instructions: Circle the best answer for each of the following questions.

1. In the manufacture of 10,000 equivalent units of product for a period, direct materials cost incurred was $200,000, direct labor cost incurred was $75,000, and applied factory overhead cost was $185,000. What was the unit conversion cost for the period?

   a. $7.50

   b. $18.50

   c. $26

   d. $46

2. The Finishing Department had 6,000 units, 1/3 completed at the beginning of the period; 16,000 units were transferred to the Finishing Department from the Sanding Department during the period; and 2,500 units were 1/5 completed at the end of the period. What is the total units to be accounted for on the cost of production report for the Finishing Department for the period?

   a. 13,500

   b. 15,500

   c. 18,500

   d. 22,000

3. Material B is added after the processing is 60% completed. There were 2,400 units completed during the period. There were 300 units in beginning inventory (50% completed) and 100 units in process at the end of the period (20% completed). What was the total equivalent units of production for Material B?

   a. 2,400

   b. 2,200

   c. 2,500

   d. 2,700

4. If the Weaving Department had 900 units, 40% completed, in process at the beginning of the period; 9,000 units were completed during the period; and 600 units were 10% completed at the end of the period, what was the number of conversion equivalent units of production for the period using the fifo cost method?

   a. 8,520

   b. 8,700

   c. 8,900

   d. 9,060

5. The number of units that could have been completed within a given accounting period is called the:
   a. equivalent units of production
   b. optimal units of production
   c. theoretical units of production
   d. processing capacity

6. The combined direct labor and factory overhead per equivalent unit is called the:
   a. prime cost per unit
   b. processing cost per unit
   c. conversion cost per unit
   d. combined cost per unit

7. The ratio of the materials output quantity to the materials input quantity is the:
   a. materials consumption ratio
   b. materials absorption ratio
   c. capacity constraint
   d. yield

8. Cards that contain information to help work centers communicate with one another in a just-in-time processing system are called:
   a. pillars
   b. kanbans
   c. JIT cards
   d. flow cards

9. Work centers in a just-in-time processing system where processing functions are combined are:
   a. JIT centers
   b. combined processing centers
   c. master cells
   d. manufacturing cells

10. There were 2,000 pounds in process at the beginning of the period in the Finishing Department. The department received 22,000 pounds from the Blending Department during the period, and 3,000 pounds were in process at the end of the period. How many pounds were completed by the Finishing Department during the period?
    a. 27,000
    b. 24,000
    c. 21,000
    d. 19,000

11. At the beginning of the period, there were 3,000 tons in process, 30% complete with respect to materials. There were 12,000 tons transferred into the process, of which 1,000 tons were remaining in work in process at the end of the period. The ending work in process was 60% complete as to materials. Materials were introduced at the beginning of the process and had a total cost of $415,000. What was the cost per equivalent unit for materials?

    a. $28.23

    b. $30.29

    c. $33.20

    d. $33.74

12. The costs per equivalent unit for materials and conversion costs were $18 and $6, respectively. The 5,000 whole units of ending work in process were 40% complete with respect to processing. Materials were added at the beginning of the process. What was the cost of the ending work in process?

    a. $48,000

    b. $102,000

    c. $108,000

    d. $120,000

TRUE/FALSE

Instructions: Indicate whether each of the following statements is true or false by placing a check mark in the appropriate column.

		True	False
1.	The number of units that could have been completed within a given accounting period is referred to as the equivalent units of production.	____	____
2.	A report prepared periodically for each processing department and which summarizes (a) the units for which the department is accountable and the disposition of those units and (b) the production costs incurred by the department and the allocation of those costs is called a cost of production report.	____	____
3.	The accumulated costs transferred from preceding departments and the costs of direct materials and direct labor incurred in each processing department are debited to the related work in process accounts.	____	____
4.	The most important use of the cost of production report is to schedule production.	____	____
5.	Direct labor and factory overhead are referred to as primary costs.	____	____
6.	Equivalent units for materials and conversion costs are usually determined separately.	____	____
7.	A cost of production report will normally list costs in greater detail to help management isolate problems and opportunities.	____	____
8.	If a material is introduced halfway through processing and the beginning inventory is 40% complete, then the equivalent units for beginning inventory for this material for the current period will be zero (assuming fifo).	____	____
9.	The first-in, first-out cost method is based on the assumption that the work in process at the beginning of the current period was started and completed during the current period.	____	____
10.	If the work in process at the beginning of the period is 400 gallons, 1,600 gallons were started during the period, and 300 gallons remained in process at the end of the period, then the units started and completed are 1,700 gallons.	____	____

EXERCISE 19-1

Instructions: Presented below is a diagram of the cost flows for Cortex Company, a process manufacturer. Cortex has two processing departments. All materials are placed into production in Department 1. In the spaces beneath the diagram identify each letter contained in the diagram.

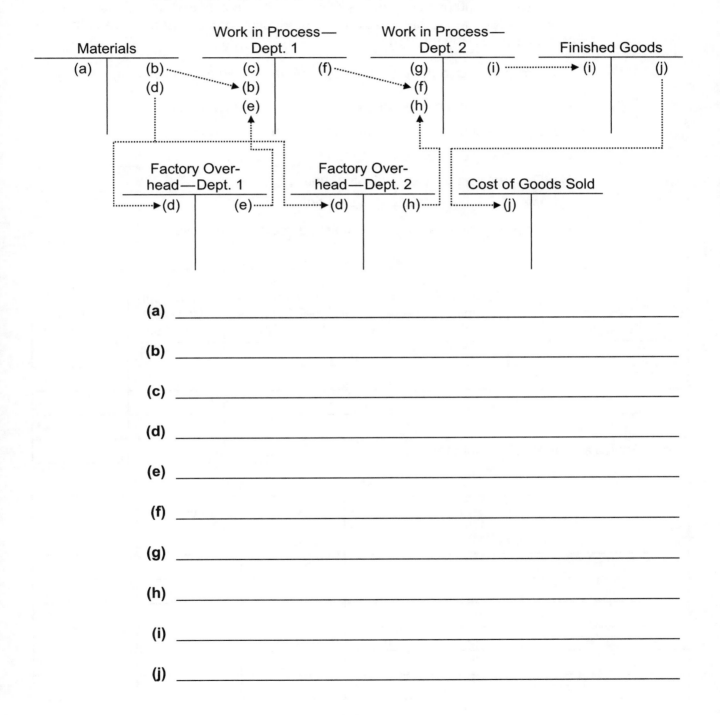

(a) _____

(b) _____

(c) _____

(d) _____

(e) _____

(f) _____

(g) _____

(h) _____

(i) _____

(j) _____

EXERCISE 19-2

Ellis Company started April with 12,000 units in process that were 30% complete at a cost of $32,600. During April, the following costs were incurred: direct materials, $148,800; direct labor, $141,000; and factory overhead, $185,400. During April, 66,000 units were completed and transferred to finished goods. There were 8,000 units in process that were 20% completed at April 30. All materials are added at the beginning of the production process and conversion costs are incurred evenly throughout.

Instructions: Use the work sheet presented below to determine the following:

(1)   Equivalent units of production for materials costs .... _____

(2)   Equivalent units of production for conversion costs .... _____

(3)   Materials cost per equivalent unit .... $ _____

(4)   Conversion cost per equivalent unit .... $ _____

(5)   Work in process inventory, April 30 .... $ _____

(6)   Cost of goods transferred to finished goods warehouse . $ _____

Units	Total Whole Units	% Material to be Completed in April	% Conversion to be Completed in April	(1) Equivalent Units for Materials	(2) Equivalent Units for Conversion
Total Equivalent Units to Account for					

Costs	(3) Direct Materials	(4) Conversion Costs	Total
(6)			
(5)			
Total Costs Charged to Department			

EXERCISE 19-3

The following work in process account information was obtained from the Cooking Department of Southern Soup Company. All direct materials are introduced at the beginning of the process, and conversion costs are incurred evenly throughout the process. The beginning inventory consists of $75,600 of direct materials and $20,160 of conversion costs

ACCOUNT   *Work In Process—Cooking Dept.*   ACCOUNT NO. _____

DATE		ITEM	DEBIT	CREDIT	BALANCE DEBIT	BALANCE CREDIT
April	1	Bal., 4,200 units, 40% completed			95 7 6 0	
	30	Direct materials, 35,000 units	647 5 0 0		743 2 6 0	
	30	Direct labor	202 1 0 0		945 3 6 0	
	30	Factory overhead	247 7 2 0		1193 0 8 0	
	30	Goods transferred, 36,000 units		1104 4 8 0	88 6 0 0	
	30	Bal., 3,200 units, 75% completed			88 6 0 0	

Instructions: Determine the cost per equivalent unit of direct materials and conversion costs.

	WHOLE UNITS	EQUIVALENT UNITS DIRECT MATERIALS	EQUIVALENT UNITS CONVERSION

	COSTS DIRECT MATERIALS	COSTS CONVERSION

PROBLEM 19-1

Mirror Inc. is a small manufacturing company that uses a process cost accounting system. The firm has two processing departments.

Instructions: Record the following transactions in the journals provided on the following pages. Any indirect cost such as indirect labor or indirect material incurred by a department should be charged to the department's overhead account. (Omit dates and explanations.)

(1) Materials purchased on account, $210,000.

(2) The following materials were requisitioned: Department 10, direct, $18,000; Department 10, indirect, $2,100; Department 20, direct, $24,000; Department 20, indirect, $600.

(3) The labor used by factory departments was as follows: Department 10, direct, $25,000; Department 10, indirect, $2,700; Department 20, direct, $20,000; Department 20, indirect, $2,700.

(4) The following other costs and expenses were incurred on account: factory overhead, Department 10, $1,500; factory overhead, Department 20, $2,250.

(5) Depreciation expenses were as follows: Department 10, $4,200; Department 20, $3,150.

(6) Factory overhead costs were applied to work in process on the basis of 102% of the direct labor cost of Department 10 and 75% of the direct labor cost of Department 20. (See transaction 3.)

(7) There was no beginning or ending inventory in Department 10. All costs accumulated in Department 10 work in process were transferred to Department 20.

(8) The work in process in Department 20 at the end of the period amounted to $12,500. The balance (representing 25,000 units) was transferred to finished goods. (There was no beginning inventory of work in process.)

(9) Sales of 21,000 units for $160,000 on account were made during the month. The cost of goods sold was $122,000.

JOURNAL

	DATE		DESCRIPTION	POST. REF.	DEBIT	CREDIT	
1							1
2							2
3							3
4							4
5							5
6							6
7							7
8							8
9							9
10							10
11							11
12							12
13							13
14							14
15							15
16							16
17							17
18							18
19							19
20							20
21							21
22							22
23							23
24							24
25							25
26							26
27							27
28							28
29							29
30							30
31							31
32							32
33							33
34							34
35							35
36							36

JOURNAL   PAGE

	DATE		DESCRIPTION	POST. REF.	DEBIT	CREDIT	
1							1
2							2
3							3
4							4
5							5
6							6
7							7
8							8
9							9
10							10
11							11
12							12
13							13
14							14
15							15
16							16
17							17
18							18
19							19
20							20
21							21
22							22
23							23
24							24
25							25

PROBLEM 19-2

Instructions: Prepare a cost of production report for the Polishing Department of Ivy Inc. for March of the current fiscal year using the fifo cost method and the following data:

Inventory, March 1, 5,000 units, 30% completed	$ 37,025
Materials from the Cutting Department, 21,000 units	105,000
Direct labor for March	176,140
Factory overhead for March	120,000
Inventory, March 31, 6,000 units, 60% completed	—

Ivy Inc.

Cost of Production Report—Polishing Department

For the Month Ended March 31, 20--

UNITS	WHOLE UNITS	EQUIVALENT UNITS	
		DIRECT MATERIALS	CONVERSION

Ivy Inc.

Cost of Production Report—Polishing Department (Concluded)

For the Month Ended March 31, 20--

COSTS	COSTS		
	DIRECT MATERIALS	CONVERSION	TOTAL COSTS

20 Cost Behavior and Cost-Volume-Profit Analysis

QUIZ AND TEST HINTS

The following hints may be helpful to you in preparing for a quiz or a test over the material covered in Chapter 20.

1. Many new terms are introduced in this chapter. You can expect true/false, multiple-choice, or matching questions testing your knowledge of these terms. Review the key terms in the next section by completing the Matching exercises.

2. Expect some multiple-choice questions related to the behavior of costs. For example, you might be required to classify various types of costs (direct materials, for example) as variable, fixed, or mixed for the activity of units produced. You might also have to use the high-low method to separate a mixed cost into its variable and fixed costs components.

3. The major focus of this chapter is the computation of break-even sales (units) and sales (units) required to achieve a target profit. These computations are based upon the contribution margin concept. In your studying, focus on the mathematical approach to cost-volume-profit analysis. Instructors often do not require preparation of a cost-volume-profit or a profit-volume chart.

4. The special cost-volume-profit relationships (margin of safety and operating leverage) and the assumptions of cost-volume-profit analysis often appear in the form of true/false or multiple-choice questions on tests.

MATCHING

Instructions: Match each of the statements below with its proper term. Some terms may not be used.

A.	absorption costing	**K.**	margin of safety
B.	activity bases (drivers)	**L.**	mixed cost
C.	break-even point	**M.**	operating leverage
D.	contribution margin	**N.**	profit-volume chart
E.	contribution margin ratio	**O.**	relevant range
F.	cost behavior	**P.**	sales mix
G.	cost-volume-profit analysis	**Q.**	unit contribution margin
H.	cost-volume-profit chart	**R.**	variable costing
I.	fixed costs	**S.**	variable costs
J.	high-low method		

_____ **1.** Costs that vary in total dollar amount as the level of activity changes.

_____ **2.** Sales less variable cost of goods sold and variable selling and administrative expenses.

_____ **3.** A measure of activity that is thought to cause a cost; used in analyzing and classifying cost behavior.

_____ **4.** The percentage of each sales dollar that is available to cover the fixed costs and provide income from operations.

_____ **5.** Costs that tend to remain the same in amount, regardless of variations in the level of activity.

_____ **6.** The range of activity over which changes in cost are of interest to management.

_____ **7.** A technique that uses the highest and lowest total cost as a basis for estimating the variable cost per unit and the fixed cost component of a mixed cost.

_____ **8.** The level of business operations at which revenues and expired costs are equal.

_____ **9.** The systematic examination of the relationships among costs, expenses, sales, and operating profit or loss.

_____ **10.** The manner in which a cost changes in relation to its activity base (driver).

_____ **11.** A chart used to assist management in understanding the relationships among costs, expenses, sales, and operating profit or loss.

_____ **12.** The dollars available from each unit of sales to cover fixed costs and provide income from operations.

_____ **13.** A chart used to assist management in understanding the relationship between profit and volume.

____ **14.** A cost with both variable and fixed characteristics.

____ **15.** The difference between current sales revenue and the sales at the break-even point.

____ **16.** The relative distribution of sales among the various products available for sale.

____ **17.** A measure of the relative mix of a business's variable costs and fixed costs, computed as contribution margin divided by income from operations.

____ **18.** A method of reporting variable and fixed costs that includes only the variable manufacturing costs in the cost of the product.

FILL IN THE BLANK—PART A

Instructions: Answer the following questions or complete the statements by writing the appropriate words or amounts in the answer blanks.

1. Activities that are thought to cause a cost to be incurred are called

   _____ _____.

2. The range of activity over which the changes in a cost are of interest to management is referred to as the _____ _____.

3. In terms of cost behavior, direct materials and labor costs are generally classified as _____ _____.

4. Straight-line depreciation of factory equipment and insurance on factory plant are examples of _____ (variable, fixed, or mixed) costs.

5. Rental of equipment at $2,000 per month plus $1 for each machine hour used over 10,000 hours is a type of _____ (variable, fixed, or mixed) cost.

6. The high-low method is a cost estimate technique that may be used to separate _____ (variable, fixed, or mixed) costs.

7. A management accounting reporting system that includes only variable manufacturing costs in the product cost is known as variable costing or

   _____ _____.

8. _____-_____-_____ analysis is the systematic examination of the relationship among selling prices, sales and production volume, costs, expenses, and profits.

9. Sales minus variable costs divided by sales is the calculation of the

   _____ _____ _____.

10. Given a selling price per unit of $20, variable costs per unit of $10, and fixed costs of $95,000, the break-even point in sales units is _____.

11. An increase in fixed costs will cause the break-even point to _____.

12. Increases in the price of direct materials and the wages of factory workers will cause the break-even point to _____.

13. If fixed costs are $200,000 and the unit contribution margin is $40, the sales volume in units needed to earn a target profit of $100,000 is _____.

14. A cost-volume-profit chart is also called a(n) _____-_____ chart.

15. On a cost-volume-profit chart, units of sales are plotted along the _____ axis.

16. The _____-_____ chart is a graphic approach to cost-volume-profit analysis that focuses on profits.

17. With computers, managers can vary assumptions regarding selling prices, costs, and volume and can see immediately the effects on the break-even point. This is known as _____ _____ _____.

18. The relative distribution of sales among the various products sold by a business is called the _____ _____.

19. The difference between the current sales revenue and the sales at the break-even point is called the _____ _____ _____.

20. _____ _____ is computed by dividing the contribution margin by the operating income.

FILL IN THE BLANK—PART B

Instructions: Answer the following questions or complete the statements by writing the appropriate words or amounts in the answer blanks.

1. Activities that are thought to cause a cost to be incurred are called activity bases or _____ _____.

2. _____ _____ vary in proportion to changes in the level of activity.

3. The salary of a factory supervisor is an example of a _____ (fixed/variable) cost.

4. _____ _____ remain the same in total dollar amount as the level of activity changes.

5. The rental cost of a piece of office equipment is $2,000 per month plus $1.00 for each machine hour used over 1,500 hours. This is an example of a(n) _____ cost.

6. Mixed costs are sometimes called semivariable or _____ costs.

7. In the high-low method, the difference in total cost divided by the difference in production equals the _____ _____ _____ _____.

8. The _____ _____ is the excess of sales revenue over variable costs.

9. The contribution margin ratio is also called the _____-_____ _____.

10. The _____ _____ ratio measures the effect on operating income of an increase or decrease in sales volume.

11. The unit contribution margin is the dollars from each unit of sales available to cover _____ _____ and provide operating profits.

12. The _____-_____ _____ is the level of operations at which a business's revenues and costs are exactly equal.

13. Increases in property tax rates will cause the break-even point to _____.

14. Decreases in the unit selling price will cause the break-even point to _____.

15. Increases in the unit selling price will cause the break-even point to _____.

16. The vertical axis of a break-even chart depicts _____ and _____.

17. Analyzing the effects of changing selling prices, costs, and volume on the break-even point and profit is called "what if" analysis or _____ _____.

18. The sales volume necessary to break even or to earn a target profit for a business selling two or more products depends upon the _____ _____.

19. If the contribution margin is $200,000 and operating income is $50,000, the operating leverage is _____.

20. An important assumption of cost-volume-profit analysis is that total sales and total costs can be represented by _____ _____.

MULTIPLE CHOICE

Instructions: Circle the best answer for each of the following questions.

1. Which of the following statements describes fixed costs?
   a. costs that remain constant on a per unit basis as the activity base changes
   b. costs that vary in total in direct proportion to changes in the activity base
   c. costs that remain constant on a per unit basis, but vary in total as the activity level changes
   d. costs that remain constant in total dollar amount as the level of activity changes

2. What term is used to describe a cost which has characteristics of both a variable and fixed cost?
   a. variable cost
   b. fixed cost
   c. mixed cost
   d. sunk cost

3. If Berkson Inc.'s costs at 150,000 units of production are $240,000 (the high point of production) and $152,500 at 80,000 units of production (the low point of production), the variable cost per unit using the high-low method of cost estimation is:
   a. zero
   b. $1.25
   c. $1.60
   d. $1.91

4. Which of the following changes would have the effect of increasing the break-even point for a business?
   a. a decrease in fixed costs
   b. a decrease in unit variable cost
   c. a decrease in unit selling price
   d. none of the above

5. Which of the following costs will be classified as a fixed cost in cost-volume-profit analysis?
   a. direct materials
   b. real estate taxes
   c. direct labor
   d. supplies

6. If the contribution margin is $16 and fixed costs are $400,000, what is the break-even point in units?

    a. 25,000

    b. 250,000

    c. 400,000

    d. 6,400,000

7. If sales are $300,000 and sales at the break-even point are $250,000, what is the margin of safety?

    a. 17%

    b. 20%

    c. 83%

    d. 120%

8. If for Jones Inc. the contribution margin is $200,000 and operating income is $40,000, what is the operating leverage?

    a. 240,000

    b. 160,000

    c. 5

    d. 0.2

9. In cost-volume-profit analysis, variable costs are costs that:

    a. increase per unit with an increase in the activity level

    b. decrease per unit with a decrease in the activity level

    c. remain the same in total at different activity levels

    d. remain the same per unit at different activity levels

10. CM Inc.'s sales are 40,000 units at $12 per unit, variable costs are $8 per unit, and fixed costs are $50,000. What is CM's contribution margin ratio?

    a. 23%

    b. 33%

    c. 50%

    d. 67%

11. B-E Co.'s fixed costs are $120,000, unit selling price is $30, and unit variable cost is $18. What is B-E's break-even point in units?

    a. 4,000

    b. 6,667

    c. 10,000

    d. none of the above

12. Which of the following is a primary assumption of cost-volume-profit analysis?
   a. within the relevant range, the efficiency of operations does not change
   b. costs can be accurately divided into fixed and variable components
   c. sales mix is constant
   d. all of the above

TRUE/FALSE

Instructions: Indicate whether each of the following statements is true or false by placing a check mark in the appropriate column.

	True	False
1. Most operating decisions by management focus on a range of activity, known as the relevant range, within which management plans to operate.	____	____
2. Mixed costs, sometimes referred to as semi-variable or semi-fixed costs, are costs that are mostly variable.	____	____
3. The high-low method can be used to estimate the fixed cost and variable cost components of a mixed cost.	____	____
4. Using the high-low method, the fixed costs will differ at the highest and lowest levels of activity.	____	____
5. The point in the operations of a business at which revenues and expired costs are equal is called the break-even point.	____	____
6. The data required to compute the break-even point are (1) total estimated fixed costs for a future period and (2) the unit contribution margin.	____	____
7. Decreases in the unit selling price will decrease the break-even point.	____	____
8. Decreases in fixed costs will increase the break-even point.	____	____
9. The operating leverage is determined by dividing the income from operations by the sales dollars at break-even.	____	____
10. A primary assumption of cost-volume-profit analysis is that the quantity of units in the beginning inventory is equal to the quantity of units in the ending inventory.	____	____

EXERCISE 20-1

Data for the highest and lowest levels of production for Evans Company are as follows:

	Total Costs	Total Units Produced
Highest level	$550,000	50,000 units
Lowest level	$250,000	20,000

Instructions:

(1) Determine the differences between total costs and total units produced at the highest and lowest levels of production.

(2) Using the high-low method of cost estimation, estimate the variable cost per unit and the fixed cost for Evans Company.

(3) Based on (2), estimate the total costs for 80,000 units of production.

Exercise 20-2

Instructions: Name the following chart and identify the items represented by the letters *a* through *f*.

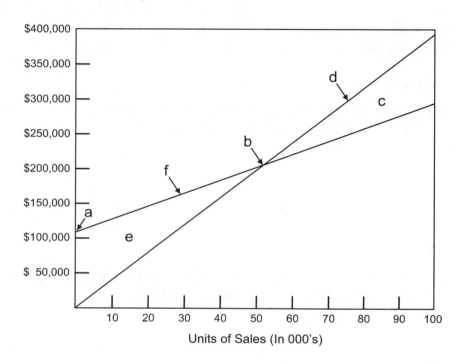

Chart: _____

(a) _____

(b) _____

(c) _____

(d) _____

(e) _____

(f) _____

EXERCISE 20-3

Instructions: In each of the following cases, use the appropriate formula (margin of safety or operating leverage ratio) to determine the answer.

(1) Sales are $2,000,000.
Break-even sales would be $1,700,000.
The margin of safety as a percentage of sales is ......   _____%

(2) Sales are $150,000.
Break-even sales would be $100,000.
The margin of safety as a percentage of sales is ......   _____%

(3) Operating income is $175,000.
The contribution margin is $300,000.
The operating leverage is ....   _____

(4) Sales are $700,000.
Variable costs are $300,000.
Operating income is $200,000.
The operating leverage is ....   _____

PROBLEM 20-1

Larson Co. produces telephone answering machines. At March 1, Larson estimates fixed costs related to production to be $700,000. The unit selling price, unit variable cost, and unit contribution margin for Larson Co. are as follows:

Unit selling price $75
Unit variable cost 25
Unit contribution margin $50

Instructions: Perform the following calculations assuming the facts given above, unless otherwise indicated. (Round to the nearest dollar.)

(1) Calculate the break-even point in units for Larson Co.

(2) Assume Larson Co. is contemplating paying $2,000 more to each of five factory supervisors. What would the new break-even point be if such a plan were put into action?

(3) What would the break-even point be if the cost of direct materials increased by $1.00 per unit?

(4) What would the break-even point be if the selling price increased to $77 per telephone answering machine?

(5) What is the sales volume necessary to earn a target profit of $300,000?

PROBLEM 20-2

Data related to the expected sales of products A and B for Galla Inc. for the current year, which is typical of recent years, are as follows.

Product	Selling Price per Unit	Variable Cost per Unit	Sales Mix
A	$180	$140	80%
B	$280	$190	20%

The estimated fixed costs for the current year are $400,000.

Instructions:

(1) Determine the estimated sales in units and dollars to reach the break-even point for the current year.

(2) Prove the validity of the answer in (1) by completing the following condensed income statement.

	Product A	Product B	Total
Sales:			
_____ units × $180	_____	_____	_____
_____ units × $280	_____	_____	_____
Total sales	_____	_____	_____
Variable costs:			
_____ units × $140	_____	_____	_____
_____ units × $190	_____	_____	_____
Total variable costs	_____	_____	_____
Contribution margin			_____
Fixed costs			_____
Operating profit			_____

21

Budgeting

QUIZ AND TEST HINTS

The following hints may be helpful to you in preparing for a quiz or a test over the material covered in Chapter 21.

1. Many new terms are introduced in this chapter. You can expect true/false, multiple-choice, or matching questions testing your knowledge of these terms. Review the key terms by completing the Matching exercises.

2. A major emphasis of this chapter is budgeting for manufacturing operations. You should be familiar with all the budgets illustrated in the chapter. The order in which the budgets are normally prepared is the same as that presented in the chapter. For example, the sales budget is normally presented first, followed by the production budget, etc. You may be required to prepare one of these budgets on a test.

3. The cash budget, or elements thereof, such as the budgeted cash receipts or cash disbursements, will often be the subject of an exam question.

4. You can also expect to see some multiple-choice questions that require the computation of the amount of materials to be purchased, units to be produced, cash receipts for a month, and so on, as part of the budgeting process.

MATCHING

Instructions: Match each of the statements below with its proper term. Some terms may not be used.

A.   budget
B.   budgetary slack
C.   capital expenditures budget
D.   cash budget
E.   continuous budgeting
F.   cost of goods sold budget
G.   direct materials purchases budget

H.   flexible budget
I.   goal conflict
J.   master budget
K.   production budget
L.   responsibility center
M.   sales budget
N.   static budget
O.   zero-based budgeting

_____   1.   The comprehensive budget plan linking all the individual budgets related to sales, cost of goods sold, operating expenses, projects, capital expenditures, and cash.

_____   2.   A method of budgeting that provides for maintaining a twelve-month projection into the future.

_____   3.   A concept of budgeting that requires all levels of management to start from zero and estimate budget data as if there had been no previous activities in their units.

_____   4.   An accounting device used to plan and control resources of operational departments and divisions.

_____   5.   A budget that uses the production budget as a starting point.

_____   6.   The budget summarizing future plans for acquiring plant facilities and equipment.

_____   7.   A budget of the estimated direct materials, direct labor, and factory overhead consumed by sold products.

_____   8.   A budget of estimated unit production.

_____   9.   A budget that does not adjust to changes in activity levels.

_____   10.   A budget that adjusts for varying rates of activity.

_____   11.   A budget of estimated cash receipts and payments.

_____   12.   An organizational unit for which a manager is assigned responsibility over costs, revenues, or assets.

_____   13.   Excess resources set within a budget to provide for uncertain events.

FILL IN THE BLANK—PART A

Instructions: Answer the following questions or complete the statements by writing the appropriate words or amounts in the answer blanks.

1. The document that charts a course of future action for a business by outlining the plans of the business in financial terms is the
   _____.

2. Establishing specific goals for future operations is part of the
   _____ function of management.

3. The budgetary units of an organization are called _____
   _____.

4. Comparing actual results to the plan to help prevent unplanned expenditures is part of the _____ function of management.

5. A budget that establishes lower goals than may be possible is said to contain budgetary _____.

6. When individual objectives are opposed to those that are in the best interests of the business, the situation can be described as a(n)
   _____ _____.

7. The length of time for which the operating budget normally is prepared is a(n) _____ _____.

8. Budgets are usually monitored and summarized by the
   _____ Department.

9. A(n) _____ budget shows the expected results of a responsibility center for only one activity level.

10. When constructing a flexible budget, the planner must begin by identifying _____ _____ _____.

11. Manufacturing operations require a series of budgets that are linked together in a(n) _____ _____.

12–13. The budget process is started by preparing a sales budget. For each product, the sales budget normally indicates the:

12. _____ _____ _____ _____, and

13. _____ _____ _____ _____.

14. The following data are available from the production budget of O'Connor Inc. for Product X:

Expected units of sales	615,000
Estimated units in beginning inventory	73,500
Total units to be produced	705,500

    The desired units in ending inventory are _____.

15. The _____ budget is the starting point for determining the estimated quantities of direct materials to be purchased.

16. The budgets that are used by managers to plan financing, investing, and cash objectives are the _____ _____ _____.

17. The _____ budget presents the expected receipts (inflow) and payments (outflow) of cash for a period of time.

18. The _____ _____ budget summarizes plans for acquiring fixed assets.

19–20. The Townsend Co. production budget for Product X is 300,000 units. Product X is manufactured in two departments. Direct labor in Department 1 is 0.2 hour per unit at an hourly pay rate of $17. Department 2 direct labor requirements for Product X are 0.08 hour per unit at an hourly pay rate of $20.

19. Total hours required for production of Product X are _____.

20. Total direct labor cost is _____.

FILL IN THE BLANK—PART B

Instructions: Answer the following questions or complete the statements by writing the appropriate words or amounts in the answer blanks.

1. Executing actions to meet the goals of the business is the _____ function of management.

2. Giving information to employees about their performance relative to the goals they helped establish is called _____.

3. The budget becomes less effective as a tool for planning or controlling operations if employees view budget goals as unachievable. This occurs when the budget is set too _____.

4. When budgets establish lower goals than may be possible, they are said to be "padded" or to contain _____ _____.

5. The manager of the transportation department was directed to stay within the department budget. To accomplish this goal, the manager stopped shipping to customers for an entire month. This manager's behavior is said to exhibit _____ _____.

6. A variation of fiscal-year budgeting that seeks to maintain a twelve-month projection into the future is called _____ _____.

7. _____-_____ budgeting requires managers to estimate sales, production, and other operating data as though operations are being started for the first time.

8. XYZ Motor Co. establishes its budget at only one level of activity. This type of budget is called a(n) _____ _____.

9. PDQ Construction Co. prepares its budgets based on 8,000, 9,000, and 10,000 units of production. This type of budget is known as a(n) _____ _____.

10. _____ budgeting systems speed up and reduce the cost of preparing budgets.

11. The budget process begins by estimating _____.

12. The production budgets are used to prepare the direct materials purchases, direct labor cost, and _____ _____ _____ budgets.

13. The direct materials purchases, direct labor cost, and factory overhead cost budgets are used to develop the _____ _____ _____ _____ budget.

14. Two major budgets comprising the budgeted balance sheet are the cash budget and the _____ _____ budget.

15. The starting point often used in estimating the quantity of sales for each product in the sales budget is _____ _____ _____.

16. The number of units to be manufactured to meet budgeted sales and inventory needs is set forth in the _____ budget.

17. The _____ _____ _____ budget is prepared based on the production budget and the estimated labor requirements for each unit of product.

18. The _____ _____ _____ allows management to assess the effects of the individual budgets on profits for the year.

19–20. Goldman Inc. uses a flexible budgeting system to plan for its manufacturing operations. The static budget for 9,000 units of production provides for direct labor at $5 per unit and variable electric at $0.60 per unit. Fixed costs are electric power, $1,000, and supervisor salaries of $17,500.

19. Variable costs for 10,000 units of production are _____.

20. Fixed costs for 10,000 units of production are _____.

MULTIPLE CHOICE

Instructions: Circle the best answer for each of the following questions.

1. Which of the following budgets provides the starting point for preparing the direct labor cost budget?
    a. direct materials purchases budget
    b. cash budget
    c. production budget
    d. cost of goods sold budget

2. The budget which provides data on the quantities of direct materials purchases necessary to meet production needs is the:
    a. direct materials purchases budget
    b. sales budget
    c. production budget
    d. direct labor cost budget

3. This budget summarizes future plans for the acquisition of plant facilities and equipment.
    a. budgeted balance sheet
    b. production budget
    c. cash budget
    d. capital expenditures budget

4. A series of budgeted amounts for varying levels of activity is called a:
    a. variable budget
    b. continuous budget
    c. flexible budget
    d. zero-based budget

5. Which of the following budgets is used most frequently for administrative functions?
    a. phased budget
    b. zero-based budget
    c. static budget
    d. flexible budget

6. Assume 80% of sales are collected in the month of sale, with the remainder the following month. Sales for October and November were $640,000 and $860,000, respectively. What are the cash receipts from accounts receivable collections for November?
    a. $684,000
    b. $816,000
    c. $812,000
    d. $860,000

7. A method of budgeting which requires managers to estimate sales, production, and other operating data as though operations were being started for the first time is called:

a. zero-based budgeting

b. master budgeting

c. flexible budgeting

d. continuous budgeting

8. A method of budgeting which maintains a twelve-month projection into the future is called:

a. annual budgeting

b. continuous budgeting

c. perpetual budgeting

d. dynamic budgeting

9. An organizational unit with a manager who has authority and responsibility for the unit's performance is called a(n):

a. economic unit

b. profit center

c. budgetary center

d. responsibility center

10. Assume estimated sales for the coming year is 280,000 units. The estimated inventory at the beginning of the year is 25,000 units, and the desired inventory at the end of the year is 35,000 units. The total production indicated in the production budget is:

a. 290,000 units

b. 270,000 units

c. 305,000 units

d. 315,000 units

11. The direct materials purchases budget totals $1,200,000, while the direct labor cost budget totals $650,000. The factory overhead is budgeted at $900,000. The budgeted inventory information is as follows:

	Beginning Inventory	Ending Inventory
Materials	$45,000	$40,000
Finished goods	$80,000	$95,000

What is the cost of goods sold budgeted for the period?

a. $2,730,000

b. $2,740,000

c. $2,750,000

d. $2,760,000

12. Manufacturing costs are estimated to be $360,000 and $450,000 for July and August, respectively. These amounts include $30,000 of monthly depreciation plant and equipment expense. Cash payments are paid such that 60% are paid in the month incurred and 40% are paid in the following month. What are the budgeted cash payments for August?

 a. $252,000

 b. $366,000

 c. $384,000

 d. $414,000

TRUE/FALSE

Instructions: Indicate whether each of the following statements is true or false by placing a check mark in the appropriate column.

	True	False
1. A zero-based budget is actually a series of budgets for varying rates of activity..	_____	_____
2. A budgeting method which provides for maintenance of a twelve-month projection into the future is called continuous budgeting.	_____	_____
3. Computers are seldom used in the budget process, although computers can reduce the cost of budget preparation.	_____	_____
4. The number of units of each commodity expected to be manufactured to meet budgeted sales and inventory requirements is set forth in the production budget................	_____	_____
5. A schedule of collections from sales is useful for developing a cash budget..	_____	_____
6. The amount of the expenditures for fixed assets such as machinery and equipment usually remains fairly constant from year to year.	_____	_____
7. Minimum cash balances are maintained to serve as a safety buffer for variations in estimates and for unexpected emergencies...	_____	_____
8. The budgeted balance sheet brings together the projection of all profit-making phases of operations.	_____	_____
9. The first budget usually prepared is the cash budget.	_____	_____
10. The sales budget normally indicates for each product the quantity of estimated sales and the expected unit selling price.	_____	_____

EXERCISE 21-1

Texier Inc. manufactures two products, C and Q. It is estimated that the May 1 inventory will consist of 8,000 units of C and 21,000 units of Q. Estimated sales for May by sales territory are as follows:

East: Product C—60,000 units at $15 per unit
       Product Q—75,000 units at $8 per unit
West: Product C—80,000 units at $20 per unit
       Product Q—50,000 units at $10 per unit

An ending inventory of 20% of May sales is desired.

Instructions: Complete the following sales and production budgets for the month of May.

Texier Inc.

Sales Budget

For the Month of May, 20--

PRODUCT AND AREA	UNIT SALES VOLUME	UNIT SELLING PRICE	TOTAL SALES
Product C:			
East area			
West area			
Total			
Product Q:			
East area			
West area			
Total			
Total revenue from sales			

Texier Inc.

Production Budget

For the Month of May, 20--

| | UNITS | |
	PRODUCT C	PRODUCT Q
Sales		
Plus desired inventory, May 31		
Total		
Less estimated inventory, May 1		
Total production		

EXERCISE 21-2

Instructions: Complete the following factory overhead cost budget for Nathalie Inc. for the month of January. The items listed as variable costs are assumed to vary directly with the units of product. The items listed as fixed costs are assumed to remain constant regardless of units produced.

Nathalie Inc.

Factory Overhead Cost Budget

For the Month of January, 20--

	30,000	60,000	90,000
Units of product			
Variable cost:			
Indirect factory wages ($.80 per unit)	$ 24 0 0 0		
Indirect materials ($.45 per unit)	13 5 0 0		
Electric power ($.60 per unit)	18 0 0 0		
Total variable cost	$ 55 5 0 0		
Fixed cost:			
Supervisory salaries	$ 30 0 0 0		
Depreciation of plant and equipment	18 0 0 0		
Property taxes	12 0 0 0		
Insurance	7 5 0 0		
Electric power	4 5 0 0		
Total fixed cost	$ 72 0 0 0		
Total factory overhead cost	$127 5 0 0		

EXERCISE 21-3

The Gyro Company budgeted sales of 500,000 units of Product A. Each unit of Product A requires 0.5 pounds of Material XX and 1.2 pounds of Material ZZ. Estimated and desired inventory information is as follows:

	Estimated Beginning Inventory	Desired Ending Inventory
Product A	12,000	10,000
Material XX	8,000	14,000
Material ZZ	20,000	25,000

Instructions:

(1) Prepare a production budget.

Gyro Company

Production Budget

	PRODUCT A

(2) Prepare a direct materials purchases budget, assuming a price per pound of $4 and $6 for Materials XX and ZZ, respectively.

Gyro Company

Direct Materials Purchases Budget

	MATERIAL XX	MATERIAL ZZ

(3) If each unit of Product A requires 0.25 hours of Assembly Department labor at a cost of $12 per hour, what would be the direct labor budget amount?

PROBLEM 21-1

The treasurer of Amant Inc. has accumulated the following budget information for the next two months:

	March	April
Sales	$240,000	$200,000
Merchandise costs	150,000	120,000
Operating expenses	60,000	40,000
Capital expenditures	—	125,000

The company expects to sell about 40% of its merchandise for cash. Of sales on account, 80% are expected to be collected in full in the month of the sale and the remainder in the month following the sale. One-third of the merchandise costs are expected to be paid in the month in which they are incurred and the other two-thirds in the following month. Depreciation, insurance, and property taxes represent $20,000 of the probable monthly operating expenses. Insurance is paid in December and a $5,000 installment on property taxes is expected to be paid in March. Of the remainder of the operating expenses, 60% are expected to be paid in the month in which they are incurred and the balance in the following month. Capital expenditures of $125,000 are expected to be paid in April.

Current assets as of March 1 are composed of cash of $24,000 and accounts receivable of $45,000. Current liabilities as of March 1 are composed of accounts payable of $90,000 ($80,000 for merchandise purchases and $10,000 for operating expenses). Management desires to maintain a minimum cash balance of $50,000 at the end of March and April.

Instructions: Prepare a monthly cash budget for March and April.

Amant, Inc.

Cash Budget

For Two Months Ending April 30, 20--

	MARCH	APRIL

PROBLEM 21-2

The Fernandez Furniture Company produces two products, Product A and Product B. The management wishes to budget the sales, production, direct material, and direct labor for the upcoming year. In order to meet this request you have obtained information from various managers throughout the organization. The sales budget was provided by the Sales Department as follows:

Product	Unit Sales Volume	Unit Sales Price	Total Sales
Product A	168,000	$4.20	$ 705,600
Product B	324,000	$8.80	2,851,200
Total			$3,556,800

Information about the inventories for Product A and Product B was obtained by the production manager:

	Product A	Product B
Estimated units in beginning inventory	12,000	24,000
Desired units in ending inventory	8,000	36,000

The materials manager provided information about the materials used in production. There are three different materials used to manufacture Fernandez products: Material X, Material Y, and Material Z. The standard number of pounds required for each unit of Product A and B was determined from the bill of materials:

Standard material pounds per unit	Product A	Product B
Material X	0.6 pounds	1.8 pounds
Material Y		3.4 pounds
Material Z	1.2 pounds	

The purchasing manager provided the standard price per pound for each of the materials:

Material	Price per Pound
Material X	$0.40
Material Y	$0.50
Material Z	$0.60

The materials manager was responsible for the materials inventories and provided the following inventory information:

	Product		
	Material X	Material Y	Material Z
Estimated units in beginning inventory	16,000	5,600	12,400
Desired units in ending inventory	14,500	8,700	9,800

Products A and B are manufactured in two departments, 1 and 2. The industrial engineers provided standard direct labor information from the routing files.

Standard hours per unit	Dept. 1	Dept. 2
Product A	0.20 hours	0.15 hours
Product B	0.05 hours	0.10 hours

The labor rates in each department were provided by the department supervisor for each department.

	Dept. 1	Dept. 2
Labor cost per hour	$14.00	$18.00

Instructions: Construct the following budgets for Fernandez Furniture Company:

(1)   Production budget

(2)   Direct materials purchases budget

(3)   Direct labor cost budget

(1)   *Fernandez Furniture Company*

Production Budget

	PRODUCT A	PRODUCT B

(2) _Fernandez Furniture Company_

Direct Materials Purchases Budget

	MATERIAL X	MATERIAL Y	MATERIAL Z	TOTAL

(3) _Fernandez Furniture Company_

Direct Labor Cost Budget

	DEPARTMENT 1	DEPARTMENT 2	TOTAL

22 Performance Evaluation Using Variances from Standard Costs

QUIZ AND TEST HINTS

The following hints may be helpful to you in preparing for a quiz or a test over the material covered in Chapter 22.

1. Many new terms are introduced in this chapter. You can expect true/false, multiple-choice, or matching questions testing your knowledge of these terms. As a review of the key terms, do the Matching exercises included in this Study Guide.

2. The major emphasis of this chapter is standard costing. You should be able to compute the six variances illustrated in the chapter. The Illustrative Problem at the end of the chapter is a good study aid for the computation of variances.

3. You also should be able to perform variance analysis based on a flexible budget.

4. Depending upon whether your instructor emphasized standards in the accounts in lecture or through homework, you may be required to prepare journal entries for incorporating standards in the accounts. If your instructor did not cover this topic in class, then do not spend much time studying this section of the chapter.

MATCHING

Instructions: Match each of the statements below with its proper term. Some terms may not be used.

A. budget performance report
B. controllable variance
C. cost variance
D. currently attainable standards
E. direct labor rate variance
F. direct labor time variance
G. direct materials price variance

H. direct materials quantity variance
I. ideal standards
J. nonfinancial performance measures
K. standard cost
L. standard cost systems
M. volume variance

_____ 1. Standards that represent levels of operation that can be obtained with reasonable effort.

_____ 2. The cost associated with the difference between the standard quantity and the actual quantity of direct materials used in producing a commodity.

_____ 3. A report comparing actual results with budget figures.

_____ 4. Standards that represent levels of performance that can be achieved only under perfect operating conditions.

_____ 5. A detailed estimate of what a product should cost.

_____ 6. The difference between the budgeted fixed overhead at 100% of normal capacity and the standard fixed overhead for the actual production achieved during the period.

_____ 7. The cost associated with the difference between the standard hours and the actual hours of direct labor spent producing a commodity.

_____ 8. The difference between the actual amount of variable factory overhead cost incurred and the amount of variable factory overhead budgeted for actual production.

_____ 9. The cost associated with the difference between the standard price and the actual price of direct materials used in producing a commodity.

_____ 10. The difference between the actual cost and the standard cost at actual volumes.

_____ 11. The cost associated with the difference between the standard rate and the actual rate paid for direct labor used in producing a commodity.

_____ 12. Accounting systems that use standards for each manufacturing cost entering into the finished product.

FILL IN THE BLANK—PART A

Instructions: Answer the following questions or complete the statements by writing the appropriate words or amounts in the answer blanks.

1. Accounting systems that use standards for each element of manufacturing cost entering into the finished product are called _____ _____ _____.

2. When actual costs are compared with standard costs, only variances are reported for cost control. This reporting philosophy is known as the _____ _____ _____.

3. Standards that allow for no idle time, no machine breakdowns, and no materials spoilage are called _____ standards.

4. _____ _____ standards can be attained with reasonable effort and allow for normal production difficulties and mistakes.

5. Standards for direct materials, direct labor, and factory overhead are separated into two components: a price standard and a(n) _____ standard.

6. The _____ department is responsible for the direct materials price per square yard.

7. The difference between the actual cost and the standard cost at the actual volume is called a(n) _____ _____.

8. The sum of the direct materials cost variance, direct labor cost variance, and factory overhead cost variance is the _____ _____ cost variance.

9. The difference between the actual quantity used and the standard quantity at actual production, multiplied by the standard price per unit is the _____ _____ _____ _____.

10. If the actual quantity of materials used was 7,000 units at an actual price of $5 per unit and the standard quantity was 6,800 units at a standard price of $5.10 per unit, the materials price variance is _____.

11. The difference between the actual hours worked and the standard hours at actual production, multiplied by the standard rate per hour results in the _____ _____ _____ _____.

12. If the actual hours worked are 3,000 at an actual rate per hour of $12 and the standard hours are 3,100 at $11 per hour, the total direct labor cost variance is _____.

13. The _____ variance measures the efficiency of using variable overhead resources.

14. If actual variable factory overhead is $11,400, actual fixed factory overhead is $13,000, and budgeted variable factory overhead for the actual amount produced is $14,400, the controllable variance is _____.

15. The difference between the budgeted fixed overhead at 100% of normal capacity and the standard fixed overhead for actual production achieved is called the _____ _____.

16. The difference between the actual factory overhead and the total overhead applied to production is the _____ _____ _____ _____ variance.

17. The factory overhead cost variance can be verified for each variable factory overhead cost and fixed factory overhead cost element in the _____ _____ _____ _____ _____.

18. A favorable direct materials quantity variance is recorded by crediting _____ _____ _____ _____.

19. At the end of the fiscal year, minor standard cost variances are usually transferred to the _____ _____ _____ _____ account.

20. A way to bring broader perspectives, such as quality of work, to evaluating performance is to supplement financial performance measures with _____ _____ measures.

21. Nonfinancial measures can be either a(n) _____ or _____ of an activity or process.

FILL IN THE BLANK—PART B

Instructions: Answer the following questions or complete the statements by writing the appropriate words or amounts in the answer blanks.

1. A management accounting system that enables management to determine how much a product should cost, how much it does cost, and the causes of any difference is called a(n) _____ _____ _____.

2. Standard setting normally requires the joint efforts of accountants, managers, and _____.

3. Standards that can only be achieved under perfect operating conditions are called _____ _____.

4. Duva Co. assumes normal production difficulties in its standard setting process. These standards are known as _____ _____ standards.

5. The control function of the management process requires actual performance to be compared against the budget. This is known as

   _____ _____ _____.

6. The actual costs, standard amounts for the actual level of production achieved, and the differences between the two amounts are summarized in the _____ _____ report.

7. When actual cost exceeds budgeted cost at actual volumes, the result is a(n) _____ (favorable/unfavorable) variance.

8. The difference between the actual price per unit and the standard price per unit, multiplied by the actual quantity of materials is the _____

   _____ _____ _____.

9. Excessive amounts of direct materials were used by the Hawk Shirt Manufacturing Co. because equipment used in production was not properly maintained and operated. The variance that resulted was a(n) _____

   _____ _____ _____.

10. The actual price of direct materials used to manufacture Product B was $0.03 per unit. The standard materials price was established at $0.02. The department responsible for the variance is the _____

    _____.

11. If the actual quantity of materials used was 7,000 units at an actual price of $5 per unit and the standard quantity was 6,800 units at a standard price of $5.10 per unit, the total materials cost variance is _____.

12. The difference between the actual rate per hour and the standard rate per hour, multiplied by the actual hours worked is the _____

    _____ _____ _____.

13. If the actual hours worked are 3,000 at an actual rate per hour of $12 and the standard hours are 3,100 at $11 per hour, the direct labor time variance is _____.

14. Controlling direct labor cost is normally the responsibility of the _____ _____.

15. The impact of changing production on fixed and variable factory overhead costs can be determined by using a(n) _____ budget.

16. The difference between the actual variable overhead incurred and the budgeted variable overhead for actual production is the variable factory overhead _____ _____.

17. The efficiency of using variable overhead resources is measured by the _____ _____.

18. If budgeted fixed overhead is $12,000, standard fixed overhead for the actual production achieved is $13,000, and actual variable overhead is $13,700, the volume variance is _____.

19. An unfavorable direct materials price variance is recorded by debiting _____ _____ _____ _____.

20. Measuring both financial and _____ performance helps employees consider multiple performance objectives.

21. A chain of nonfinancial inputs and outputs can be _____ across a set of connected activities.

MULTIPLE CHOICE

Instructions: Circle the best answer for each of the following questions.

1. Standard costs serve as a device for measuring:
   a. efficiency
   b. nonfinancial performance
   c. volume
   d. quantity

2. Woodson Inc. produced 6,000 light fixtures in May of the current year. Each unit requires 0.75 standard hours. The standard labor rate is $10 per hour. Actual direct labor for May was 4,800 hours. What is the direct labor time variance?
   a. $3,000 favorable
   b. $6,000 unfavorable
   c. $3,000 unfavorable
   d. $9,000 favorable

3. The following data relate to direct materials cost for May:

   Standard costs (5,000 lbs. at $2 per lb.) $10,000
   Actual costs (5,100 lbs. at $3 per lb.)   15,300

   What is the direct materials quantity variance?
   a. $200 favorable
   b. $200 unfavorable
   c. $300 favorable
   d. $300 unfavorable

4. Lloyd Company produces music boxes. The standard factory overhead cost at 100% of normal capacity is $100,000 (20,000 hours at $5: $3 variable, $2 fixed). If 700 hours were unused, the fixed factory overhead volume variance would be:
   a. $700 favorable
   b. $1,400 favorable
   c. $2,100 unfavorable
   d. $1,400 unfavorable

5. The Hill Company produced 5,000 units of X. The standard time per unit is 0.25 hours. The actual hours used to produce 5,000 units of X were 1,350 hours. The standard labor rate is $12 per hour. The actual labor cost was $18,900. What is the total direct labor cost variance?
   a. $1,200 unfavorable
   b. $3,900 unfavorable
   c. $1,400 unfavorable
   d. $2,700 unfavorable

6. The cost associated with the difference between the standard quantity and the actual quantity of direct materials used in producing a commodity is called the:
   a. direct materials quantity variance
   b. direct materials price variance
   c. direct materials volume variance
   d. controllable materials variance

7. The cost associated with the difference between the standard hours and the actual hours of direct labor spent producing a commodity is called the:
   a. direct labor quantity variance
   b. direct labor volume variance
   c. direct labor rate variance
   d. direct labor time variance

8. The difference between the budgeted fixed overhead at 100% of normal capacity and the standard fixed overhead for the actual production achieved during the period is called the:
   a. efficiency variance
   b. controllable variance
   c. volume variance
   d. total overhead variance

9. An unfavorable volume variance might be caused by which of the following factors?
   a. an uneven work flow
   b. machine breakdowns
   c. repairs leading to work stoppages
   d. all of the above

10. Which of the following is an example of a nonfinancial performance measure?
    a. number of customer complaints
    b. direct labor time variance
    c. controllable overhead variance
    d. all of the above

11. A quantity of 1,200 gallons of Material X is purchased at a price of $4.50 per gallon. The standard price is $4.00 per gallon. The journal entry for this purchase will include a:
    a. debit to Materials for $5,400
    b. debit to Direct Materials Price Variance for $600
    c. credit to Direct Materials Price Variance for $600
    d. debit to Work in Process for $4,800

12. Factory overhead is applied at a rate of $9 per labor hour, of which $6 is variable. The actual variable factory overhead is $32,000. In the current period, 2,500 units are produced at a standard time of 2 labor hours per unit. These units require 5,500 actual labor hours. What is the controllable variance?
    a. $2,000 favorable
    b. $2,000 unfavorable
    c. $1,000 favorable
    d. $1,000 unfavorable

TRUE/FALSE

Instructions: Indicate whether each of the following statements is true or false by placing a check mark in the appropriate column.

	True	False
1. Differences between the standard costs of a department or product and the actual costs incurred are termed variances.	____	____
2. If the actual unit price of the materials differs from the standard price, there is a quantity variance.	____	____
3. If the actual direct labor hours spent producing a product differ from the standard hours, there is a direct labor time variance.	____	____
4. The difference between the actual factory overhead and the budgeted factory overhead for the level of production achieved is called the volume variance.	____	____
5. Factory overhead costs are more difficult to manage than are direct labor and materials costs.	____	____
6. At the end of the year, the variances from standard are usually transferred to the work in process account.	____	____
7. A standard level of operation that can be attained with reasonable effort is called an ideal standard.	____	____
8. A useful means of reporting standard factory overhead cost variance data is through a factory overhead cost variance report.	____	____
9. Standards should only be applied in factory settings.	____	____
10. An example of nonfinancial performance measures is the number of customer complaints.	____	____

EXERCISE 22-1

The following data relate to the direct materials and direct labor costs for the production of 10,000 units of product:

Direct Materials
Actual: 77,000 pounds at $1.82 .... $140,140
Standard: 75,000 pounds at $1.80   135,000

Direct Labor
Actual: 42,500 hours at $19.75 .... $839,375
Standard: 42,000 hours at $20.00   840,000

Instructions:

(1) Compute the price variance, quantity variance, and total direct materials cost variance.

Price variance:

Quantity variance:

Total direct materials cost variance $_____

(2) Compute the rate variance, time variance, and total direct labor cost variance.

Rate variance:

Time variance:

Total direct labor cost variance $_____

EXERCISE 22-2

The following data relate to factory overhead cost for the production of 20,000 units of product:

Actual:	Variable factory overhead	$153,500
	Fixed factory overhead	120,000
Standard:	30,000 hours at $8	240,000

Productive capacity of 100% was 40,000 hours, and the factory overhead cost budgeted at the level of 30,000 standard hours was $270,000.

Instructions: Compute the fixed factory overhead volume variance, variable factory overhead controllable variance, and total factory overhead cost variance. The fixed factory overhead rate was $3 per hour.

Volume variance:

Controllable variance:

Total factory overhead cost variance $ _____

EXERCISE 22-3

During January, Nathalie Inc. manufactured 60,000 units, and the factory overhead costs were indirect factory wages, $50,500; electric power, $39,500 (included both variable and fixed components); indirect materials, $27,600; supervisory salaries, $30,000; depreciation of plant and equipment, $18,000; property taxes, $12,000; and insurance, $7,500.

Instructions: Prepare a budget performance report for factory overhead for January based on the above data and the factory overhead cost budget shown below.

Nathalie Inc.

Budget Performance Report—Factory Overhead Cost

For Month Ended January 31, 20--

	BUDGET	ACTUAL	UNFAVORABLE	FAVORABLE
Variable cost:				
Indirect factory wages	4 8 0 0 0			
Indirect materials	2 7 0 0 0			
Electric power	3 6 0 0 0			
Total variable cost	11 1 0 0 0			
Fixed cost:				
Supervisory salaries	3 0 0 0 0			
Depr. of plant and equipment	1 8 0 0 0			
Property taxes	1 2 0 0 0			
Insurance	7 5 0 0			
Electric power	4 5 0 0			
Total fixed cost	7 2 0 0 0			
Total factory overhead cost	18 3 0 0 0			

EXERCISE 22-4

Each year, a regional IRS office processes thousands of individual tax returns. The standard for processing returns was broken into two types as follows:

Type of Return	Standard Time to Complete Processing
Traditional paper return	45 min.
Return filed electronically	8 min.

By filing their tax returns electronically, individuals reduce the amount of processing time required by the IRS employees.

The regional office employs 30 full-time people (40 hrs./wk.) at $16.00 per hour. For the most recent week, the office processed 1,300 traditional returns and 225 electronically filed returns.

Instructions:

(1) Compute the amount spent on labor for the week.

(2) Determine the flexible budget in hours for the actual volume for the week.

(3) Compute the time variance.

PROBLEM 22-1

Haley Inc. has established the following standard unit costs:

Materials: 10 lbs. @ $6 per lb.	$ 60.00
Labor: 3 hrs. @ $15 per hr.	45.00
Factory overhead: 3 hrs. @ $3.50 per hr.	10.50
Total standard cost per unit	$115.50

The factory overhead budget includes the following data:

	85%	100%
Percent of capacity	85%	100%
Direct labor hours	76,500	90,000
Variable costs	$153,000	$180,000
Fixed costs	135,000	135,000
Total factory overhead cost	$288,000	$315,000
Variable overhead rate per hour		$ 2.00
Fixed overhead rate per hour		1.50
Total overhead rate per hour		$ 3.50

Actual manufacturing costs incurred:

Materials: 250,000 lbs. @ $6.20	$1,550,000
Labor: 77,400 hrs. @ $14.60	1,130,040
Factory overhead (including $135,000 fixed)	295,000
Total actual cost for 25,500 units	$2,975,040
Standard cost of 25,500 units (standard time, 76,500 hrs.) .	2,945,250
Overall variance to be analyzed (unfavorable)	$ 29,790

Instructions:

(1) Determine the price variance and quantity variance for the direct materials cost. Beside the amount of each variance, write the letter F or U to indicate whether the variance is favorable or unfavorable.

Direct Materials Cost Variances

Variance

Price variance:

Actual price .... $_____ per lb.

Standard price .... _____ per lb.

Variance .... $_____ per lb. × actual qty., _____ lbs. $_____

Quantity variance:

Actual quantity .... _____ lbs.

Standard quantity ..... _____ lbs.

Variance .... _____ lbs. × standard price, $_____ _____

Total direct materials cost variance .... $_____

(2) Determine the rate variance and time variance for the direct labor cost. Beside the amount of each variance, write the letter F or U to indicate whether the variance is favorable or unfavorable.

<u>Direct Labor Cost Variances</u>

<u>Variance</u>

Rate variance:

    Actual rate .... $ _____ per hr.

    Standard rate .... _____ per hr.

        Variance .... $ _____ per hr. × actual time, _____ hrs. $ _____

Time variance:

    Actual time .... _____ hrs.

    Standard time .... _____ hrs.

        Variance .... _____ hrs. × standard rate, $ _____ _____

Total direct labor cost variance .... $ _____

(3) Determine the controllable variance and the volume variance for the factory overhead cost. Beside the amount of each variance, write the letter F or U to indicate whether the variance is favorable or unfavorable.

<u>Factory Overhead Cost Variances</u>

<u>Variance</u>

Controllable variance:

    Actual variable factory overhead cost incurred .... $ _____

    Budgeted variable factory overhead for actual product produced .... _____

        Variance .... $ _____

Volume variance:

    Budgeted hours at 100% of normal capacity .... _____ hrs.

    Standard hours for amount produced .... _____ hrs.

    Productive capacity not used .... _____ hrs.

    Standard fixed factory overhead cost rate .... $ _____

        Variance .... _____

Total factory overhead cost variance .... $ _____

PROBLEM 22-2

The following data were taken from the records of Piazza Company Inc. for January of the current year:

Administrative expenses	$ 42,000
Selling expenses	68,000
Cost of goods sold (at standard)	812,000
Fixed factory overhead volume variance—unfavorable	10,000
Variable factory overhead controllable variance—favorable ...	4,000
Direct materials quantity variance—unfavorable	1,500
Direct materials price variance—unfavorable	500
Direct labor time variance—favorable	3,000
Direct labor rate variance—unfavorable	1,200
Sales	995,000

Instructions: Prepare an income statement for presentation to management.

Piazza Company, Inc.

Income Statement

For the Month Ended January 31, 20--

23 Performance Evaluation for Decentralized Operations

QUIZ AND TEST HINTS

The following hints may be helpful to you in preparing for a quiz or a test over the material covered in Chapter 23.

1. Many new terms are introduced in this chapter. You can expect true/false, multiple-choice, or matching questions testing your knowledge of these terms. Review the key terms in the next section using the Matching exercises.

2. The major focus of this chapter is responsibility accounting. Budget performance reports for cost centers have been discussed in earlier chapters, therefore, expect some multiple-choice questions on cost centers. You will probably not have to prepare a budget performance report. You can expect questions requiring you to determine the amount of service department expenses to charge to a profit center, and to calculate income from operations.

3. For investment centers, you should be able to compute rate of return on investment (including the profit margin and investment turnover) and residual income. Be prepared to use the DuPont formula. The Illustrative Problem at the end of the chapter is a good study aid for these computations.

4. This chapter also discusses transfer pricing. Most instructors use multiple-choice questions to cover this topic on tests and quizzes.

MATCHING

Instructions: Match each of the statements below with its proper term. Some terms may not be used.

A.   balanced scorecard
B.   controllable expenses
C.   cost center
D.   cost price approach
E.   decentralization
F.   division
G.   DuPont formula
H.   income from operations
I.   investment center
J.   investment turnover

K.   market price approach
L.   negotiated price approach
M.   profit center
N.   profit margin
O.   rate of return on investment
P.   residual income
Q.   responsibility accounting
R.   service department charges
S.   transfer price

_____   **1.**   A measure of managerial efficiency in the use of investments in assets, computed as income from operations divided by invested assets.

_____   **2.**   An approach to transfer pricing that uses the price at which the product or service transferred could be sold to outside buyers as the transfer price.

_____   **3.**   Revenues less operating expenses and service department charges for a profit or investment center.

_____   **4.**   The costs of services provided by an internal service department and transferred to a responsibility center.

_____   **5.**   An approach to transfer pricing that uses cost as the basis for setting the transfer price.

_____   **6.**   A decentralized unit in which the manager has the responsibility and authority to make decisions that affect not only costs and revenues but also the fixed assets available to the center.

_____   **7.**   Costs that can be influenced by the decisions of a manager.

_____   **8.**   An approach to transfer pricing that allows managers of decentralized units to agree (negotiate) among themselves as to the transfer price.

_____   **9.**   A component of the rate of return on investment, computed as the ratio of income from operations to sales.

_____   **10.**   The price charged one decentralized unit by another for the goods or services provided.

_____   **11.**   The separation of a business into more manageable operating units.

_____   **12.**   The excess of divisional income from operations over a "minimum" acceptable income from operations.

___ **13.** A decentralized unit in which the manager has the responsibility and the authority to make decisions that affect both costs and revenues (and thus profits).

___ **14.** A decentralized unit that is structured around a common function, product, customer, or geographical territory.

___ **15.** The process of measuring and reporting operating data by areas of responsibility.

___ **16.** A decentralized unit in which the department or division manager has responsibility for the control of costs incurred and the authority to make decisions that affect these costs.

___ **17.** A component of the rate of return on investment, computed as the ratio of sales to invested assets.

___ **18.** A performance evaluation approach that incorporates multiple performance dimensions by combining financial and nonfinancial measures.

FILL IN THE BLANK—PART A

Instructions: Answer the following questions or complete the statements by writing the appropriate words or amounts in the answer blanks.

1. A business operating structure in which all major planning and operating decisions are made by top management can be described as

   _____.

2. Decentralized operating units of a business over which a manager has responsibility are referred to as _____ _____.

3. The process of measuring and reporting operating data by responsibility center is called _____ _____.

4. A responsibility center in which the manager is not required to make decisions concerning sales or the amount of fixed assets invested in the center is called a(n) _____ _____.

5. The principal difference in the responsibility accounting reports provided to higher levels of management is that these reports are _____ (more/less) summarized than for lower levels of management.

6. In a profit center, the manager has the responsibility and authority to make decisions that affect both costs and _____.

7. Costs that can be influenced by the decisions of profit center managers are said to be _____.

8. The costs of services charged to a profit center, based on its use of those services, are called _____ _____ _____.

9. A measure of the services performed by a service department, which serves as a basis for charging profit centers, is called the _____ _____.

10. The payroll department processed a total of 50,000 payroll checks and had total expenses of $240,000. If H Division has 10,000 payroll checks for the period, it should be charged _____ for payroll services.

11. If sales are $400,000, cost of goods sold is $235,000, selling expenses are $70,000, and service department charges are $42,000, income from operations is _____.

12. A segment of a business in which the manager has responsibility and authority to make decisions regarding costs, revenues, and invested assets is known as a(n) _____ _____.

13. Income from operations divided by invested assets equals _____ _____ _____ _____ _____.

14. The ratio of income from operations to sales is called the _____ _____.

15–17. Income from operations is $70,000, invested assets are $280,000, and sales are $875,000.

15. The profit margin is _____.

16. The investment turnover is _____.

17. The rate of return on investment is _____.

18. The rate of return on investment is the product of the profit margin and the investment turnover, otherwise known as the _____ _____.

19. The excess of income from operations over a minimum amount of desired income from operations is termed _____ _____.

20. Transfer prices can be set as low as the variable cost per unit or as high as the _____ _____.

21. The _____ _____ approach allows the managers of decentralized units to agree among themselves as to the transfer price.

22. The _____ _____ is a set of financial and nonfinancial measures that reflect multiple performance dimensions of a business.

FILL IN THE BLANK—PART B

Instructions: Answer the following questions or complete the statements by writing the appropriate words or amounts in the answer blanks.

1. Separating a business into divisions or operating units and delegating responsibility for these units to managers is called _____.

2. A manager's area of responsibility is called a(n) _____ _____.

3. Three common types of responsibility centers are cost centers, profit centers, and _____ _____.

4. Responsibility accounting for cost centers focuses on _____.

5. Responsibility accounting reports for a supervisor of the mail room would contain _____ (more/less) detailed information than the report issued to the vice-president of administration.

6. A division over which the manager has the responsibility and the authority to make decisions that affect both costs and revenues is known as a(n) _____ _____.

7. The manager of the Suit Department of Macy's can influence the amount of salaries paid to departmental personnel. These expenses are said to be _____.

8. The costs of services provided by the Payroll Department to a profit center within the same company are called _____ _____ _____.

9. Service department charges are _____ (direct/indirect) expenses to a profit center.

10. The payroll department processed a total of 50,000 payroll checks and had total expenses of $240,000. If J Division has 8,000 payroll checks for the period, it should be charged _____ for payroll services.

11. If sales are $400,000, cost of goods sold is $220,000, selling expenses are $70,000, and service department charges are $42,000, income from operations is _____ .

12. Three measures used to evaluate the performance of investment center managers are income from operations, rate of return on investments, and _____ _____.

13. ROI is calculated by dividing income from operations by _____ _____.

14. The ratio of sales to invested assets is called the _____ _____.

15–17. Income from operations is $70,000, invested assets are $350,000, and sales are $875,000.

15. The profit margin is _____.

16. The investment turnover is _____.

17. The rate of return on investment is _____.

18. Measures of product quality, customer complaints, and warranty expenses are examples of _____ _____ _____.

19. Division A manufactures a radio that is used in the automobile produced in Division B. The charge to Division B for the product is called a(n) _____ _____.

20. Using the _____ _____ approach, the transfer price is the price at which the product or service could be sold to outside buyers.

21. The balanced scorecard consists of the innovation and learning, _____, _____, and _____ _____ dimensions.

MULTIPLE CHOICE

Instructions: Circle the best answer for each of the following questions.

1. When the manager has responsibility and authority to make decisions that affect costs, but no responsibility or authority over revenues and assets invested in the department, the department is referred to as:

   a. cost center

   b. a profit center

   c. an investment center

   d. none of the above

2. If a selling division organized as a profit center has excess capacity, the most appropriate approach to setting the transfer price is:

   a. market price

   b. negotiated price

   c. cost price

   d. marginal price

3. Which of the following expressions is frequently referred to as the profit margin factor in determining the rate of return on investment?

   a. income from operations divided by invested assets

   b. sales divided by invested assets

   c. income from operations divided by sales

   d. DuPont formula

4. The manager of which of the following centers has the most authority and responsibility?

   a. cost center

   b. profit center

   c. data center

   d. investment center

5. Division F has sales of $750,000; cost of goods sold of $450,000; operating expenses of $228,000; and invested assets of $300,000. What is the rate of return on investment of Division F?

   a. 9.6%

   b. 10%

   c. 20%

   d. 24%

6. Division F has sales of $750,000; cost of goods sold of $450,000; operating expenses of $228,000; and invested assets of $300,000. What is the investment turnover of Division F?

   a. 1.7

   b. 2.5

   c. 4.2

   d. 10.4

7. The profit margin for Division Q is 15% and the investment turnover is 1.2. What is the rate of return on investment for Division Q?

   a. 12.5%

   b. 15%

   c. 18%

   d. 20%

8. Which of the following is considered an advantage of decentralization?

   a. Decentralized decision making provides excellent training for managers.

   b. Decisions made by different managers all positively affect the overall profitability of the company.

   c. Assets and costs are duplicated across operating divisions.

   d. all of the above

9. Which of the following is an example of a service department?
   a. information systems
   b. purchasing
   c. payroll
   d. all of the above

10. A good example of a nonfinancial performance measure is:
   a. residual income
   b. income from operations
   c. customer retention rate
   d. investment turnover

11. The Payroll Department has a budget of $130,000. It is estimated that the company has 100 employees paid on a weekly (52 weeks per year) basis. The Video Division has 30 employees. Payroll Department service costs are charged to divisions on the basis of payroll checks. What would be the February Payroll Department service department charge to the Video Division?
   a. $750
   b. $3,000
   c. $3,250
   d. $39,000

12. The Collection Department has an annual budget of $180,000. The Publishing Division has an outstanding balance of $500,000 of accounts receivable, representing 1,200 invoices and 300 different customers. The Collection Department collects approximately 10,000 invoices per month, of which 4,000 are related to the Publishing Division. Collection Department service costs are charged to divisions on the basis of invoices. What would be the monthly Collection Department service department charge to the Publishing Division?
   a. $1,800
   b. $6,000
   c. $7,800
   d. $72,000

TRUE/FALSE

Instructions: Indicate whether each of the following statements is true or false by placing a check mark in the appropriate column.

<table>
<tr><td></td><td></td><td>**True**</td><td>**False**</td></tr>
<tr><td>1.</td><td>A primary disadvantage of decentralized operations is that decisions made by one manager may negatively affect the profitability of the entire company.</td><td>____</td><td>____</td></tr>
<tr><td>2.</td><td>In an investment center, the manager has responsibility and authority to make decisions that affect not only costs and revenues, but also the assets available to the center...</td><td>____</td><td>____</td></tr>
<tr><td>3.</td><td>Responsibility accounting reports for cost centers contain the same amount of detail, regardless of the level of operations to which the report is addressed.</td><td>____</td><td>____</td></tr>
<tr><td>4.</td><td>The primary responsibility accounting report for a cost center is the income statement.</td><td>____</td><td>____</td></tr>
<tr><td>5.</td><td>Three measures of investment center performance are rate of return on investment, residual income, and income from operations.</td><td>____</td><td>____</td></tr>
<tr><td>6.</td><td>Rate of return on investment as a measure of investment center performance reflects not only the revenues and costs of the division, but also the amount of invested assets.</td><td>____</td><td>____</td></tr>
<tr><td>7.</td><td>The rate of return on investment is computed by dividing sales by invested assets.</td><td>____</td><td>____</td></tr>
<tr><td>8.</td><td>If the rate of return on investment is 18% and the investment turnover is 3, the profit margin is 9%.</td><td>____</td><td>____</td></tr>
<tr><td>9.</td><td>If the divisional profit margin decreases and the investment turnover remains unchanged, the rate of return on investment will decrease.</td><td>____</td><td>____</td></tr>
<tr><td>10.</td><td>The market approach to transfer pricing should be used when the transferring division has excess capacity.</td><td>____</td><td>____</td></tr>
</table>

EXERCISE 23-1

Condensed income statements for Divisions M and N of Perlita Inc. and the amount invested in each division are as follows:

	Division M		Division N
Sales	$ 500,000	(c) $	
Cost of goods sold	(a) _____		275,000
Gross profit	$ 220,000		$ 245,000
Operating expenses and service department charges	100,000	(d)	
Income from operations	(b) $ _____		$ 110,000
Invested assets	$ 750,000		$ 500,000

Instructions:

(1) Insert the amounts of the missing items (a)–(d) in the condensed divisional income statements above.

(2) Determine the rate of return on investment for each division.

Division M:

Division N:

(3) On the basis of income from operations, which division is more profitable?

(4) On the basis of rate of return on investment, which division is more profitable?

EXERCISE 23-2

Based on the data in Exercise 23-1, assume that Perlita Inc. has established a minimum rate of return for invested assets at 12%.

Instructions:

(1) Determine the residual income for each division of Perlita.

Division M:

Division N:

(2) On the basis of residual income, which division is more profitable?

EXERCISE 23-3

One item is omitted from each of the following computations of the rate of return on investment using the DuPont formula:

Rate of Return on Investment	=	Profit Margin	×	Investment Turnover
16%		10%		**(a)** _____
17.5%		**(b)** _____		1.4
(c) _____		21%		0.9
21.6%		**(d)** _____		1.2
24%		16%		**(e)** _____

Instructions: Determine the missing items.

PROBLEM 23-1

The budget for Department F of Plant 7 for the current month ended July 31 is as follows:

Factory wages	$65,000
Materials	39,500
Supervisory salaries	15,000
Power and light	8,900
Depreciation of plant and equipment	7,500
Maintenance	4,300
Insurance and property taxes	2,000

During July, the costs incurred in Department F of Plant 7 were factory wages, $73,600; materials, $37,700; supervisory salaries, $15,000; power and light, $9,600; depreciation of plant and equipment, $7,500; maintenance, $3,900; and insurance and property taxes, $2,000.

Instructions: Prepare a budget performance report for the supervisor of Department F, Plant 7, for the month of July, using the following form:

Budget Performance Report—Supervisor, Department F, Plant 7

For Month Ended July 31, 20--

	BUDGET	ACTUAL	OVER	UNDER

PROBLEM 23-2

Instructions: Using the following information, complete the income statement for Divisions J and K of Firefly Co. on the following page.

(1) Division J sales $280,000
    Division K sales 420,000

(2) Cost of J sales 122,500
    Cost of K sales 227,500

(3) Division J operating expenses 48,000
    Division K operating expenses 72,000

The following service department expenses should be charged to the two divisions on the following bases:

(4) Corporate Service Department	Amount	Basis for Charging
Payroll accounting	$60,000	Number of payroll checks
Central purchasing	88,000	Number of requisitions
Brochures	50,000	Number of brochure pages

	Number of Payroll Checks	Number of Requisitions	Number of Brochure Pages
Division J	400	2,200	500
Division K	600	1,800	300
Total	1,000	4,000	800

Firefly Co.

Income Statement—Divisions J and K

For the Year Ended May 31, 20--

	DIVISION J	DIVISION K	TOTAL
Net sales			
Cost of goods sold			
Gross profit			
Operating expenses			
Income from operations before service			
department charges			
Less service department charges:			
Payroll accounting			
Purchasing			
Brochure advertising			
Total service department charges			
Income from operations			

PROBLEM 23-3

TP Co. has two manufacturing divisions, X and Y. Division X currently purchases 10,000 units of materials from an outside supplier at $30 per unit. The same materials are produced by Division Y at a variable cost of $22 per unit. Division Y is operating at full capacity of 40,000 units and can sell all it produces either to outside buyers at $30 or to Division X.

Instructions:

(1) Assume that Division Y sells 10,000 units of its product to Division X rather than to outside buyers. If the sale is made at a market price of $30, what will be the effect on:

    (a) Division X's income from operations?

          _____ increase by $_____

          _____ decrease by $_____

          _____ no effect

    (b) Division Y's income from operations?

          _____ increase by $_____

          _____ decrease by $_____

          _____ no effect

(2) Assume that Division Y sells 40,000 units of product at $30 to outside buyers and still has excess capacity of 10,000 units. If 10,000 units of product are sold to Division X at a negotiated transfer price of $27, what will be the effect on:

    (a) Division X's income from operations?

          _____ increase by $_____

          _____ decrease by $_____

          _____ no effect

    (b) Division Y's income from operations?

          _____ increase by $_____

          _____ decrease by $_____

          _____ no effect

(3) Assume the same facts as in (2), but use a negotiated transfer price of $20. What will be the effect on:

    (a) Division X's income from operations?

          _____ increase by $_____

          _____ decrease by $_____

          _____ no effect

    (b) Division Y's income from operations?

          _____ increase by $_____

          _____ decrease by $_____

          _____ no effect

24 Differential Analysis and Product Pricing

QUIZ AND TEST HINTS

The following hints may be helpful to you in preparing for a quiz or a test over the material covered in Chapter 24.

1. Many new terms are introduced in this chapter. You can expect true/false, multiple-choice, or matching questions testing your knowledge of these terms. Review the key terms in the next section by completing the Matching exercises.

2. You can expect short problems testing your ability to perform differential analysis for one or more of the six types of differential analysis illustrations presented in the chapter. Part 5 of the Illustrative Problem at the end of the chapter is a useful study aid for differential analysis of accepting additional business at a special price.

3. You also are likely to see a short problem applying the cost-plus approach to setting product prices. Remember that there are three versions of the cost-plus approach: total cost, product cost, and variable cost. You may find the Illustrative Problem to be a useful study aid.

4. If your instructor emphasized product pricing under production bottlenecks, you might also see a short problem in that area. At least be able to compute the contribution margin per bottleneck hour and describe how this information is used to adjust the product price.

MATCHING

Instructions: Match each of the statements below with its proper term. Some terms may not be used.

A. activity-based costing
B. bottleneck
C. differential analysis
D. differential cost
E. differential revenue
F. markup
G. opportunity cost

H. product cost concept
I. sunk cost
J. target costing
K. theory of constraints (TOC)
L. total cost concept
M. variable cost concept

_____ 1. The amount of income forgone from an alternative to a proposed use of cash or its equivalent.

_____ 2. A condition that occurs when product demand exceeds production capacity.

_____ 3. A concept used in applying the cost-plus approach to product pricing in which all the costs of manufacturing the product plus the selling and administrative expenses are included in the cost amount to which the markup is added.

_____ 4. A cost that is not affected by subsequent decisions.

_____ 5. The area of accounting concerned with the effect of alternative courses of action on revenues and costs.

_____ 6. A concept used in applying the cost-plus approach to product pricing in which only the variable costs are included in the cost amount to which the markup is added.

_____ 7. The amount of increase or decrease in revenue expected from a particular course of action as compared with an alternative.

_____ 8. A cost allocation method that identifies activities causing the incurrence of costs and allocates these costs to products (or other cost objects), based upon activity drivers (bases).

_____ 9. The amount of increase or decrease in cost expected from a particular course of action compared with an alternative.

_____ 10. A manufacturing strategy that attempts to remove the influence of bottlenecks (constraints) on a process.

_____ 11. A concept used in applying the cost-plus approach to product pricing in which only the costs of manufacturing the product, termed the product cost, are included in the cost amount to which the markup is added.

___ **12.** A concept used to design and manufacture a product at a cost that will deliver a target profit for a given market-determined price.

___ **13.** An amount that is added to a "cost" amount to determine product price.

FILL IN THE BLANK—PART A

Instructions: Answer the following questions or complete the statements by writing the appropriate words or amounts in the answer blanks.

1. The amount of increase or decrease in revenue expected from a course of action as compared with an alternative is called _____ _____.

2. The amount of increase or decrease in cost that is expected from a course of action as compared with an alternative is called the _____ _____.

3. In the lease or sell decision regarding a piece of equipment, the book value of the equipment would be considered a(n) _____ _____.

4. In using differential analysis, two additional factors that often need to be considered besides the basic differential revenue and costs are (1) differential revenue from investing the funds generated by the alternatives, and (2) any _____ _____ _____.

5. Product A has a loss from operations of $18,000 and fixed costs of $25,000. All remaining products have income from operations of $75,000 and fixed costs of $30,000. The estimated income from operations if Product A is discontinued would be _____.

6. Part Z can be purchased for $30 per unit or manufactured internally for $8 of direct materials, $9 of direct labor, and $15 of factory overhead ($7 of which is fixed). The cost savings from manufacturing Part Z internally would be _____.

7. The amount of income that is forgone from an alternative use of cash is called _____ _____.

8. McKeon Gas Co. is deciding whether to sell one of its products at an intermediate stage of development or process it further. The decision will rest on differential revenues and the differential costs of _____ _____.

9. H. Hoch and Co. is considering doing additional business at a special price. If Hoch is operating below full capacity, the differential costs of the additional production are the _____ manufacturing costs.

10. In deciding whether to accept business at a price lower than the normal price, the minimum short-run price should be set high enough to cover all _____ _____.

11–12. The two market methods of setting the normal selling price are:

11. _____-_____.

12. _____-_____.

13. The markup percentage for the total cost concept is determined by dividing desired profit by _____ _____.

14. The markup percentage for the variable cost concept is determined by dividing desired profit plus _____ _____ _____ by total variable costs.

15–17. Product M has total cost per unit of $60, including $20 per unit of selling and administrative costs. Total variable cost is $36 per unit, and desired profit is $6 per unit.

15. The markup percentage based on total cost is _____.

16. The markup percentage based on product cost is _____.

17. The markup percentage based on variable cost is _____.

18. The difference between the existing product cost and the target cost is termed the _____.

19. A method of more accurately measuring costs of producing and selling product and focusing on identifying and tracing activities to specific products is known as _____-_____ _____.

20. When the demand for the company's product exceeds its ability to produce the product, the resultant difficulty is referred to as a(n) _____ _____.

21. The manufacturing strategy that focuses on reducing the influence of bottlenecks on a process is the _____ _____ _____.

FILL IN THE BLANK—PART B

Instructions: Answer the following questions or complete the statements by writing the appropriate words or amounts in the answer blanks.

1. A method of decision making that focuses on the effect of alternative courses of action on the relevant revenues and costs is

   _____ _____.

2. Costs that have been incurred in the past that are not relevant to the decision are called _____ _____.

3. The difference between the differential revenue and differential costs is called the _____ _____.

4. The relevant financial factors to be considered in a lease or sell decision are differential costs and _____ _____.

5. Product B has a loss from operations of $12,000 and fixed costs of $8,000. All remaining products have income from operations of $75,000 and fixed costs of $30,000. The estimated income from operations if Product B is discontinued would be _____.

6. Make or buy options often arise when a manufacturer has excess _____.

7. A net cash outlay of $225,000 for a new piece of equipment could alternatively be invested to earn 10%. The $22,500 forgone by not investing the funds is called a(n) _____ _____.

8. Product K is produced for $4 per gallon and can be sold without additional processing for $5 per gallon. Product K can be processed further into Product G at a cost of $2 per gallon ($.80 fixed). Product G can be sold for $6.50 per gallon. The differential income per gallon from processing Product K into Product G is _____.

9. The law that prohibits price discrimination within the United States, unless differences in prices can be justified by different costs of serving different customers, is the _____-_____

   _____.

10–12. The three cost concepts used in applying the cost-plus approach to setting normal product prices are:

   10. _____ _____.

   11. _____ _____.

   12. _____ _____.

13. Under the _____ _____ concept, all costs of manufacturing a product plus the selling and administrative expenses are included in the cost amount to which the markup is added.

14. Contractors who sell products to government agencies often use the _____ _____ concept of applying the cost-plus approach to product pricing.

15. The markup percentage for the product cost concept is determined by dividing desired profit plus total selling and administrative expenses by _____ _____ _____.

16–18. Product N has total cost per unit of $40, including $15 per unit of selling and administrative costs. Total variable cost is $30 per unit, and desired profit is $5 per unit.

16. The markup percentage based on total cost is _____.

17. The markup percentage based on product cost is _____.

18. The markup percentage based on variable cost is _____.

19. A cost reduction concept, pioneered by the Japanese, that assumes that the selling price is set by the marketplace is _____ _____.

20. The term used to describe a situation when the demand for a company's product exceeds the ability of the company to produce it is _____ _____.

MULTIPLE CHOICE

Instructions: Circle the best answer for each of the following questions.

1. The area of accounting concerned with the effect of alternative courses of action on revenues and costs is called:

    a. gross profit analysis

    b. capital investment analysis

    c. differential analysis

    d. cost-volume-profit analysis

2. A business received an offer from an exporter for 10,000 units of product at $18 per unit. The acceptance of the offer will not affect normal production or the domestic sales price. The following data are available:

    Domestic sales price $25
    Unit manufacturing costs:
        Variable   16
        Fixed   4

    What is the amount of gain or loss from acceptance of the offer?

    a. $20,000 gain

    b. $20,000 loss

    c. $70,000 gain

    d. $70,000 loss

3. The amount of income that is forgone from the best available alternative to the proposed use of cash or its equivalent is called:

    a. sunk cost

    b. opportunity cost

    c. differential cost

    d. opportunity revenue

4. For which cost concept used in applying the cost-plus approach to product pricing are total selling and general expenses and desired profit allowed for in the determination of markup?

    a. total cost

    b. product cost

    c. variable cost

    d. none of the above

5. A business produces Product A in batches of 5,000 gallons, which can be sold for $3 per gallon. The business has been offered $5 per finished gallon to process two batches of Product A further into Product B. Product B will require additional processing costs of $7,800 per batch, and 10% of the gallons of Product A will evaporate during processing. What is the amount of gain or loss from further processing of Product A?

   a. $7,200 gain

   b. $4,400 gain

   c. $2,400 gain

   d. $600 loss

6. Which of the following cost concepts is not used in applying the cost-plus approach to setting the selling price?

   a. product cost

   b. total cost

   c. variable cost

   d. fixed cost

7. Which of the following concepts accepts a product price as given by the marketplace as the first step in determining the markup?

   a. total cost plus markup concept

   b. variable cost plus markup concept

   c. target costing

   d. product cost plus markup concept

8. The Majestic Company's casting operation is a production bottleneck. Majestic produces three products with the following per unit characteristics.

	Product A	Product B	Product C
Sales price	$100	$120	$200
Variable cost per unit	40	50	120
Contribution margin per unit	60	70	80
Fixed cost per unit	10	30	50
Net profit per unit	50	40	30
Casting time	3.5 hrs.	3 hrs.	4 hrs.

   Which product is the most profitable to the company?

   a. Product A

   b. Product B

   c. Product C

   d. Products A and C

9. Which of the following is a market method of setting the selling price?
   a. competition-based
   b. total cost-based
   c. variable cost-based
   d. product cost-based

10. Management is considering replacing its blending equipment. The annual costs of operating the old equipment are $250,000. The annual costs of operating the new equipment are expected to be $220,000. The old equipment has a book value of $35,000 and can be sold for $25,000. The cost of the new equipment would be $260,000. Which of these amounts should be considered a sunk cost in deciding whether to replace the old equipment?
   a. $250,000
   b. $220,000
   c. $35,000
   d. $25,000

11. A business has been purchasing 5,000 units of a part from an outside supplier for $40 per unit. In addition to the purchase price, there are import duties of 10% of the purchase price. A proposal was received to manufacture the part internally using excess manufacturing capacity. The per-unit cost for the part was estimated as follows:

Direct materials $21
Direct labor 15
Variable factory overhead 5
Fixed factory overhead 9
   Total cost per unit $50

What is the differential income or loss from manufacturing the part, rather than purchasing it from the outside supplier?
   a. $15,000 income
   b. $5,000 loss
   c. $30,000 loss
   d. $50,000 loss

12. A business has three product lines: small, medium, and large speakers. The small speaker line has a loss from operations of $25,000, while the medium and large speaker lines have a combined income from operations of $100,000. The total fixed costs of $50,000 are allocated on the basis of sales volume across the three product lines. The small product line has 30% of the sales volume. What is the differential income or loss from discontinuing the small speaker product line?

    a. $10,000 income

    b. $25,000 income

    c. $10,000 loss

    d. $15,000 loss

13. A business currently sells mobile phones in the domestic market for $80. The cost of the phones includes $50 variable cost per unit and $20 fixed cost per unit. A bid is received from an overseas customer for 1,000 phones at a price of $60 per phone. An additional 10% export fee on price would be assessed to the mobile phone company for overseas sales. What would be the differential income or loss from accepting the overseas bid?

    a. $4,000 loss

    b. $14,000 loss

    c. $4,000 income

    d. $10,000 income

TRUE/FALSE

Instructions: Indicate whether each of the following statements is true or false by placing a check mark in the appropriate column.

		True	False
1.	In deciding whether to replace fixed assets, the book values of the fixed assets being replaced are sunk costs and are irrelevant.	____	____
2.	The amount of increase or decrease in cost that is expected from a particular course of action as compared with an alternative is called opportunity cost.	____	____
3.	In deciding whether to accept business at a special price, a company that is operating below full capacity will decrease its operating income if the special price does not exceed all costs.	____	____
4.	Discontinuing an unprofitable segment of business will usually eliminate all of the related fixed costs.	____	____
5.	The amount of income that would result from the best available alternative to the proposed use of cash or its equivalent is called differential cost.	____	____
6.	Using the total cost concept of applying the cost-plus approach to product pricing, all costs of manufacturing the product plus the selling and administrative expenses are included in the cost amount to which the markup is added.	____	____
7.	In differential analysis, two additional factors to be considered in making a lease or sell decision are (1) differential revenue from investing funds generated by alternatives and (2) any income tax differential.	____	____
8.	Using the cost-plus approach to product pricing, managers determine product prices by adding a markup to a cost amount.	____	____
9.	Contractors who sell to government agencies often use the total cost approach to product pricing.	____	____
10.	The best way to measure product profitability in a production bottleneck environment is with contribution margin per unit.	____	____

EXERCISE 24-1

Walden Transportation Inc. has a truck that it no longer needs. The truck can be sold for $18,000 or it can be leased for a period of 5 years at $4,000 per year. At the end of the lease, the truck is expected to be sold for a negligible amount. The truck cost $50,000 four years ago, and $35,000 depreciation has been taken on it to date. To be sold for $18,000, the truck must first be repainted at a cost of $900. If the truck is to be leased for the 5-year period, Walden must provide the licenses, which cost $220 per year. The lessee must provide insurance at an annual cost of $200, tires at an estimated annual cost of $600, and repairs that are expected to amount to $2,000 during the 5-year period.

Instructions: Complete the following form to determine which alternative is more advantageous to Walden Transportation Inc. and to determine the amount of that advantage. (Ignore the fact that if the truck is leased, not all of the revenue is received at once.)

Walden Transportation Inc.
Proposal to Lease or Sell Truck

Differential revenue from alternatives:

    Revenue from lease .... $_____

    Revenue from sale .... _____

        Differential revenue from lease .... $_____

Differential cost of alternatives:

    License expenses during lease .... $_____

    Repainting expense on sale .... _____

        Differential cost of leasing .... _____

Net differential income (loss) from lease alternative .... $_____

EXERCISE 24-2

Tran Inc. has been purchasing metal blades for $14 a set for use in producing food processors. The cost of manufacturing the blades is estimated at $6.75 for direct materials, $5.10 for direct labor, and $1.80 for factory overhead ($1.00 fixed and $0.80 variable). Because there is unused capacity available, there would be no increase in the total amount of fixed factory overhead costs if Tran manufactures the blades.

Instructions: Complete the following form to determine whether Tran Inc. should make or buy the blades.

Tran Inc.
Proposal to Manufacture Metal Blades

Purchase price of blades		$ _____
Differential cost to manufacture blades:		
Direct materials	$ _____	
Direct labor	_____	
Variable factory overhead	_____	_____
Cost savings (increase) from manufacturing blades ...		$ _____

EXERCISE 24-3

English Chairs Inc. produces a line of rocking chairs in one section of the plant, and stuffed chairs and recliner chairs in other sections. The controller has supplied the following condensed income statement for the year just ended:

English Chairs Inc.
Condensed Income Statement
For Year Ended December 31, 20--

	Stuffed Chairs	Recliner Chairs	Rocking Chairs	Total
Sales	$500,000	$250,000	$350,000	$1,100,000
Cost of goods sold:				
Variable costs	$250,000	$110,000	$180,000	$ 540,000
Fixed costs	50,000	30,000	90,000	170,000
Total cost of goods sold	$300,000	$140,000	$270,000	$ 710,000
Gross profit	$200,000	$110,000	$ 80,000	$ 390,000
Operating expenses:				
Variable expenses	$100,000	$ 60,000	$ 75,000	$ 235,000
Fixed expenses	60,000	25,000	43,000	128,000
Total operating expenses	$160,000	$ 85,000	$118,000	$ 363,000
Income (loss) from operations	$ 40,000	$ 25,000	$ (38,000)	$ 27,000

Instructions: Complete the following form and determine whether the rocking chairs section should be continued.

English Chairs Inc.
Proposal to Discontinue Rocking Chairs
December 31, 20--

Differential revenue from sales of rocking chairs:

Revenue from sales .... $ _____

Differential cost of sales of rocking chairs:

Variable cost of goods sold .... $ _____

Variable operating expenses .... _____ _____

Differential income (loss) from sales of rocking chairs .... $ _____

The rocking chairs section probably _____ be continued.

EXERCISE 24-4

Golub Inc. has a machine which cost $250,000 five years ago and has $155,000 accumulated depreciation to date. The company can sell the machine for $83,000 and replace it with a larger one costing $370,000. The variable annual operating cost of the present machine amounts to $65,000. The variable annual operating cost of the new machine is estimated to be $30,000. It is estimated that either machine could be used for seven years from this date, December 31, 20--, and that at the end of the seven-year period neither would have a significant residual value.

Instructions: Complete the following schedule and determine the advisability of replacing the present machine.

Golub Inc.
Proposal to Replace Machine
December 31, 20--

Annual variable costs—present machine	$_____	
Annual variable costs—new machine	_____	
Annual differential decrease (increase) in variable costs	$_____	
Number of years applicable	_____	
Total differential decrease (increase) in variable costs	$_____	
Proceeds from sale of present machine	_____	$_____
Cost of new machine		_____
Net differential decrease (increase) in cost, seven-year total		$_____
Annual net differential decrease (increase) in cost—new machine		$_____

PROBLEM 24-1

Smith Company recently began production of a new product, G, which required the investment of $500,000 in assets. The costs and expenses of producing and selling 50,000 units of Product G are as follows:

Variable costs:

Direct materials	$1.20 per unit
Direct labor	2.40
Factory overhead	.40
Selling and administrative expenses	1.00
Total	$5.00 per unit

Fixed costs:

Factory overhead	$35,000
Selling and administrative expenses	15,000

Smith Company is currently establishing a selling price for Product G. The president of Smith Company has decided to use the cost-plus approach to product pricing and has indicated that Product G must earn a 12% rate of return on invested assets.

Instructions:

(1) Determine the amount of desired profit from the production and sale of Product G.

(2) Assuming that the total cost concept is used, determine (a) the cost amount per unit, (b) the markup percentage, and (c) the selling price of Product G.

(a)

(b)

(c)

PROBLEM 24-2

Based upon the data in Problem 24-1, assume that Smith Company uses the product cost concept of product pricing.

Instructions: Determine (1) the cost amount per unit, (2) the markup percentage, and (3) the selling price of Product G. (Round to the nearest cent.)

(1)

(2)

(3)

PROBLEM 24-3

Based upon the data in Problem 24-1, assume that Smith Company uses the variable cost concept of product pricing.

Instructions: Determine (1) the cost amount per unit, (2) the markup percentage, and (3) the selling price of Product G.

(1)

(2)

(3)

PROBLEM 24-4

The Zelda Company produces three products, Products D, E, and F. All three products require heat treatment in a furnace operation. The furnace operation is a production bottleneck. The annual cost of the furnace operation is $180,000. Information about the three products is as follows:

	Product D	Product E	Product F
Sales price per unit	$750	$600	$400
Variable cost per unit	300	350	200
Contribution margin per unit	$450	$250	$200
Fixed cost per unit	200	200	150
Profit per unit	$250	$ 50	$ 50
Furnace hours per unit	15	10	8

Instructions: Determine the price for Products E and F that would generate the same profitability as Product D.

25 Capital Investment Analysis

QUIZ AND TEST HINTS

The following hints may be helpful to you in preparing for a quiz or a test over the material covered in Chapter 25.

1. Many new terms are introduced in this chapter. You can expect true/false, multiple-choice, or matching questions testing your knowledge of these terms. Review the key terms in the next section using the Matching exercises.

2. You can expect some problems requiring you to perform capital investment analysis using each of the four methods illustrated in the chapter. Often, instructors will use multiple-choice questions to test your knowledge of the average rate of return method, cash payback method, and present value index. Short problems will be used to test your knowledge of the net present value and internal rate of return methods. The chapter illustrations and the Illustrative Problem at the end of the chapter are good study aids.

3. The remaining chapter topics are tested most often using true/false or multiple-choice questions. The Key Points at the end of the chapter are a good, concise review for many of these items.

MATCHING

Instructions: Match each of the statements below with its proper term. Some terms may not be used.

A. annuity
B. average rate of return
C. capital investment analysis
D. capital rationing
E. cash payback period
F. currency exchange rate
G. inflation

H. internal rate of return method
I. net present value method
J. present value concept
K. present value index
L. present value of an annuity
M. time value of money concept

_____ 1. A method of analysis of proposed capital investments that focuses on using present value concepts to compute the rate of return from the net cash flows expected from the investment.

_____ 2. An index computed by dividing the total present value of the net cash flow to be received from a proposed capital investment by the amount to be invested.

_____ 3. A series of equal cash flows at fixed intervals.

_____ 4. The expected period of time that will elapse between the date of a capital expenditure and the complete recovery in cash (or equivalent) of the amount invested.

_____ 5. The concept that an amount of money invested today will earn income.

_____ 6. A method of analysis of proposed capital investments that focuses on the present value of the cash flows expected from the investments.

_____ 7. The sum of the present values of a series of equal cash flows to be received at fixed intervals.

_____ 8. The process by which management plans, evaluates, and controls long-term capital investments involving fixed assets.

_____ 9. A period when prices in general are rising and the purchasing power of money is declining.

_____ 10. Cash today is not the equivalent of the same amount of money to be received in the future.

_____ 11. The process by which management allocates available investment funds among competing capital investment proposals.

_____ 12. A method of evaluating capital investment proposals that focuses on the expected profitability of the investment.

_____ 13. The rate at which currency in another country can be exchanged for local currency.

FILL IN THE BLANK—PART A

Instructions: Answer the following questions or complete the statements by writing the appropriate words or amounts in the answer blanks.

1. The process by which management plans, evaluates, and controls investments in fixed assets is called _____ _____ _____.

2. Two methods for evaluating capital investment proposals using present values are the net present value method and the _____ _____ _____ _____ method.

3. The methods that ignore present value are often useful in evaluating capital investment proposals that have relatively _____ useful lives.

4. Mist Company is considering whether or not to buy a new machine costing $400,000. The machine has a useful life of 8 years, with a residual value of $28,000, and is expected to produce average yearly revenues of $53,500. The average rate of return on this machine is _____.

5. One advantage of the _____ _____ _____ _____ method is that it emphasizes accounting income, which is often used by investors and creditors in evaluating management performance.

6. The _____ _____ period is the amount of time that will pass between the date of the investment and the complete recovery of the funds invested.

7. A new machine will cost $15,000 per year to operate and is expected to generate $65,000 in revenues. The machine is expected to last for 10 years and will cost $300,000. The cash payback period on this investment is _____.

8. Managers who are primarily concerned with liquidity will prefer to use the _____ _____ method of evaluating capital investments.

9. A series of equal net cash flows at fixed intervals is called a(n) _____.

10. The _____ _____ _____ method analyzes capital investment proposals by comparing the initial cash investment with the present value of the net cash flows.

11. A project has estimated annual net cash flows of $50,000 for 5 years and is estimated to cost $180,000. Assuming a minimum rate of return of 10%, the net present value of this project is _____.

12. A present value _____ is calculated by dividing the total present value of the net cash flow by the amount to be invested.

13. An advantage of the _____ _____ _____ method is that it considers the time value of money.

14. The present value factor for an annuity is calculated by dividing the total amount to be invested by the equal _____ _____ _____ _____ created by the investment.

15. A company is using the internal rate of return method to appraise a capital investment decision. Several proposals have been ranked according to their internal rate of return. The company should choose the proposal with the _____ (highest/lowest) rate of return.

16. Factors that complicate capital investment analysis include federal income tax, unequal lives of alternative proposals, leasing, _____, changes in price levels, and qualitative factors.

17. To evaluate capital investment alternatives with different useful lives, net present values should be adjusted so that each alternative ends at the _____ time.

18. Investments designed to affect a company's long-term ability to generate profits are called _____ investments.

19. Product quality, manufacturing flexibility, employee morale, manufacturing productivity, and manufacturing control are _____ considerations affecting capital investment analysis.

20. In capital rationing, alternative proposals are initially screened by establishing _____ standards for the cash payback and the average rate of return.

FILL IN THE BLANK—PART B

Instructions: Answer the following questions or complete the statements by writing the appropriate words or amounts in the answer blanks.

1. Methods of evaluating capital investment proposals can be grouped into two categories based on whether or not they involve _____ _____.

2. Two methods for evaluating capital investment proposals that do not use present values are the average rate of return method and the _____ _____ method.

3. The _____ _____ of money concept recognizes that an amount of cash invested today will earn income and therefore has value over time.

4. The _____ _____ _____ _____ is a measure of the average income as a percent of the average investment in fixed assets.

5. The average rate of return for a project that is estimated to yield total income of $270,000 over three years, cost $680,000, and has a $40,000 residual value is _____.

6. The excess of cash flowing in (from revenues) over the cash flowing out (for expenses) is called the _____ _____ _____.

7. When annual net cash flows are not equal, the _____ _____ _____ is determined by adding the annual net cash flows until the cumulative sum equals the amount of the proposed investment.

8. Present value methods for evaluating capital investment proposals consider both the amounts and the _____ of net cash flows.

9. The sum of the present values of a series of equal net cash flows is known as the _____ _____ _____ _____ _____.

10. If the _____ _____ _____ of the cash flows expected from a proposed investment equals or exceeds the amount of the initial investment, the proposal is desirable.

11. Shine Company is using the net present value method to evaluate an investment. The investment will cost $60,000, is expected to last for 3 years, and will generate annual returns of $30,000. The desired rate of return is 12%. The net present value of this investment is _____.

12. Project X costs $50,000 and has a total present value of $72,000. The present value index is _____.

13. The _____ _____ _____ _____ method uses present value concepts to compute the rate of return from the net cash flows expected from capital investment proposals.

14. You are using the internal rate of return method to evaluate an investment alternative. You can buy new equipment costing $26,500. The equipment has a useful life of 4 years and is expected to produce annual cash flows of $10,000. Assuming a 10% rate of return, the net present value of this investment is _____.

15. A new fabricating machine will cost $79,600 and will generate equal annual revenues of $16,000. The present value factor of this machine is _____.

16. The primary advantage of the _____ _____ _____ _____ method is that the present values of the net cash flows over the entire useful life of the proposal are considered.

17. _____ allows a business to use fixed assets without spending large amounts of cash to purchase them and may be evaluated using capital investment analysis techniques.

18. A period of increasing prices, sometimes called a period of _____, can significantly affect capital investment analysis.

19. Capital _____ is the process by which management allocates funds among competing capital investment proposals.

20. Qualitative considerations in capital investment analysis are most appropriate for _____ _____.

MULTIPLE CHOICE

Instructions: Circle the best answer for each of the following questions.

1. Which of the following methods of evaluating capital investment proposals ignores present value concepts?
   a. average rate of return method
   b. discounted cash flow method
   c. discounted internal rate of return method
   d. none of the above

2. The method of evaluating capital investment proposals that determines the total present value of cash flows expected from investment proposals and compares these values with the amounts to be invested is:
   a. average rate of return method
   b. cash payback method
   c. discounted internal rate of return method
   d. net present value method

3. The method of evaluating capital investment proposals which uses present value concepts to compute the rate of return from the net cash flows expected from the proposals is:
   a. average rate of return method
   b. cash payback method
   c. internal rate of return method
   d. net present value method

4. Jones Inc. is considering the purchase of a machine that costs $360,000. The machine is expected to have a useful life of 10 years, with no salvage value, and is expected to yield an annual net cash flow of $120,000 and an annual operating income of $60,000. What is the estimated cash payback period for the machine?
   a. 2 years
   b. 3 years
   c. 5 years
   d. 6 years

5. Management is considering an $800,000 investment in a project with a 6-year life and no residual value. If the total income from the project is expected to be $600,000, the average rate of return is:
   a. 12.5%
   b. 25%
   c. 32%
   d. 44%

6. Which of the following is a qualitative consideration that may impact upon capital investment analysis?
   a. manufacturing flexibility
   b. expected net cash inflows
   c. amounts of cash to be invested
   d. timing of cash inflows

7. Genko Company has purchased a machine for $145,000. The machine is expected to generate a positive annual net cash flow of $50,000 for four consecutive years. What is the present value index, assuming a minimum rate of return of 10%?
   a. 0.942
   b. 0.915
   c. 1.093
   d. 1.379

8. The net present value method is also called the:
   a. internal rate of return method
   b. time-adjusted rate of return method
   c. average rate of discounted return method
   d. discounted cash flow method

9. A disadvantage of the cash payback method is that it:
   a. focuses on measures that are not important to bankers and other creditors
   b. emphasizes accounting income
   c. does not use present value concepts in valuing cash flows occurring in different periods
   d. cannot be used when annual net cash flows are not equal

10. Which of the following factors may have an impact on a capital investment decision?
    a. federal income taxes
    b. unequal lives of proposed investments
    c. changes in price levels
    d. all of the above

11. A business is considering the investment in a new machine that will cost $320,000 with no salvage value. The machine is expected to reduce labor costs by $70,000 per year and material scrap by $20,000 per year. The machine is expected to have a 5-year life. What is the present value of this investment, assuming a 12% interest rate?

   a. $4,450

   b. $130,000

   c. $(64,850)

   d. $(67,650)

12. A business invests $83,200 in a project that is expected to generate $20,000 in annual cash flows at the end of each of the next seven years. What is the internal rate of return on this project?

   a. 10%

   b. 12%

   c. 15%

   d. 20%

13. A machine will cost $45,000 and is expected to generate equal annual cash flows of $15,000 at the end of each of the next five years. In addition, the machine is expected to have a salvage value of $8,000 at the end of the fifth year. Determine the net present value of this investment, assuming an interest rate of 20%.

   a. $(14,850)

   b. $(135)

   c. $3,081

   d. $23,793

TRUE/FALSE

Instructions: Indicate whether each of the following statements is true or false by placing a check mark in the appropriate column.

	True	False

1. The two common present value methods used in evaluating capital investment proposals are (1) the net present value method and (2) the internal rate of return method. .... _____ _____

2. Two methods of evaluating capital investment proposals that ignore present value are (1) the average rate of return method and (2) the cash payback period method............... _____ _____

3. The expected time that will pass between the date of capital investment and the complete recovery of cash (or equivalent) of the amount invested is called the present value period.. _____ _____

4. The methods of evaluating capital investment proposals that ignore present value are especially useful in evaluating capital investments that have relatively long useful lives. .... _____ _____

5. The net present value method, sometimes called the internal rate of return or time-adjusted rate of return method, uses present value concepts to compute the rate of return from the net cash flows expected from the capital investment proposals. .... _____ _____

6. The present value index is computed by dividing the amount to be invested by the total present value of the net cash flow. .... _____ _____

7. The present value factor for an annuity of $1 is computed by dividing the amount to be invested by the equal annual net cash flow. .... _____ _____

8. Proposals that are funded in the capital rationing process are included in the capital expenditures budget to aid the planning and financing of operations. .... _____ _____

9. One advantage of the average rate of return method is that it includes the amount of income earned over the entire life of the proposal.. _____ _____

10. One disadvantage of the cash payback method is that it includes cash flows occurring after the payback period. ..... _____ _____

EXERCISE 25-1

Daily Inc. is considering the acquisition of a newly developed machine at a cost of $620,000. This machine is expected to have a useful life of 5 years and no residual value. Use of the new machine is expected to yield total income of $240,000 during the 5 years of its useful life and to provide an average annual net cash flow of $200,000. The minimum rate of return desired by Daily is 12%. The maximum cash payback period desired by Daily is 3 years.

Instructions: Using the information given, make the analyses indicated and write your answers in the spaces provided.

(1) What average rate of return (based on the average investment) can Daily expect to achieve during the useful life of this machine? .... _____ %

(2) What is the expected cash payback period for this proposed expenditure? .... _____ years

(3) Based on the analysis of average rate of return, should the management of Daily acquire the new machine? ....   yes ____   no ____

(4) Based on the expected cash payback period, should management acquire the new machine? ....   yes ____   no ____

EXERCISE 25-2

Crusty Corp. is evaluating two capital investment proposals, each requiring an investment of $250,000 and each with a six-year life and expected total net cash flows of $360,000.

Proposal 1 is expected to provide equal annual net cash flows of $60,000. Proposal 2 is expected to have the following unequal net cash flows:

Year 1	$100,000	Year 4	$45,000
Year 2	80,000	Year 5	45,000
Year 3	70,000	Year 6	20,000

Instructions: Determine the cash payback period for each proposal.

Proposal 1:

Proposal 2:

EXERCISE 25-3

Assume that Crusty Corp. is re-evaluating the two capital investment proposals described in Exercise 25-2, taking into consideration present value concepts.

Instructions: Determine the net present value for each proposal using a rate of 10%.

Proposal 1:

Proposal 2:

EXERCISE 25-4

The management of Argo Inc. has decided to use the internal rate of return method to analyze a capital investment proposal that involves an investment of $358,900 and annual net cash flows of $120,000 for each of the 5 years of useful life.

Instructions:

(1) Determine the present value factor for an annuity of $1 which can be used in determining the internal rate of return.

(2) Using the factor determined in (1) and the present value of an annuity of $1 table appearing in Chapter 25, determine the internal rate of return for the proposal.

PROBLEM 25-1

Instructions:

(1) Complete the following table using the net present value method to evaluate capital investment in new equipment.

Year	Present Value of 1 at 12%	Net Cash Flow	Present Value of Net Cash Flow
1	0.893	$ 80,000	$ _____
2	0.797	60,000	_____
3	0.712	60,000	_____
4	0.636	60,000	_____
5	0.567	60,000	_____
Total		$320,000	$ _____

Amount to be invested in equipment .... _____ 180,000

Excess of present value over amount to be invested .. $ _____

(2) Compute the present value index for the new equipment. (Round to two decimal places.)

(3) Based on the net present value method, should management acquire the new machine? .... yes ____ no ____

PROBLEM 25-2

Preston Co. is evaluating two projects which have different useful lives but which have an equal investment requirement of $180,000. The estimated net cash flows from each project are as follows:

Year	Project 1	Project 2
1	$55,000	$55,000
2	50,000	55,000
3	45,000	55,000
4	40,000	55,000
5	40,000	55,000
6	30,000	
7	15,000	

Preston Co. has selected a rate of 10% for purposes of net present value analysis. Preston also estimates that there will be no residual value at the end of each project's useful life, but at the end of the fifth year, Project 1's residual value would be $60,000.

Instructions:

(1) For each project, compute the net present value.

Project 1:

Project 2:

(2) For each project, compute the net present value, assuming that Project 1 is adjusted to a five-year life for purposes of analysis.

(3) Determine which of the two projects is more attractive based upon your findings in (2) above.

CHAPTER 12

MATCHING

1. M	4. K	7. F	10. D	13. A	16. H
2. P	5. B	8. C	11. Q	14. N	17. L
3. G	6. I	9. J	12. O	15. E	

FILL IN THE BLANK—PART A

1. stock
2. stockholders' equity
3. retained earnings
4. $995,000
5. outstanding
6. common
7. nonparticipating
8. $100,000
9. premium
10. $160,000
11. treasury
12. none
13. dividend
14. $32,500
15. retained earnings

FILL IN THE BLANK—PART B

1. stockholders
2. paid-in
3. deficit
4. stated
5. preferred
6. cumulative
7. $140,000
8. discount
9. $32,500 decrease
10. $895,000
11. stock split
12. $36
13. stock dividend
14. par
15. dividend yield

MULTIPLE CHOICE

1. a. Incorrect. Ownership represented by shares of stock is a characteristic of the corporate form of organization.
   b. Incorrect. Separate legal existence is a characteristic of the corporate form of organization.
   c. **Correct.** Unlimited liability of stockholders is not a characteristic of the corporate form of organization. Rather, stockholders of a corporation have limited liability that limits the liability to the amount invested.
   d. Incorrect. Earnings subject to the federal income tax is a characteristic of the corporate form of organization.

2. a. Incorrect. The stated value is the amount the board of directors assigns to no-par stock.
   b. Incorrect. The premium is the amount by which the issue price of a stock exceeds its par.
   c. Incorrect. The discount is the amount by which the par value of a stock exceeds its issue price.
   d. **Correct.** The amount printed on a stock certificate is known as par value.

3. a. Incorrect.
   b. Incorrect.
   c. **Correct.** The amount of preferred dividends that must be declared in the current year before a dividend can be declared on common stock is $150,000, computed as $120,000 dividends in arrears [(5,000 shares × $6) × 4 years] plus the current year dividend of $30,000 (5,000 shares × $6).
   d. Incorrect.

4. a. Incorrect.
   b. **Correct.** When a corporation purchases its own stock, Treasury Stock is debited for the cost of the stock.
   c. Incorrect.
   d. Incorrect.

5. a. Incorrect. Retained Earnings is credited for the income of a period, not for the excess of proceeds from selling treasury stock over its cost.

   b. Incorrect. Premium on Capital Stock is credited for the issuance of new stock at a price exceeding the par or stated value of the stock.

   c. Incorrect. A corporation cannot have gains and losses from trading its stock.

   d. **Correct.** The excess of the proceeds from selling treasury stock over its cost should be credited to Paid-In Capital from Sale of Treasury Stock.

6. a. Incorrect. The claims of preferred stockholders are satisfied after the claims of creditors upon liquidation of a corporation.

   b. Incorrect. The claims of preferred stockholders are satisfied after the claims of creditors upon liquidation of a corporation.

   c. Incorrect. The claims of common stockholders are satisfied last upon liquidation of a corporation

   d. **Correct.** The claims of the creditors must first be satisfied upon liquidation of a corporation.

7. a. **Correct.** The amount transferred from the retained earnings account to paid-in capital accounts as a result of the stock dividend is $36,000, computed as [(12,000 shares × 5%) × $60].

   b. Incorrect.

   c. Incorrect. The amount transferred from the retained earnings account to paid-in capital accounts as a result of the stock dividend is based upon the market price of the stock, not the par value.

   d. Incorrect.

8. a. Incorrect. 5,000 is the number of shares reacquired.

   b. **Correct.** The number of shares outstanding is 55,000 shares, determined as the 60,000 shares issued minus the 5,000 shares reacquired.

   c. Incorrect. 60,000 is the number of shares issued.

   d. Incorrect. 100,000 is the number of shares authorized.

9. a. Incorrect. Donated Capital is credited for the fair value of assets donated to a corporation as an incentive to locate or remain in a community.

   b. Incorrect. Retained Earnings is credited for the income of the period.

   c. Incorrect. Treasury Stock is credited when reacquired shares are sold.

   d. **Correct.** The entry to record the issuance of common stock at a price above par would include a credit to Paid-In Capital in Excess of Par—Common Stock.

10. a. Incorrect. The total stockholders' equity will decrease, not increase.

   b. Incorrect. The total stockholders' equity will decrease, not increase.

   c. Incorrect. The decrease is based upon the cost of the reacquired stock, not its par value.

   d. **Correct.** The effect on total stockholders' equity of purchasing 10,000 shares of its own $20 par common stock for $35 per share is a decrease of $350,000 (10,000 shares × $35).

TRUE/FALSE

1. T

2. T

3. F The two main sources of stockholders' equity are paid-in capital and retained earnings, not long-term debt.

4. F The preferred stockholders have a greater chance of receiving regular dividends than do common stockholders, not vice versa.

5. T

6. T

7. F Preferred stock for which dividend rights are limited to a certain amount is said to be nonparticipating, not noncumulative.

8. T

9. F Sales of treasury stock result in a net increase, not decrease, in paid-in capital.

10. F Expenditures incurred in organizing a corporation, such as legal fees, taxes, fees paid to the state, and promotional costs, are charged to an expense account entitled Organization Expenses, not Goodwill.

11. F A commonly used method for accounting for the purchase and resale of treasury stock is the cost method, not the derivative method.

12. F A major objective of a stock split is to reduce the market price per share of the stock. A stock split does not affect the amount of total stockholders' equity.

13. T

14. F A liability for a dividend is normally recorded in the accounting records on the date of declaration, not the date of record.

15. T

EXERCISE 12-1

(1) Cash 700,000

   Common Stock 700,000

(2) Cash 500,000

   Common Stock 500,000

(3) Cash 1,200,000

   Common Stock 1,000,000

   Paid-In Capital in Excess of Par—Common Stock 200,000

(4) Equipment 145,000

   Common Stock 100,000

   Paid-In Capital in Excess of Par—Common Stock 45,000

(5) Cash 300,000

   Preferred Stock 250,000

   Paid-In Capital in Excess of Par—Preferred Stock 50,000

EXERCISE 12-2

(1) Oct. 1   Treasury Stock 150,000

      Cash 150,000

(2) Oct. 31   Cash 65,600

      Treasury Stock 60,000

      Paid-In Capital from Sale of Treasury Stock 5,600

(3) Nov. 20   Cash 7,000

      Paid-In Capital from Sale of Treasury Stock 500

      Treasury Stock 7,500

EXERCISE 12-3

(1) Feb. 20   Cash Dividends 60,000

      Cash Dividends Payable 60,000

(2) Mar. 22   Cash Dividends Payable 60,000

      Cash 60,000

(3) Dec. 15   Stock Dividends 200,000

      Stock Dividends Distributable 160,000

      Paid-In Capital in Excess of Par—Common Stock ... 40,000

(4) Jan. 14   Stock Dividends Distributable 160,000

      Common Stock 160,000

(5) Feb. 20   None

PROBLEM 12-1

(1)

Year	Total Dividends	Preferred Dividends		Common Dividends	
		Total	Per Share	Total	Per Share
1	$ 7,000	$7,000	$7	–0–	–0–
2	9,000	9,000	9	–0–	–0–
3	28,000	8,000	8	$20,000	$ 5
4	48,000	8,000	8	40,000	10

(2)

Year	Total Dividends	Preferred Dividends		Common Dividends	
		Total	Per Share	Total	Per Share
1	$ 7,000	$7,000	$7	–0–	–0–
2	9,000	8,000	8	$ 1,000	$ .25
3	28,000	8,000	8	20,000	5.00
4	48,000	8,000	8	40,000	10.00

PROBLEM 12-2

		(1)	(2)	(3)
		Column A	Column B	Column C
		Before Any Dividend	After Cash Dividend	After Stock Dividend
a.	Total number of shares outstanding..........	100,000	100,000	105,000
b.	Total par value of shares outstanding.......	$2,500,000	$2,500,000	$2,625,000
c.	Total additional paid-in capital...................	$1,500,000	$1,500,000	$1,525,000
d.	Total retained earnings.............................	$6,440,000	$6,290,000	$6,290,000
e.	Total stockholders' equity.........................	$10,440,000	$10,290,000	$10,440,000
f.	Amount required to pay a $1.50 per share cash dividend next year	$150,000	$150,000	$157,500
g.	Percentage of total stock owned by Rafael...	1%	1%	1%
h.	Total number of shares owned by Rafael .	1,000	1,000	1,050
i.	Total par value of Rafael's shares.............	$25,000	$25,000	$26,250
j.	Total equity of Rafael's shares..................	$104,400	$102,900	$104,400

PROBLEM 12-3

Paid-in capital:
    Preferred $10 stock, $100 par (10,000 shares authorized;
        7,500 issued) .... $ 750,000
    Excess over par.. 375,000 $1,125,000
    Common stock, $25 par (150,000 shares authorized;
        100,000 issued) $2,500,000
    Excess over par.. 500,000   3,000,000
    From sale of treasury stock 4,000
    Total paid-in capital $4,129,000
Retained earnings.. 1,000,000
Total $5,129,000
Deduct treasury common stock (1,000 shares at cost) 50,000
    Total stockholders' equity.. $5,079,000

CHAPTER 13

MATCHING

1. I	**4.** A	**6.** H	**8.** J	**10.** B
2. C	**5.** G	**7.** D	**9.** L	**11.** E
3. F				

FILL IN THE BLANK—PART A

1. proprietorship
2. limited liability corporation; corporation
3. mutual agency
4. corporate
5. statement of stockholders' equity
6. equally
7. salary allowance
8. $60,000
9. current market values
10. $4,000 ($20,000 – $16,000)
11. Owens
12. capital balances
13. $9,000
14. loss; income-sharing ratio
15. venture capitalist

FILL IN THE BLANK—PART B

1. proprietorship; limited liability corporation; partnership
2. partnership agreement
3. unlimited liability
4. ease
5. statement of members' equity
6. partnership agreement
7. interest
8. $150,000
9. gain; loss
10. $18,000 ($50,000 – $32,000)
11. Long
12. realized
13. deficiency
14. $30,000
15. underwriting firm (or investment bank)

MULTIPLE CHOICE

1. a. Incorrect.
    b. ***Correct.*** If the partnership agreement is silent, then income and loss are divided equally.
    c. Incorrect.
    d. Incorrect.

2. a. Incorrect. Access to more capital *is* an advantage of a partnership.
    b. Incorrect. Partner income taxes may be less than with a corporation since partnerships are not taxed as separate entities, whereas corporations are.
    c. Incorrect. Access to more managerial skill *is* an advantage of a partnership.
    d. ***Correct.*** Partners have unlimited liability, thus, this is an incorrect statement.

3. a. Incorrect. Both are incorrect for a LLC.
    b. Incorrect. A limited life is not an advantage.
    c. ***Correct.*** A limited liability corporation has the limited liability features of a corporation and the nontaxable (flow-through) features of a partnership.
    d. Incorrect. LLCs are not taxed as separate entities.

4. a. Incorrect.
    b. Incorrect.
    c. Incorrect.
    d. ***Correct.*** When a new partner is admitted by the contribution of assets, the assets of the partnership would increase, as would the total partner capital. This would be necessary to keep the accounting equation in balance. All other answers would violate the accounting equation.

5. a. Incorrect.
    b. ***Correct.*** $40,000 – [($25,000 + $35,000 + $40,000) × 30%]
    c. Incorrect.
    d. Incorrect.

6. a. Incorrect. This would be Columbo's share.
    b. Incorrect. This would be equal sharing and would be correct only in the absence of a partnership agreement.
    c. ***Correct.*** 2/5 × $80,000
    d. Incorrect. This would be correct only if the total income were $100,000.

7. a. Incorrect. The revaluation is reflected in the capital accounts so that the newly admitted partner's relative portion of the capital equitably reflects current market values.
    b. Incorrect. This would be Haley's capital account impact.
    c. **Correct.** ($90,000 – $75,000) × 3/5; the capital account is debited for the loss in market value.
    d. Incorrect. Multiplying the loss of $15,000 by 3/2 is incorrect.

8. a. Incorrect. It is incorrect to calculate the loss as $60,000 × 1/6 since Patterson cannot be allocated deficiency.
    b. **Correct.** $60,000 × 1/3
    c. Incorrect. There is an income-sharing ratio, thus equal sharing of the deficiency cannot be assumed.
    d. Incorrect. This is Hill's allocation ($60,000 × 2/3).

9. a. Incorrect.
    b. Incorrect. Only the final distribution should be allocated on the basis of the current balances of the capital accounts.
    c. **Correct.** All gains and losses should be allocated on the basis of the income-sharing ratio.
    d. Incorrect. This is correct only when the partnership agreement is silent as to the income-sharing ratio.

10. a. Incorrect. Underwriting firms are involved in pricing and selling initial public offerings. They do not primarily invest in new businesses.
    b. Incorrect. The founders are the individuals that have the initial idea for the business.
    c. Incorrect. This is an owner of a limited liability corporation.
    d. **Correct.** Venture capitalists provide private financing for new companies. Their investments can be in partnerships, LLCs, or corporations.

TRUE/FALSE

1. F Partners are owners in a partnership, and their capital contributions are not loans to the partnership (even though they may receive credit for interest on their capital balance). Neither are partners considered employees (even though they may receive a salary allowance).
2. T
3. T
4. F Any property contributed to the partnership by a partner becomes the property of the partnership.
5. F The claim against the net assets of a partnership is measured by a partner's *current* capital balance.
6. T
7. T
8. T
9. F A partnership is a nontaxable (flow-through) entity.
10. T
11. F All of the partners must agree.
12. F No partner's interest can be disposed of without all partners in agreement, thus dissolving the partnership.
13. F The purchase price only affects the accounts of the individual partners, not the partnership.
14. T
15. T
16. T
17. F Cash from the sale of assets must first go to satisfying the claims of creditors (liabilities).
18. T
19. T

EXERCISE 13-1

Cash..	100,000	
Merchandise Inventory......................................	80,000	
Cutco, Capital		180,000

Cash..	10,000	
Land..	115,000	
Equipment...	45,000	
Merchandise Inventory......................................	5,000	
Robbs, Capital		175,000

EXERCISE 13-2

(1) June 30

Hartly, Capital	20,000	
Smetz, Capital	11,000	
Grasso, Capital	7,000	
Schafer, Capital...............................		38,000

(2) July 1

Cash...	50,000	
Hartly, Capital	7,000	
Smetz, Capital	7,000	
Grasso, Capital.......................................	7,000	
Masko, Capital		71,000

EXERCISE 13-3

(1)

Inventory..	12,750	
Arway, Capital..................................		4,250
Batts, Capital		4,250
Carlone, Capital		4,250
Carlone, Capital......................................	44,250	
Arway, Capital..................................		44,250

(2)

Inventory..	6,000	
Arway, Capital..................................		2,000
Batts, Capital		2,000
Carlone, Capital		2,000
Carlone, Capital......................................	42,000	
Cash...		42,000

PROBLEM 13-1

(1)

Bulley's share	$100,000
Scram's share	100,000
Total	$200,000

(2)

Bulley's share	$ 80,000
Scram's share	120,000
Total	$200,000

(3)

Bulley's share	$ 60,000
Scram's share	140,000
Total	$200,000

(4)

Division of Net Income	Bulley	Scram	Total
Salary allowance	$30,000	$ 50,000	$ 80,000
Remaining income	60,000	60,000	120,000
Net income	$90,000	$110,000	$200,000

(5)

Division of Net Income	Bulley	Scram	Total
Interest allowance	$15,000	$ 35,000	$ 50,000
Remaining income	75,000	75,000	150,000
Net income	$90,000	$110,000	$200,000

(6)

Division of Net Income	Bulley	Scram	Total
Salary allowance	$15,000	$ 25,000	$ 40,000
Interest allowance	15,000	35,000	50,000
Remaining income	55,000	55,000	110,000
Net income	$85,000	$115,000	$200,000

(7)

Division of Net Income	Bulley	Scram	Total
Salary allowance	$80,000	$ 78,000	$158,000
Interest allowance	15,000	35,000	50,000
Total	$95,000	$113,000	$208,000
Excess of allowances over income	4,000	4,000	8,000
Net income	$91,000	$109,000	$200,000

PROBLEM 13-2

(1)

Processing Equipment	20,000	
Baskin, member equity		15,000
Robbins, member equity		5,000

Baskin: $20,000 × 3/4   Robbins: $20,000 × 1/4

(2) (a)

Cash	100,000	
Baskin, member equity	30,000	
Robbins, member equity	10,000	
Dreyer, member equity		140,000

Supporting calculations:

Equity of Baskin (after revaluation)	$400,000
Equity of Robbins (after revaluation)	200,000
Contribution by Dreyer	100,000
Total equity after admitting Dreyer	$700,000
Dreyer's equity interest after admission	20%
Dreyer's equity after admission	$140,000
Contribution by Dreyer	100,000
Bonus paid to Dreyer	$ 40,000

Baskin: $40,000 × 3/4   Robbins: $40,000 × 1/4

(b)

Cash	180,000	
Baskin, member equity		47,250
Robbins, member equity		15,750
Dreyer, member equity		117,000

Supporting calculations:

Equity of Baskin (after revaluation)	$400,000
Equity of Robbins (after revaluation)	200,000
Contribution by Dreyer	180,000
Total equity after admitting Dreyer	$780,000
Dreyer's equity interest after admission	15%
Dreyer's equity after admission	$117,000
Contribution by Dreyer	$180,000
Dreyer's equity after admission	117,000
Bonus paid to Baskin and Robbins	$ 63,000

Baskin: $63,000 × 3/4   Robbins: $63,000 × 1/4

PROBLEM 13-3

(1)

	Cash +	Noncash Assets =	Liabilities +	Trite (30%) +	Sandpipe (50%) +	Hinkle (20%)
Balances before realization	$100,000	$300,000	$120,000	$ 90,000	$ 60,000	$130,000
Sale of noncash assets and division of gain	+400,000	−300,000		+ 30,000	+ 50,000	+ 20,000
Balances after realization	$500,000	−0−	$120,000	$120,000	$110,000	$150,000
Payment of liabilities	−120,000		−120,000			
Balances after payment of liabilities	$380,000	−0−	−0−	$120,000	$110,000	$150,000
Distribution of cash to partners	−380,000			−120,000	−110,000	−150,000
Final balances	−0−	−0−	−0−	−0−	−0−	−0−

(2)

	Cash +	Noncash Assets =	Liabilities +	Trite (30%) +	Sandpipe (50%) +	Hinkle (20%)
Balances before realization	$100,000	$300,000	$120,000	$90,000	$60,000	$130,000
Sale of noncash assets and division of loss	+130,000	−300,000		−51,000	−85,000	− 34,000
Balances after realization	$230,000	−0−	$120,000	$39,000	$25,000 Dr.	$ 96,000
Payment of liabilities	−120,000		−120,000			
Balances after payment of liabilities	$110,000	−0−	−0−	$39,000	$25,000 Dr.	$ 96,000
Receipt of deficiency	+ 25,000				25,000	
Balances	$135,000			$39,000	−0−	$ 96,000
Distribution of cash to partners	−135,000			−39,000	−0−	−96,000
Final balances	−0−	−0−	−0−	−0−	−0−	−0−

(3)	Cash	130,000	
	Loss and Gain on Realization	170,000	
	Noncash Assets		300,000
	Triste, Capital	51,000	
	Sandpipe, Capital	85,000	
	Hinkle, Capital	34,000	
	Loss and Gain on Realization		170,000
	Liabilities	120,000	
	Cash		120,000
	Cash	25,000	
	Sandpipe, Capital		25,000
	Triste, Capital	39,000	
	Hinkle, Capital	96,000	
	Cash		135,000

CHAPTER 14

MATCHING

1. U	6. A	10. X	14. L	18. E	22. O
2. V	7. S	11. B	15. K	19. P	23. D
3. F	8. C	12. W	16. H	20. T	24. N
4. J	9. I	13. Y	17. M	21. R	25. Q
5. G					

FILL IN THE BLANK—PART A

1. taxable
2. $150,000
3. restructuring charges
4. discontinued
5. extraordinary items
6. loss from discontinued operations
7. earnings per share (eps)
8. preferred dividends
9. comprehensive
10. trading
11. temporary investments
12. equity
13. consolidation
14. subsidiary
15. minority interest

FILL IN THE BLANK—PART B

1. temporary
2. $25,000
3. fixed asset impairment
4. extraordinary item
5. stockholders' equity
6. equity
7. available-for-sale
8. unrealized
9. cost
10. merger
11. investments
12. parent
13. accumulated other comprehensive income
14. consolidated
15. price-earnings

MULTIPLE CHOICE

1. a. *Correct.* The amount of income tax deferred to future years is $40,000 [($300,000 − $200,000) × 40%].
   b. Incorrect.
   c. Incorrect.
   d. Incorrect.

2. a. Incorrect. A method of recognizing revenue when the sale is made is used for financial statements, and a method of recognizing revenue at the time the cash is collected is used for tax reporting *does* result in a temporary difference.
   b. Incorrect. Warranty expense is recognized in the year of sale for financial statements and when paid for tax reporting *does* result in a temporary difference.

c. Incorrect. An accelerated depreciation method is used for tax reporting, and the straight-line method is used for financial statements *does* result in a temporary difference.

d. **Correct.** Interest income on municipal bonds is recognized for financial statements and not for tax reporting *does not* result in a temporary difference.

3. a. Incorrect. A correction of an error in the prior year's financial statements is a prior-period adjustment and would be reported in the statement of retained earnings.

b. Incorrect. A gain resulting from the sale of fixed assets is not an extraordinary item, but it is reported as other income on the income statement.

c. Incorrect. A loss on sale of temporary investments is not an extraordinary item, but it is reported as other income or loss on the income statement.

d. **Correct.** A loss on condemnation of land is an extraordinary item on the income statement.

4. a. Incorrect. Earnings per share is not required to be presented on the face of the income statement for extraordinary items.

b. Incorrect. Earnings per share is not required to be presented on the face of the income statement for discontinued operations.

c. **Correct.** Earnings per share is required to be presented on the face of the income statement for income from continuing operations and net income.

d. Incorrect.

5. a. Incorrect.

b. **Correct.** All changes in stockholders' equity during a period except those resulting from investments by stockholders and dividends is the definition of comprehensive income.

c. Incorrect.

d. Incorrect.

6. a. Incorrect. Under the equity method, the receipt of cash dividends on a long-term investment in common stock is accounted for as a debit to Cash and a credit to the investment account, not Dividend Revenue.

b. Incorrect.

c. **Correct.** Under the cost method, the receipt of cash dividends on a long-term investment in common stock is accounted for as a debit to Cash and a credit to Dividend Revenue.

d. Incorrect.

7. a. **Correct.** Under the equity method, the receipt of cash dividends on a long-term investment in common stock is accounted for as a debit to Cash and a credit to Investment in Spacek Inc.

b. Incorrect.

c. Incorrect. Under the cost method, the receipt of cash dividends on a long-term investment in common stock is accounted for as a debit to Cash and a credit to Dividend Revenue, not a credit to Investment in Spacek Inc.

d. Incorrect.

8. a. Incorrect.

b. **Correct.** The amount of net increase in the Investment in Subsidiary account for the year is $112,500, determined as [($200,000 × 75%) − ($50,000 × 75%)].

c. Incorrect.

d. Incorrect.

9. a. **Correct.** The amount of loss on the sale is $1,000, determined as [($96,000 / 800 shares) − $115] × 200 shares sold.

b. Incorrect. A loss, not gain, was incurred on the sale.

c. Incorrect.

d. Incorrect.

10. a. Incorrect.
    b. Incorrect.
    c. **Correct.** The balance of the account Investment in Subsidiary would appear in the investments section of the parent company's balance sheet.
    d. Incorrect.

11. a. Incorrect.
    b. **Correct.** The beginning balance of $12,000 would be reduced by the $5,000 loss to $7,000.
    c. Incorrect.
    d. Incorrect. The accumulated other comprehensive amount wasn't a deficit of $12,000 at the beginning of the period.

TRUE/FALSE

1. F   Income that is exempt from federal taxes, such as interest income on municipal bonds, is not an example of a temporary tax difference since it will not reverse or turn around in later years. Instead, such differences are sometimes called permanent differences.

2. F   Only extraordinary items, discontinued items, and cumulative effects of changes in accounting principle have separate earnings per share disclosures.

3. T

4. T

5. T

6. F   Over the life of a business, temporary differences do *not* reduce the total amount of tax paid. Rather, temporary differences only affect when the taxes are paid.

7. T

8. F   The accumulated other comprehensive income should be disclosed in the stockholders' equity section of the balance sheet.

9. F   Under the cost method of accounting for investments in stocks, the investor records its share of cash dividends as an increase in Dividend Revenue, not a decrease in the investment account. The cash account is also increased for the dividends received.

10. T

11. T

12. F   When two or more corporations transfer their assets and liabilities to a corporation that has been created for the purpose of the takeover, the combination is called a consolidation, not a merger. A merger is when one corporation acquires all the assets and liabilities of another corporation, which is then dissolved.

13. T

14. T

15. T

EXERCISE 14-1

(1)	Income Tax	220,000	
	Income Tax Payable		128,000
	Deferred Income Tax Payable		92,000
(2)	Income Tax	200,000	
	Deferred Income Tax Payable	40,000	
	Income Tax Payable		240,000

EXERCISE 14-2

(1) Income Tax.. 62,500
       Cash..   62,500

(2) Income Tax.. 30,000
       Income Tax Payable   30,000

PROBLEM 14-1

(1)

Emory Corporation
Balance Sheet (selected items)
December 31, 200X

Current Assets

Temporary investments in marketable securities as cost	$40,000	
Add: Unrealized gain net of applicable income tax of $900	5,100	$45,100

(2)

Emory Corporation
Balance Sheet (selected items)
December 31, 200X

Stockholders' Equity

Retained earnings	$645,000
Accumulated other comprehensive income	8,100

(3)

Emory Corporation
Statement of Comprehensive Income

Net income	$124,000
Other comprehensive income:	
Unrealized gain on temporary investments in marketable	
securities net of applicable income tax of $1,200	4,800
Comprehensive income	$128,800

PROBLEM 14-2

(1) (a) Investment in Norris Inc. Stock................................... 600,000
            Cash   600,000

    (b) Cash (40,000 × $.75)... 30,000
            Investment in Norris Inc. Stock   30,000

    (c) Investment in Norris Inc. Stock ($900,000 × 25%)....... 225,000
            Income of Norris Inc.   225,000

(2) (a) Investment in Kline Inc... 150,000
            Cash   150,000

    (b) Cash... 5,000
            Dividend Revenue..   5,000

    (c) None

PROBLEM 14-3

Wess Corp.
Income Statement
For Year Ended March 31, 20--

Sales	$2,700,000
Cost of merchandise sold	1,800,000
Gross profit	$ 900,000
Operating expenses	100,000
Restructuring charge	200,000
Income from continuing operations before income tax	$ 600,000
Income tax	176,000
Income from continuing operations	$ 424,000
Loss on discontinued operations, net of applicable income tax of $20,000	(50,000)
Income before extraordinary item and cumulative effect of a change in accounting principle	$ 374,000
Extraordinary item:	
Loss from earthquake, net of applicable income tax of $48,000	(192,000)
Cumulative effect on prior years of changing to a different depreciation method, net of applicable income tax of $18,000	62,000
Net income	$ 244,000
Earnings per common share:	
Income from continuing operations	$ 8.48
Loss on discontinued operations	(1.00)
Income before extraordinary item and cumulative effect of a change in accounting principle	$ 7.48
Extraordinary item	(3.84)
Cumulative effect on prior years of changing to a different depreciation method	1.24
Net income	$ 4.88

CHAPTER 15

MATCHING

1. C	**4.** A	**7.** L	**9.** O	**11.** F	**13.** N
2. E	**5.** Q	**8.** H	**10.** R	**12.** M	**14.** K
3. G	**6.** P				

FILL IN THE BLANK—PART A

1. bond indenture (or trust indenture)
2. callable
3. debenture bonds
4. contract (or coupon)
5. premium
6. future value
7. $909.09 ($1,000 × 0.90909)
8. $17,125 ($10,000 × 1.71252)
9. straight-line
10. effective interest rate
11. sinking fund
12. carrying amount
13. $388,000 ($400,000 − $12,000)
14. $2,030,000
15. $103,650 [($100,000 × 1.03) + $650]
16. Interest Revenue
17. Investment in Bonds
18. $2,000 (loss)
19. held-to-maturity security
20. 12.6 [(29,000,000 + 2,500,000) / 2,500,000]

FILL IN THE BLANK—PART B

1. term
2. convertible
3. discount
4. $712.99 ($1,000 × .71299)
5. $67,803 ($12,000 × 5.65022)
6. annuity
7. $10,000 (gain)
8. Investments
9. Long-term liabilities
10. Long-term liabilities
11. Investments
12. $73,850 [($75,000 × .98) + $350]
13. $5,045,000
14. $240,000 ($4,000,000 × .12 × 6/12)
15. $28,000 ($280,000 / 10 periods)
16. $120,000 ($4,000,000 × .12 × 3/12)
17. remains the same
18. number of times interest charges earned
19. 8.33 [(60,500,000 + 8,250,000) / 8,250,000]
20. present value

MULTIPLE CHOICE

1. a. **Correct.** A bond that gives the bondholder a right to exchange the bond for other securities under certain conditions is called a convertible bond.
   b. Incorrect. A bond sinking fund is a special fund in which amounts are set aside for the payment of a bond issue at its maturity date.
   c. Incorrect. Term bonds refers to bonds of an issue that all mature at the same time.
   d. Incorrect. Bonds issued on the basis of the general credit of the corporation are called debenture bonds.

2. a. Incorrect.
   b. **Correct.** The present value of $2,000 to be paid in one year at a current interest rate of 6% is $1,887 ($2,000 / 1.06).
   c. Incorrect. The present value must be less than the amount to be received at the end of one year.
   d. Incorrect. The present value must be less than the amount to be received at the end of one year.

3. a. Incorrect.
   b. **Correct.** The entry to record the amortization of a discount on bonds payable is a debit to Interest Expense and a credit to Discount on Bonds Payable.
   c. Incorrect.
   d. Incorrect.

4. a. Incorrect.
   b. Incorrect.
   c. **Correct.** Under the straight-line method of bond discount amortization, as a bond payable approaches maturity, the total yearly amount of interest expense will remain the same.
   d. Incorrect.

5. a. Incorrect. The cost of the bond is more than its face value, since it was purchased at a premium.
   b. Incorrect. The cost of the bond also includes the brokerage commission.
   c. **Correct.** The total cost to be debited to the investment account is $1,048 [($1,000 × 1.04) + $8].
   d. Incorrect.

6. a. Incorrect.
   b. Incorrect.
   c. Incorrect.
   d. **Correct.** The interest method of amortizing bond discount or premium is required by generally accepted accounting principles.

7. a. Incorrect.
   b. Incorrect. Investments in bonds or other debt securities that management intends to hold to their maturity are called held-to-maturity securities.
   c. Incorrect. Sinking-bond funds are special funds in which amounts are set aside for the payment of bond issues at their maturity dates.
   d. **Correct.** Bonds that do not provide for any interest payments are called zero-coupon bonds.

8. a. Incorrect. The present value is the value today of an amount to be received at a future date.
　 b. Incorrect. The estimated worth in the future of an amount of cash on hand today invested at a fixed rate of interest is the future value.
　 c. **Correct.** The principal of each bond is also called the face value.
　 d. Incorrect.

9. a. **Correct.** A special fund accumulated over the life of a bond issue and kept separate from other assets in order to provide for payment of bonds at maturity is called a sinking fund.
　 b. Incorrect.
　 c. Incorrect.
　 d. Incorrect.

10. a. Incorrect.
　 b. **Correct.** Held-to-maturity securities are classified on the balance sheet as investments.
　 c. Incorrect.
　 d. Incorrect.

TRUE/FALSE

1. F The interest rate specified on the bond indenture is called the contract rate. It is not called the effective rate, which is sometimes called the market rate.

2. F If the market rate is lower than the contract rate, the bonds will sell at a premium, not a discount.

3. T

4. T

5. F Bonds that may be exchanged for other securities under certain conditions are called convertible bonds, not callable bonds. Callable bonds are bonds that a corporation reserves the right to redeem before their maturity.

6. F When cash is transferred to the sinking fund, it is recorded in an account called Sinking Fund Cash, not Sinking Fund Investments. When investments are purchased with the sinking fund cash, the investments are recorded in Sinking Fund Investments.

7. T

8. T

9. T

10. T

EXERCISE 15-1

(1)	June	1	Cash...	500,000	
			Bonds Payable		500,000
	Dec.	1	Interest Expense...	30,000	
			Cash		30,000
(2)	Apr.	1	Cash...	942,645	
			Discount on Bonds Payable...........................	57,355	
			Bonds Payable		1,000,000
	Oct.	1	Interest Expense...	57,868	
			Discount on Bonds Payable ($57,355 / 20)		2,868
			Cash		55,000

(3) Mar. 1   Cash..   743,625*

　　　　　　　Premium on Bonds Payable....................................   43,625

　　　　　　　Bonds Payable   700,000

　　　*$700,000 × .3769 (present value of $1 for 20 periods at 5%)   263,830

　　　$38,500 × 12.4622 (present value of an annuity of $1 for 20 periods at 5%)   479,795

　　　Total present value of bonds   743,625

　　Sept. 1   Interest Expense...   36,319

　　　　　　　Premium on Bonds Payable ($43,625 / 20)....................   2,181

　　　　　　　Cash..   38,500

EXERCISE 15-2

(1)   Bonds Payable   5,000,000

　　Loss on Redemption of Bonds Payable.............................   50,000

　　　Cash...   5,050,000

(2)   Bonds Payable   5,000,000

　　　Cash...   4,900,000

　　　Gain on Redemption of Bonds Payable   100,000

EXERCISE 15-3

(1) Oct. 1   Investment in Elgin Inc. Bonds ($400,000 × .99)..............   396,000

　　　　　　Interest Revenue   10,000

　　　　　　　Cash..   406,000

(2) Dec. 31   Cash..   20,000

　　　　　　　Interest Revenue...   20,000

(3) Dec. 31   Investment in Elgin Inc. Bonds   120

　　　　　　　Interest Revenue...   120

(4) Dec. 1   Cash..   424,667

　　　　　　　Investment in Elgin Inc. Bonds...............................   397,040

　　　　　　　Interest Revenue...   16,667

　　　　　　　Gain on Sale of Investments   10,960

PROBLEM 15-1

(1) (a)   Present value of $1 at compound interest of 5½% in 20

　　　　semiannual periods 3427

　　　Face amount of bonds..   × $2,000,000 $ 685,400

　　　Present value of annuity of $1 for 20 periods at 5½%....................   11.9504

　　　Semiannual interest payments ....   × $ 110,000   1,314,544

　　　Proceeds of bonds (present value)... $1,999,944

　　Note: The difference of $56 between the face value of the
　　bonds and the present value is due to rounding.

(b)   There is no premium or discount on the bond issuance.

(2) (a) Present value of $1 at compound interest of 6% in 20
   semiannual periods .... .3118
   Face amount of bonds .... × $2,000,000 $ 623,600

   Present value of annuity of $1 for 20 periods at 6%...................... 11.4699
   Semiannual interest payments .... × $ 110,000   1,261,689

   Proceeds of bonds (present value)....................................... $1,885,289

(b) The discount is $114,711 on the bond issuance.

(3) (a) Present value of $1 at compound interest of 5% in 20
   semiannual periods .... .3769
   Face amount of bonds .... × $2,000,000 $ 753,800

   Present value of annuity of $1 for 20 periods at 5%...................... 12.4622
   Semiannual interest payments .... × $ 110,000   1,370,842

   Proceeds of bonds (present value)....................................... $2,124,642

(b) The premium is $124,642 on the bond issuance.

PROBLEM 15-2

(1) Dec. 31   Cash... 531,161
   Bonds Payable   500,000
   Premium on Bonds Payable..........................   31,161

(2) June 30   Interest Expense ($27,500 − $1,558) 25,942
   Premium on Bonds Payable ($31,161 / 20)... 1,558
   Cash   27,500

(3) Dec. 31   Interest Expense ($27,500 − $1,558) 25,942
   Premium on Bonds Payable ($31,161 / 20)... 1,558
   Cash   27,500

(4) Dec. 31   Bonds Payable.. 250,000
   Premium on Bonds Payable [($31,161 − $1,558 − $1,558) / 2] 14,023
   Gain on Redemption of Bonds.....................   6,523
   Cash   257,500

PROBLEM 15-3

(1) Jan. 1   Cash... 885,295
   Discount on Bonds Payable.......................... 114,705
   Bonds Payable   1,000,000

(2) June 30   Interest Expense ($50,000 + $5,735) 55,735
   Discount on Bonds Payable ($114,705 / 20) ...   5,735
   Cash   50,000

(3) Dec. 31   Interest Expense ($50,000 + $5,735) 55,735
   Discount on Bonds Payable ($114,705 / 20) ...   5,735
   Cash   50,000

(4) Dec. 31   Bonds Payable.. 500,000
   Loss on Redemption of Bonds 41,618
   Discount on Bonds Payable [($114,705 − $5,735 − $5,735) / 2].....   51,618
   Cash   490,000

CHAPTER 16

MATCHING

1. B   **3.** H   **5.** E   **7.** G
2. C   **4.** A   **6.** D   **8.** F

FILL IN THE BLANK—PART A

1. statement of cash flows
2. direct; indirect
3. operating
4. investing
5. investing
6. financing
7. investing
8. increased
9. decreased
10. decreased
11. $34,250
12. $102,000
13. $195,000
14. $60,000
15. $49,500
16. $1,040,000
17. $330,000
18. financing
19. $60,000
20. cash flow per share

FILL IN THE BLANK—PART B

1. indirect
2. operating
3. direct
4. financing
5. financing
6. operating
7. financing
8. investing
9. noncash
10. deducted from
11. added to
12. $330,000
13. $746,250
14. $3,125,000
15. $46,000
16. $20,000
17. retained earnings
18. $51,000
19. operating
20. free cash flow

MULTIPLE CHOICE

1. a. Incorrect. The cash flows from financing activities is a major section of the statement of cash flows.
b. **Correct.** The cash flows from selling activities is not a major section of the statement of cash flows.
c. incorrect. The cash flows from operating activities is a major section of the statement of cash flows.
d. Incorrect. The cash flows from investing activities is a major section of the statement of cash flows.

2. a. Incorrect. Noncash investing and financing activities are not reported within the statement of cash flows because cash is not affected by these transactions.
b. **Correct.** Although noncash investing and financing activities do not affect cash, these transactions are disclosed in a separate schedule that accompanies the statement of cash flows. This helps users interpret major investing and financing transactions that involve stock swaps, asset swaps, and other noncash events.
c. Incorrect. Noncash investing and financing activities are not reported within the statement of retained earnings because this statement shows the events that influence retained earnings, such as net income and dividends.
d. Incorrect. Noncash investing and financing activities are not reported in the footnotes to the balance sheet.

3. a. Incorrect. Depreciation is added to net income in deriving cash flows from operating activities under the indirect method.
b. Incorrect. Decreases in current assets are added to net income in deriving cash flows from operating activities under the indirect method.
c. **Correct.** Decreases in current liabilities are subtracted from net income in deriving cash flows from operating activities under the indirect method. This is because expenses have been accrued but not paid. Thus, the expenses overstate the amount of cash that has been spent on operating activities.
d. Incorrect. A loss on sale of equipment is added to net income in deriving cash flows from operating activities under the indirect method.

4. a. Incorrect.
b. Incorrect.
c. Incorrect.
d. **Correct.** The cash paid for dividends is $40,000 declared plus the difference between the beginning and ending dividend payable ($12,000 – $10,000), or $40,000 + $12,000 – $10,000.

5. a. Incorrect. The increase in accrued expenses is deducted from operating expenses under the direct method.
   b. Incorrect. The decrease in prepaid expenses is deducted from operating expenses under the direct method.
   c. Incorrect. The increase in income taxes payable is deducted from operating expenses under the direct method.
   d. **Correct.** The increase in prepaid expenses is added to operating expenses under the direct method. The increase in a prepaid expense causes cash to be paid before the expense is recorded; hence, the increase must be added to the expense to reflect the cash outflow.

6. a. Incorrect. The receipt of cash from the sale of land is a cash flow from an investing activity.
   b. Incorrect. The receipt of cash from the collection of accounts receivable is a cash flow from operating activities.
   c. **Correct.** The payment of cash for the acquisition of treasury stock is a cash flow from a financing activity.
   d. Incorrect. The payment of cash for new machinery is a cash flow from an investing activity.

7. a. Incorrect. The retained earnings does not appear on the statement of cash flows.
   b. **Correct.** Cash received from customers is the first line when preparing the statement of cash flows under the direct method.
   c. Incorrect. The net income appears first when preparing the statement of cash flows under the indirect method.
   d. Incorrect. Depreciation is added to net income in the statement of cash flows under the indirect method, but it does not even appear under the direct method.

8. a. **Correct.** The withdrawal of cash by the owner of a business is a financing activity, similar to a dividend.
   b. Incorrect. The issuance of common stock to retire long-term debt is a transaction that exchanges long-term debt for capital stock, so it is a noncash investing and financing activity.
   c. Incorrect. The acquisition of a manufacturing plant by issuing bonds exchanges a fixed asset for long-term debt, so it is a noncash investing and financing activity.
   d. Incorrect. The issuance of common stock in exchange for convertible preferred stock exchanges two types of capital stock, so it is a noncash investing and financing activity.

9. a. **Correct.** The increase in inventories uses more cash than is shown by the cost of goods sold; thus, the increase in inventories must be added to cost of goods sold to reflect the payment of cash for merchandise.
   b. Incorrect. The increase in accounts payable uses less cash than is shown by the cost of goods sold; thus, the increase in accounts payable must be deducted from cost of goods sold to reflect the payment of cash for merchandise.
   c. Incorrect. The decrease in inventories uses less cash than is shown by the cost of goods sold; thus, the decrease in inventories must be deducted from cost of goods sold to reflect the payment of cash for merchandise.
   d. Incorrect. The decrease in accounts receivable does not impact the cash paid for merchandise, but it impacts the cash received from customers.

10. a. Incorrect.
    b. Incorrect.
    c. **Correct.** The cash paid for income taxes is part of the cash flow from operating activities under the direct method.
    d. Incorrect.

11. a. Incorrect. The loss should not be added to the book value of the land.
    b. Incorrect. The loss should not be deducted from net income on the statement of cash flows.
    c. **Correct.** The loss should be deducted from the book value of the land in determining the cash flow from investing activities.
    d. Incorrect. The loss should not be deducted from net income on the statement of cash flows.

12. a. Incorrect.
   b. ***Correct.*** $290,000 - $32,000 - $40,000. Free cash flows are the cash flows available after paying dividends and replacing productive capacity. The depreciation expense would not be used in the calculation since it is known that $40,000 was required to maintain productive capacity.
   c. Incorrect.
   d. Incorrect.

TRUE/FALSE

1. T
2. T
3. T
4. F Only cash receipts and payments from operations are evaluated under the direct method; thus, depreciation is not analyzed under the direct method.
5. F Increases in current liabilities are added to net income under the indirect method because expense accruals exceed cash payments when current liabilities increase.
6. T
7. T
8. T
9. F Both the direct and indirect methods report the same cash flows from operating activities; thus, neither method is more accurate than the other.
10. T

EXERCISE 16-1

Item	Cash Flows From			Schedule of Noncash Investing and Financing Activities
	Operating Activities	Investing Activities	Financing Activities	
1. Decrease in prepaid expenses	✔			
2. Retirement of bonds			✔	
3. Proceeds from sale of investments		✔		
4. Increase in inventories	✔			
5. Issuance of common stock			✔	
6. Purchase of equipment		✔		
7. Cash dividends paid			✔	
8. Acquisition of building in exchange for bonds				✔
9. Amortization of patents	✔			
10. Amortization of discount on bonds payable	✔			

EXERCISE 16-2

Cash flows from operating activities:

Net income, per income statement...		$150,000
Add: Depreciation..	$45,000	
Decrease in prepaid expenses	2,625	
Increase in accounts payable	17,000	64,625
		$214,625
Deduct: Increase in trade receivables...................................	$10,000	
Increase in inventories..	15,625	
Decrease in salaries payable....................................	3,000	28,625
Net cash flow from operating activities.....................................		$186,000

EXERCISE 16-3

Cash flows from operating activities:

Cash received from customers...		$520,000
Deduct: Cash payments for merchandise	$128,625	
Cash payments for operating expenses	160,375	
Cash payments for income tax	45,000	334,000
Net cash flow from operating activities.....................................		$186,000

Supporting calculations:

Sales (reported on income statement)...	$530,000
Less increase in trade receivables..	(10,000)
Cash received from customers	$520,000
Cost of merchandise sold	$130,000
Plus increase in inventories	15,625
Less increase in accounts payable..	(17,000)
Cash payments for merchandise	$128,625
Operating expenses (other than depreciation)	$160,000
Less decrease in prepaid expenses	(2,625)
Plus decrease in salaries payable	3,000
Cash payments for operating expenses	$160,375

PROBLEM 16-1

Stellar Inc.
Statement of Cash Flows
For Year Ended December 31, 2006

Cash flows from operating activities:		
Net income, per income statement..		$114,000
Add: Depreciation...	$48,000	
Decrease in inventories	6,000	
Decrease in prepaid expenses	2,400	
Increase in accounts payable	7,200	63,600
		$177,600
Deduct: Increase in trade receivables......................................	$12,000	
Gain on sale of land	18,000	30,000
Net cash flow from operating activities......................................		$147,600
Cash flows from investing activities:		
Cash received from land sold....................................	$ 54,000	
Less cash paid for purchase of equipment	96,000	
Net cash flow used for investing activities.................................		(42,000)
Cash flows from financing activities:		
Cash used to retire bonds payable..	$ 60,000	
Cash paid for dividends...	27,600*	
Net cash flow used for financing activities		(87,600)
Increase in cash...		$ 18,000
Cash, January 1, 2006...		66,000
Cash, December 31, 2006		$ 84,000

*30,000 + 21,600 – 24,000

Schedule of Noncash Investing and Financing Activities:

Acquisition of land by issuance of common stock...	$ 20,000

PROBLEM 16-2

Stellar Inc.
Statement of Cash Flows
For Year Ended December 31, 2006

Cash flows from operating activities:			
Cash received from customers...		$563,000	
Deduct: Cash payments for merchandise	$211,800		
Cash payments for operating expenses	169,600		
Cash payments for income tax	34,000	415,400	
Net cash flow from operating activities...			$147,600
Cash flows from investing activities:			
Cash received from land sold...		$ 54,000	
Less cash paid for purchase of equipment		96,000	
Net cash flow used for investing activities...................................			(42,000)
Cash flows from financing activities:			
Cash used to retire bonds payable...		$ 60,000	
Cash paid for dividends		27,600*	
Net cash flow used for financing activities.................................			(87,600)
Increase in cash...			$ 18,000
Cash, January 1, 2006...			66,000
Cash, December 31, 2006			$ 84,000

*30,000 + 21,600 – 24,000

Schedule of Noncash Investing and Financing Activities:

Acquisition of land by issuance of common stock	$ 20,000

Schedule Reconciling Net Income with Cash Flows from Operating Activities:

Net income, per income statement..		$114,000
Add: Depreciation	$48,000	
Decrease in inventories	6,000	
Decrease in prepaid expenses	2,400	
Increase in accounts payable	7,200	63,600
		$177,600
Deduct: Increase in trade receivables	$12,000	
Gain on sale of land	18,000	30,000
Net cash flow provided by operating activities		$147,600

Supporting calculations:

Sales (reported on income statement)..	$575,000
Less increase in trade receivables...	(12,000)
Cash received	$563,000
Cost of merchandise sold	$225,000
Less decrease in inventories	(6,000)
Less increase in accounts payable..	(7,200)
Cash payments for merchandise	$211,800
Operating expenses (other than depreciation)	$172,000
Less decrease in prepaid expenses	(2,400)
Cash payments for operating expenses	$169,600

CHAPTER 17

MATCHING

1. H	**5.** M	**8.** C	**11.** U	**14.** Y	**17.** I
2. Q	**6.** A	**9.** T	**12.** G	**15.** S	**18.** P
3. L	**7.** J	**10.** O	**13.** B	**16.** D	**19.** K
4. X					

FILL IN THE BLANK—PART A

1. vertical analysis
2. profitability analysis
3. current position analysis
4. solvency
5. common-size
6. current
7. net sales to assets
8. quick
9. earnings per share on common stock
10. working capital
11. accounts receivable turnover
12. inventory turnover
13. liabilities to stockholders' equity
14. preferred dividends are earned
15. income from operations
16. stockholders' equity
17. dividends
18. independent audit
19. fixed assets to long-term liabilities
20. net sales

FILL IN THE BLANK—PART B

1. horizontal analysis
2. dividend yield
3. independent auditors'
4. number of days' sales in receivables
5. number of days' sales in inventory
6. interest charges earned
7. rate earned on total assets
8. rate earned on stockholders' equity
9. leverage
10. price-earnings
11. management discussion and analysis (MDA)
12. quick assets
13. common-size
14. solvency analysis
15. bankers'
16. number of days' sales in inventory
17. earnings per share (on common stock)
18. common-size
19. receivables
20. internal control

MULTIPLE CHOICE

1. a. Incorrect.
   b. Incorrect. Horizontal statements are one type of statement that uses both relative comparisons and dollar amounts.
   c. Incorrect. Vertical statements are one type of statement that uses both relative comparisons and dollar amounts.
   d. **Correct.** In common-size statements, all items are expressed in percentages.

2. a. Incorrect. The rate of return on total assets is a profitability ratio.
   b. Incorrect. The price-earnings ratio is a profitability ratio.
   c. **Correct.** The accounts receivable turnover is a measure of solvency (short-term).
   d. Incorrect. The ratio of net sales to assets is a profitability ratio.

3. a. Incorrect.
   b. Incorrect.
   c. **Correct.** $4,000,000 / [$250,000 + $345,000) / 2]
   d. Incorrect.

4. a. Incorrect.
   b. **Correct.** $6,500,000 / [($175,000 + $297,000) / 2]
   c. Incorrect.
   d. Incorrect.

5. a. Incorrect. The independent auditor's report attests to the fairness of financial statements.
  b. Incorrect. The footnotes provide additional descriptive details of the financial statements, but they rarely include forward-looking statements by management.
  c. Incorrect. This is a new management assertion required by the Sarbanes-Oxley Act on the effectiveness of internal controls, but it does not include forward-looking statements about prospects and risks.
  d. *Correct.* The management discussion and analysis provides an in-depth discussion of prior results and statements regarding future prospects and business risks.

6. a. Incorrect. The working capital ratio provides a measure of the short-term, debt-paying ability.
  b. Incorrect. The quick ratio provides a measure of the short-term, debt-paying ability.
  c. Incorrect. The receivables to inventory ratio is not an interpretable financial ratio.
  d. *Correct.* The number of days' sales in receivables is a measure of the efficiency in collecting receivables.

7. a. Incorrect.
  b. Incorrect.
  c. *Correct.* ($510,000 + $30,000) / $30,000
  d. Incorrect.

8. a. *Correct.* ($27,000 + $23,000 + $90,000) / $70,000
  b. Incorrect.
  c. Incorrect.
  d. Incorrect.

9. a. Incorrect.
  b. *Correct.* In a vertical analysis balance sheet, items are expressed as a percentage of total assets.
  c. Incorrect.
  d. Incorrect.

10. a. Incorrect.
  b. Incorrect.
  c. *Correct.* ($460,000 − $50,000) / 50,000 shares
  d. Incorrect.

11. a. Incorrect. A high-dividend yield is usually associated with low P/E companies, since most of the shareholder return is in the form of predictable dividends, rather than share appreciation.
  b. *Correct.* High P/E firms are usually associated with high-growth companies.
  c. Incorrect. Debt position is not usually associated with the P/E ratio.
  d. Incorrect. Current position is not usually associated with the P/E ratio.

12. a. Incorrect.
  b. Incorrect.
  c. Incorrect.
  d. *Correct.* ($240,000 + $120,000) / $1,000,000

TRUE/FALSE

1. F This statement is true for a vertical analysis, not a horizontal analysis.
2. T
3. F The net sales to assets ratio is a profitability ratio that shows how effectively and efficiently assets are used to generate sales.
4. T
5. F The accounts receivable turnover is determined by dividing the net sales by the average accounts receivable outstanding during the period.
6. T
7. F The rate earned on total assets is determined by adding interest expense to net income, then dividing this sum by average total assets during the period.
8. T
9. T
10. F Working capital is the excess of current assets over current liabilities.

EXERCISE 17-1

	2007	Percent	2006	Percent
Revenues	$450,000	100%	$389,000	100%
Costs and expenses:				
Cost of sales	$200,000	44%	$176,000	45%
Selling and administrative expenses	100,000	23%	73,000	19%
Total costs and expenses	$300,000	67%	$249,000	64%
Earnings before income taxes	$150,000	33%	$140,000	36%
Income taxes	34,500	8%	32,200	8%
Net earnings	$115,500	25%	$107,800	28%

EXERCISE 17-2

	2007	2006	Increase (Decrease) Amount	Percent
Current assets	$250,000	$219,500	$ 30,500	14%
Fixed assets	435,000	401,600	33,400	8%
Intangible assets	43,700	46,000	(2,300)	−5%
Current liabilities	88,000	80,000	8,000	10%
Long-term liabilities	225,000	250,000	(25,000)	−10%
Common stock	214,000	167,600	46,400	28%
Retained earnings	200,000	170,000	30,000	18%

PROBLEM 17-1

Nordic Inc.
Comparative Income Statement
For Years Ended December 31, 2007 and 2006

	2007	2006	Increase (Decrease) Amount	Percent
Sales	$690,500	$585,000	$105,500	18.0%
Sales returns and allowances	25,500	23,000	2,500	10.9%
Net sales	$665,000	$562,000	$103,000	18.3%
Cost of goods sold	420,000	330,000	90,000	27.3%
Gross profit	$245,000	$232,000	$ 13,000	5.6%
Selling expenses	$ 43,000	$ 47,700	$ (4,700)	−9.9%
Administrative expenses	31,000	31,000	0	0.0%
Total operating expenses	$ 74,000	$ 78,700	$ (4,700)	−6.0%
Operating income	$171,000	$153,300	$ 17,700	11.5%
Other income	13,000	16,400	(3,400)	−20.7%
	$184,000	$169,700	$ 14,300	8.4%
Other expense	58,000	53,500	4,500	8.4%
Income before income taxes	$126,000	$116,200	$ 9,800	8.4%
Income taxes	34,000	32,400	1,600	4.9%
Net income	$ 92,000	$ 83,800	$ 8,200	9.8%

Nordic Inc.
Comparative Balance Sheet
December 31, 2007 and 2006

Assets	2007	2006	Increase (Decrease) Amount	Percent
Cash	$ 76,000	$ 69,000	$ 7,000	10.1%
Marketable securities	98,900	130,000	(31,100)	−23.9%
Accounts receivable (net)	199,000	195,000	4,000	2.1%
Inventory	450,000	375,000	75,000	20.0%
Prepaid expenses	28,000	26,300	1,700	6.5%
Long-term investments	35,000	35,000	0	0.0%
Fixed assets (net)	871,000	835,000	36,000	4.3%
Intangible assets	18,000	22,800	(4,800)	−21.1%
Total assets	$1,775,900	$1,688,100	$ 87,800	5.2%
Liabilities				
Current liabilities	$ 129,000	$ 107,000	$ 22,000	20.6%
Long-term liabilities	420,000	440,000	(20,000)	−4.5%
Total liabilities	$ 549,000	$ 547,000	$ 2,000	0.4%
Stockholders' Equity				
Preferred 3% stock, $100 par	$ 102,000	$ 93,000	$ 9,000	9.7%
Common stock, $50 par	549,900	530,100	19,800	3.7%
Retained earnings	575,000	518,000	57,000	11.0%
Total stockholders' equity	$1,226,900	$1,141,100	$ 85,800	7.5%
Total liabilities and stockholders' equity	$1,775,900	$1,688,100	$ 87,800	5.2%

PROBLEM 17-2

Voyageur Inc.
Comparative Balance Sheet
December 31, 2006 and 2005

	2006 Amount	2006 Percent	2005 Amount	2005 Percent
Assets				
Cash	$ 500,000	5.3%	$ 425,000	5.4%
Marketable securities	200,000	2.1%	185,000	2.4%
Accounts receivable (net)	680,000	7.3%	575,000	7.3%
Inventory	860,000	9.2%	740,000	9.4%
Prepaid expenses	104,000	1.1%	95,000	1.2%
Long-term investments	450,000	4.8%	410,000	5.2%
Fixed assets (net)	6,556,000	70.1%	5,420,000	69.0%
Total assets	$9,350,000	100.0%	$7,850,000	100.0%
Liabilities				
Current liabilities	$1,090,000	11.7%	$1,050,000	13.4%
Long-term liabilities	2,150,000	23.0%	2,050,000	26.1%
Total liabilities	$3,240,000	34.7%	$3,100,000	39.5%
Stockholders' Equity				
Preferred 5% stock, $100 par	$ 350,000	3.7%	$ 350,000	4.5%
Common stock, $10 par	2,550,000	27.3%	2,550,000	32.5%
Retained earnings	3,210,000	34.3%	1,850,000	23.5%
Total stockholders' equity	$6,110,000	65.3%	$4,750,000	60.5%
Total liabilities and stockholders' equity	$9,350,000	100.0%	$7,850,000	100.0%

Voyageur Inc.
Income Statement
For Year Ended December 31, 2006

	Amount	Percent
Sales	$12,800,000	102.4%
Sales returns and allowances	300,000	2.4%
Net sales	$12,500,000	100.0%
Cost of goods sold	7,550,000	60.4%
Gross profit	$ 4,950,000	39.6%
Selling expenses	$ 1,550,000	12.4%
Administrative expenses	825,000	6.6%
Total operating expenses	$ 2,375,000	19.0%
Operating income	$ 2,575,000	20.6%
Other income	125,000	1.0%
	$ 2,700,000	21.6%
Other expense (interest)	150,000	1.2%
Income before income taxes	$ 2,550,000	20.4%
Income taxes	937,000	7.5%
Net income	$ 1,613,000	12.9%

PROBLEM 17-3

		Calculation	Final Result
a.	Working capital	$2,344,000 - $1,090,000	1,254,000
b.	Current ratio	$$\frac{\$2,344,000}{\$1,090,000}$$	2.2
c.	Quick ratio	$$\frac{\$1,380,000}{\$1,090,000}$$	1.3
d.	Accounts receivable turnover	$$\frac{\$12,500,000}{\left(\frac{\$680,000 + \$575,000}{2}\right)}$$	19.9
e.	Number of days' sales in receivables	$$\frac{\$12,500,000}{365} = \$34,247 \qquad \frac{\$680,000}{\$34,247}$$	19.9
f.	Inventory turnover	$$\frac{\$7,550,000}{\left(\frac{\$860,000 + \$740,000}{2}\right)}$$	9.4
g.	Number of days' sales in inventory	$$\frac{\$7,550,000}{365} = \$20,685 \qquad \frac{\$860,000}{\$20,685}$$	41.6
h.	Ratio of fixed assets to long-term liabilities	$$\frac{\$6,556,000}{\$2,150,000}$$	3.0
i.	Ratio of liabilities to stockholders' equity	$$\frac{\$3,240,000}{\$6,110,000}$$	0.5
j.	Number of times interest charges earned	$$\frac{\$2,550,000 + \$150,000}{\$150,000}$$	18.0
k.	Number of times preferred dividends earned	$$\frac{\$1,613,000}{\$17,500}$$	92.2
l.	Ratio of net sales to assets	$$\frac{\$12,500,000}{\left(\frac{\$8,900,000 + \$7,440,000}{2}\right)}$$	1.5
m.	Rate earned on total assets	$$\frac{\$1,613,000 + \$150,000}{\left(\frac{\$9,350,000 + \$7,850,000}{2}\right)}$$	20.5%
n.	Rate earned on stockholders' equity	$$\frac{\$1,613,000}{\left(\frac{\$6,110,000 + \$4,750,000}{2}\right)}$$	29.7%
o.	Rate earned on common stockholders' equity	$$\frac{\$1,613,000 - \$17,500}{\left(\frac{\$5,760,000 + \$4,400,000}{2}\right)}$$	31.4%

		Calculation	Final Result
p.	Earnings per share on common stock	$\dfrac{\$1,613,000 - \$17,500}{255,000}$	$6.26
q.	Price-earnings ratio	$\dfrac{\$29.75}{\$6.26}$	4.8
r.	Dividends per share of common stock	$\dfrac{\$250,000}{255,000}$	$.98
s.	Dividend yield	$\dfrac{\left(\dfrac{\$250,000}{255,000 \text{ shares}}\right)}{\$29.75}$	3.3%

CHAPTER 18

MATCHING

1. C
2. L
3. Q
4. E
5. F
6. P
7. K
8. J
9. I
10. D
11. Y
12. BB
13. O
14. T
15. R
16. H
17. S
18. Z
19. AA
20. G
21. A
22. W
23. U
24. B
25. N
26. M
27. V
28. X

FILL IN THE BLANK—PART A

1. financial
2. staff
3. cost
4. direct labor
5. factory overhead
6. factory overhead
7. job order
8. crediting, debiting
9. time tickets
10. allocation
11. $42
12. activity-based
13. overapplied (or overabsorbed)
14. rate
15. cost of goods sold
16. materials requisitions
17. stock ledger
18. period
19. administrative
20. service

FILL IN THE BLANK—PART B

1. managerial
2. line
3. controller
4. direct materials
5. indirect labor
6. product prices
7. debited, credited
8. requisitions
9. job cost
10. time tickets
11. activity driver
12. $5,625
13. $66
14. work in process
15. underapplied (or underabsorbed)
16. time tickets
17. finished goods
18. $100,975 {[($175,000 / 20,000) × (12,000 – 3,500)] + $26,600}
19. selling
20. cost of services

MULTIPLE CHOICE

1. a. Incorrect. The building contractor should use a job order cost system to accumulate construction costs.
   b. **Correct.** The cookie processor should use a process cost system.
   c. Incorrect. The plumber should use a job order cost system to accumulate job costs.
   d. Incorrect. The textbook publisher should use a job order cost system to accumulate costs by textbook title.

2. a. Incorrect. A receiving report records the receipt of material to the storeroom.
   b. Incorrect. A purchase order is delivered to a supplier requesting the purchase of an item.
   c. Incorrect. A purchase requisition is not a term used in business.
   d. **Correct.** A materials requisition is used to request and release material from the storeroom for use in a job.

3. a. Incorrect. A clock card accumulates the amount of time an employee spends in the factory.
   b. **Correct.** A time ticket accumulates the amount of time an employee spends on a job.
   c. Incorrect. An in-and-out card accumulates the amount of time an employee spends in the factory.
   d. Incorrect. A labor requisition is not a term used in business.

4. a. Incorrect. An oil refinery would use a process cost system.
   b. Incorrect. A meat processor would use a process cost system.
   c. Incorrect. A hotel would accumulate costs by hotel property, which is not a "job."
   d. **Correct.** A textbook publisher would use a job order cost system.

5. a. Incorrect. The work in process ledger contains the individual accounts for the jobs (products) in process.
   b. **Correct.** The finished goods ledger includes the individual accounts of the products *produced*.
   c. Incorrect. The factory overhead ledger is not a term used in business.
   d. Incorrect. The materials ledger includes the individual accounts of the raw materials used to produce products.

6. a. Incorrect. The property taxes on the factory building is considered part of factory overhead costs.
   b. Incorrect. The insurance on the factory building is considered part of factory overhead costs.
   c. **Correct.** Sales salaries would be considered selling expenses, which are a period cost.
   d. Incorrect. Depreciation on the factory plant and equipment is considered part of factory overhead costs.

7. a. Incorrect. Managerial accounting need not adhere strictly to GAAP.
   b. Incorrect. The focus of financial accounting is on the information needs of external decision makers.
   c. **Correct.** Managerial accounting focuses on the decision needs of management.
   d. Incorrect.

8. a. **Correct.** If the actual factory overhead exceeds the amount applied, then the factory overhead is under-applied.
   b. Incorrect. This term is not used in business.
   c. Incorrect. Factory overhead is overapplied if the actual overhead incurred is less than the amount applied.
   d. Incorrect. Excess capacity is a different issue than determining under- or overapplied factory overhead.

9. a. Incorrect. Variable costing relates to the practice of including only variable cost in cost of goods sold.
   b. Incorrect. Flexible costing is a made-up term.
   c. **Correct.** Activity-based costing uses many overhead rates in allocating factory overhead to products.
   d. Incorrect. Service function allocation is a made-up term.

10. a. **Correct.** The controller is a staff function.
   b. Incorrect. The plant manager is a line function.
   c. Incorrect. The regional sales manager is a line function.
   d. Incorrect.

11. a. Incorrect. This is the factory overhead rate ($360,000 / 15,000 hours).
   b. Incorrect. This is the direct labor ($12 per hour × 16 hours).
   c. **Correct.** ($360,000 / 15,000 hours) × 16 hours
   d. Incorrect. This is b and c summed together.

TRUE/FALSE

1. T
2. F The process cost system accumulates cost by department, not by separate jobs.
3. F A publishing company would use a job cost system to accumulate costs for each title.
4. T
5. F Materials are released to the factory floor in response to materials requisitions.
6. T
7. F A debit balance in the factory overhead account means the factory overhead is underapplied.

8. T

9. F There is no such restriction. Indeed, many companies use both the job order and process costs systems for different products within the company.

10. T

EXERCISE 18-1

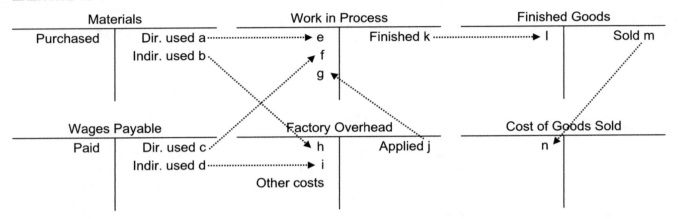

EXERCISE 18-2

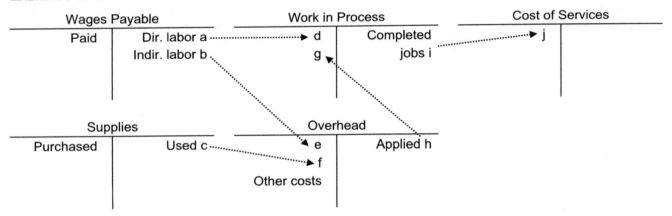

EXERCISE 18-3

(1) $3.25 per machine hour ($65,000 / 20,000 hours)

(2) 42% of direct labor cost ($243,600 / $580,000)

(3)

Work in Process—Factory 1	5,850	
Factory Overhead—Factory 1		5,850
($3.25 × 1,800)		
Work in Process—Factory 2	20,370	
Factory Overhead—Factory 2		20,370
(42% × $48,500)		

(4) Factory 1—$200 debit (underapplied)
Factory 2—$270 credit (overapplied)

EXERCISE 18-4

(1)

Client	Service	Job Costs	Billable Hours	Job Cost per Billable Hour
Astor Co.	Audit	$11,040	240	$46
Brown, Inc.	Audit	11,750	250	47
Singhal Co.	Audit	14,880	310	48
Martinez Co.	Compilation	1,875	75	25
Ng, Inc.	Compilation	2,040	85	24
Wrigley Co.	Compilation	2,185	95	23
Zane, Inc.	Compilation	4,950	110	45
Howard Co.	Tax	10,395	165	63
McNelly Co.	Tax	9,000	150	60

(2) The table indicates that tax services have the highest cost per billable hour, while compilation services have the lowest cost per billable hour. Since the professional labor cost is the largest part of the job cost, different levels of staff working on the different service assignments likely caused this result. It appears that the highest paid staff work on tax services, while the lowest paid staff work on compilation services (audit is in the middle). This is not surprising in that compilation services can be handled by bookkeepers who are not compensated at the level of experienced CPAs. In addition, the table indicates that the Zane compilation is an outlier from what would be expected. The higher cost per billable hour may be the result of higher compensated employees working on this assignment. For example, it is possible that some audit practice professionals were assigned to this job, either because the job was late or audit professional capacity was available. An alternative explanation would be the use of extensive overtime to finish this job. Regardless, there is some indication that something out of the ordinary caused the cost per hour to be higher for this job than expected.

(3) Cost of Services 68,115
      Work in Process.. 68,115

PROBLEM 18-1

(1) Materials 60,000
    Prepaid Expenses 5,300
      Accounts Payable 65,300

(2) Work in Process 23,200
    Factory Overhead 1,200
      Materials 24,400

(3) Work in Process 35,900
    Factory Overhead 2,700
      Wages Payable 38,600

(4) Factory Overhead 12,200
    Selling Expenses 21,950
    Administrative Expenses 15,300
      Accounts Payable 49,450

(5) Factory Overhead 5,000
    Selling Expenses 800
    Administrative Expenses 600
      Prepaid Expenses 6,400

(6)	Work in Process	25,130	
	Factory Overhead		25,130
(7)	Finished Goods	53,000	
	Work in Process		53,000
(8)	Accounts Receivable	160,000	
	Sales		160,000
	Cost of Goods Sold	110,000	
	Finished Goods		110,000

PROBLEM 18-2

Cash			
Bal.	135,400	**(1)**	78,000
		(4)	12,500

Finished Goods		
Bal.	50,800	
(6)	164,000	

Work In Process			
Bal.	33,800	**(6)**	164,000
(2)	56,000		
(3)	70,000		
(5)	24,000		

Materials			
Bal.	18,000	**(2)**	58,400
(1)	78,000		

Factory Overhead			
Bal.	3,000	**(5)**	24,000
(2)	2,400		
(3)	5,000		
(4)	12,500		

Wages Payable		
	(3)	75,000

CHAPTER 19

MATCHING

1.	H	**4.**	D	**6.**	A	**8.**	F
2.	I	**5.**	B	**7.**	K	**9.**	E
3.	C						

FILL IN THE BLANK—PART A

1. job order
2. process
3. factory overhead
4. allocating
5. physical
6. credited
7. units to be assigned costs
8. 34,500 (58,500 − 24,000)
9. equivalent
10. 18,300 [(8,000 × 60%) + (18,500 − 8,000) + (7,500 × 40%)]
11. $98,820 ($32,500 + $66,320)

12. $56,700 ($5.40 × 10,500)
    ($98,820 / 18,300 = $5.40 per unit)
    (18,500 − 8,000 = 10,500; the units started and completed)
13. $16,200 ($5.40 × 7,500 × 40%)
14. cost per equivalent unit
15. $531.25 ($68,000 / 128)
16. 18,600 (solve for $99,510 / X = $5.35)
17. cost of production
18. yield
19. just-in-time
20. manufacturing cells

FILL IN THE BLANK—PART B

1. process
2. job order
3. department
4. direct labor, factory overhead
5. conversion
6. fifo (first-in, first-out)
7. partially completed
8. ending in-process inventory
9. 600
10. whole
11. March
12. evenly
13. 510
14. $25
15. 8,800
16. multiplying
17. $10,350
18. $1,590
19. $11,940
20. kanbans

MULTIPLE CHOICE

1. a. Incorrect.
   b. Incorrect.
   c. **Correct.** ($75,000 + $185,000) / 10,000 units
   d. Incorrect.

2. a. Incorrect.
   b. Incorrect.
   c. Incorrect.
   d. **Correct.** 16,000 + 6,000; note that the total units to be accounted for are expressed as "whole units" and do not reflect equivalency.

3. a. **Correct.** The equivalent units for Material B include all 300 units of beginning inventory, since they are 50% complete. But the material is added at the 60% completion point, plus another 2,100 units started and completed during the period (2,400 − 300).
   b. Incorrect.
   c. Incorrect.
   d. Incorrect.

4. a. Incorrect.
   b. **Correct.** Beginning Inventory + Started and Completed + Ending Inventory, or (900 × 60%) + (9,000 − 900) + (600 × 10%)
   c. Incorrect.
   d. Incorrect.

5. a. **Correct.** Equivalent units are what could have been completed within a given accounting period. For a particular resource (material or conversion cost), equivalent units are what was incurred in production during the accounting period.
   b. Incorrect. This term is not used in business.
   c. Incorrect. This term may refer to the rated machine capacity of a particular process, but it is unrelated to what could have been completed.
   d. Incorrect. This term may refer to the rated machine capacity of a particular process, but it is unrelated to what could have been completed.

6. a. Incorrect. Prime cost is the direct labor and direct materials costs.
   b. Incorrect. The processing cost includes direct labor, direct materials, and factory overhead costs.
   c. **Correct.** The conversion cost per unit is the direct labor and factory overhead costs divided by the equivalent units of production.
   d. Incorrect. This is not a business term.

7. a. Incorrect. This is not a term used in business.
   b. Incorrect. This is not a term used in business.
   c. Incorrect. A capacity constraint is a machine or other resource that runs slower than the demand rate for the product.
   d. **Correct.** The yield is the ratio of the materials output quantity to the materials input quantity.

8. a. Incorrect. This is not a term used in business.
   b. **Correct.** Kanbans, a Japanese term for "cards," are used as material control signals in a just-in-time system.

    c. Incorrect. This is not a term used in business.
    d. Incorrect. This is not a term used in business.

9. a. Incorrect. This is not a term used in business.
    b. Incorrect. This is not a term used in business.
    c. Incorrect. This is not a term used in business.
    d. **Correct.** Work centers that are combined in just-in-time processing are termed manufacturing cells. None of the other terms in this question are typically used in business.

10. a. Incorrect.
    b. Incorrect.
    c. **Correct.** 2,000 + (22,000 – 3,000), or the beginning inventory plus the pounds started and completed.
    d. Incorrect.

11. a. Incorrect.
    b. **Correct.** $415,000 / [(3,000 \times 70\%) + 11,000 + (1,000 \times 60\%)]$
    c. Incorrect.
    d. Incorrect.

12. a. Incorrect.
    b. **Correct.** $(5,000 \times 40\% \times \$6) + (5,000 \times \$18)$
    c. Incorrect.
    d. Incorrect.

TRUE/FALSE

1. T

2. T

3. T

4. F The cost of production report is used to control costs.

5. F Direct labor and factory overhead are referred to as conversion costs.

6. T

7. T

8. F All the material will be introduced during the current period, since the material is introduced at the half-way point in production and the process is only 40% complete at the beginning of the period.

9. F Work in process at the beginning of the period was started in the previous period but completed this period.

10. F The units started and completed are the 1,600 started gallons, less the 300 gallons in process at the end of the period, or 1,300 gallons.

EXERCISE 19-1

(a) Purchases

(b) Direct materials

(c) Direct labor

(d) Indirect materials

(e) Factory overhead applied

(f) Costs transferred out / Costs transferred in

(g) Direct labor

(h) Factory overhead applied

(i) Costs transferred out to Finished Goods

(j) Cost of goods sold

EXERCISE 19-2

Units	Total Whole Units	% Material to be Completed in April	% Conversion to be Completed in April	(1) Equivalent Units for Materials	(2) Equivalent Units for Conversion
Beginning Inventory	12,000	0%	70%	0	8,400
Started and Completed (66,000 – 12,000)	54,000	100%	100%	54,000	54,000
Transferred Out	66,000			54,000	62,400
Ending Inventory	8,000	100%	20%	8,000	1,600
Total Equivalent Units to Account for				62,000	64,000

Costs	(3) Direct Materials	(4) Conversion Costs	Total
Total Costs Incurred this Period	$148,800	$326,400	
Cost per Equivalent Unit	$2.40 ($148,800 ÷ 62,000)	$5.10 ($326,400 ÷ 64,000)	
Beginning Inventory—Balance			$ 32,600
Beginning Inventory—Completed (Equiv. Units × Rate)	0	$ 42,840	42,840
Started and Completed (Equiv. Units × Rate)	$129,600	275,400	405,000
Transferred Out (6)			$480,440
Ending Inventory (Equiv. Units × Rate) (5)	$ 19,200	$ 8,160	27,360
Total Costs Charged to Department..			$507,800

EXERCISE 19-3

	Whole Units	Equivalent Units	
		Direct Materials	Conversion
Inventory in process, April 1 (40% completed)	4,200	0	2,520
Started and completed in April	31,800	31,800	31,800
Transferred to next department in April	36,000	31,800	34,320
Inventory in process, April 30 (75% complete)	3,200	3,200	2,400
Total units	39,200	35,000	36,720

	Costs	
	Direct Materials	Conversion
Total costs for April in Cooking Department	$647,500	$449,820
Total equivalent units (from above)	÷ 35,000	÷ 36,720
Cost per equivalent unit	$ 18.50	$ 12.25

PROBLEM 19-1

(1)	Materials	210,000	
	Accounts Payable		210,000

(2)	Factory Overhead—Department 10	2,100	
	Factory Overhead—Department 20	600	
	Work in Process—Department 10	18,000	
	Work in Process—Department 20	24,000	
	Materials		44,700
(3)	Factory Overhead—Department 10	2,700	
	Factory Overhead—Department 20	2,700	
	Work in Process—Department 10	25,000	
	Work in Process—Department 20	20,000	
	Wages Payable		50,400
(4)	Factory Overhead—Department 10	1,500	
	Factory Overhead—Department 20	2,250	
	Accounts Payable		3,750
(5)	Factory Overhead—Department 10	4,200	
	Factory Overhead—Department 20	3,150	
	Accumulated Depreciation—Fixed Assets		7,350
(6)	Work in Process—Department 10	25,500	
	Work in Process—Department 20	15,000	
	Factory Overhead—Department 10		25,500
	Factory Overhead—Department 20		15,000
(7)	Work in Process—Department 20	68,500	
	Work in Process—Department 10		68,500
(8)	Finished Goods	115,000	
	Work in Process—Department 20		115,000
(9)	Accounts Receivable	160,000	
	Sales		160,000
	Cost of Goods Sold	122,000	
	Finished Goods		122,000

PROBLEM 19-2

Ivy Inc.
Cost of Production Report—Polishing Department
For the Month Ended March 31, 20--

		Equivalent Units	
Units	Whole Units	Direct Materials	Conversion
Units charged to production:			
Inventory in process, March 1	5,000		
Received from Cutting	21,000		
Total units accounted for by Polishing Dept.	26,000		
Units to be assigned costs:			
Inventory in process, March 1 (30% completed)	5,000	0	3,500
Started and completed in March	15,000	15,000	15,000
Transferred to finished goods in March	20,000	15,000	18,500
Inventory in process, March 31 (60% completed)	6,000	6,000	3,600
Total units to be assigned cost	26,000	21,000	22,100

Ivy Inc.
Cost of Production Report—Polishing Department (Concluded)
For the Month Ended March 31, 20--

| | Costs | | |
Costs	Direct Materials	Conversion	Total Costs
Unit costs:			
Total cost for March in Polishing	$105,000	$296,140	
Total equivalent units (from above)	÷ 21,000	÷ 22,100	
Cost per equivalent unit	$ 5.00	$ 13.40	
Costs charged to production:			
Inventory in process, March 1			$ 37,025
Costs incurred in March			401,140
Total costs accounted for by Polishing Dept.			$438,165
Costs allocated to completed and partially completed units:			
Inventory in process, March 1—balance			$ 37,025
To complete inventory in process, March 1	$ 0	$ 46,900 [a]	46,900
Started and completed in March	75,000 [b]	201,000 [c]	276,000
Transferred to finished goods in March			$359,925
Inventory in process, March 31	30,000 [d]	48,240 [e]	78,240
Total costs assigned by Polishing Dept.			$438,165

[a] 3,500 × $13.40 = $46,900
[b] 15,000 × $5.00 = $75,000
[c] 15,000 × $13.40 = $201,000
[d] 6,000 × $5.00 = $30,000
[e] 3,600 × $13.40 = $48,240

CHAPTER 20

MATCHING

1. S	4. E	7. J	10. F	13. N	16. P
2. D	5. I	8. C	11. H	14. L	17. M
3. B	6. O	9. G	12. Q	15. K	18. R

FILL IN THE BLANK—PART A

1. activity bases (or activity drivers)
2. relevant range
3. variable costs
4. fixed
5. mixed
6. mixed
7. direct costing
8. cost-volume-profit
9. contribution margin ratio
10. 9,500
11. increase
12. increase
13. 7,500
14. break-even
15. horizontal
16. profit-volume
17. "what if" analysis (or sensitivity analysis)
18. sales mix
19. margin of safety
20. operating leverage

FILL IN THE BLANK—PART B

1. activity drivers
2. variable costs
3. fixed
4. fixed costs
5. mixed
6. semifixed
7. variable cost per unit
8. contribution margin
9. profit-volume ratio
10. contribution margin
11. fixed costs
12. break-even point
13. increase
14. increase
15. decrease
16. sales, costs
17. sensitivity analysis
18. sales mix
19. 4
20. straight lines

MULTIPLE CHOICE

1. a. Incorrect. The per unit fixed costs change with changes in the underlying activity base.
   b. Incorrect. This describes a variable cost.
   c. Incorrect. Costs that vary in total with changes in the activity base are variable costs.
   d. *Correct.* The total dollar amount of fixed costs remains constant with changes in the activity base.

2. a. Incorrect.
   b. Incorrect.
   c. *Correct.* A mixed cost has the characteristics of both a variable and fixed cost.
   d. Incorrect. A sunk cost is a cost that is not affected by subsequent decisions.

3. a. Incorrect.
   b. *Correct.* ($240,000 – $152,500) / (150,000 – 80,000)
   c. Incorrect.
   d. Incorrect.

4. a. Incorrect. A decrease in fixed costs would decrease the break-even point.
   b. Incorrect. A decrease in unit variable cost would decrease the break-even point.
   c. *Correct.* A decrease in the unit selling price would increase the break-even point.
   d. Incorrect.

5. a. Incorrect. Direct materials are a variable cost.
   b. *Correct.* Real estate taxes are a fixed cost in a break-even analysis.
   c. Incorrect. Direct labor is a variable cost.
   d. Incorrect. Supplies are a variable cost.

6. a. *Correct.* $400,000 / $16
   b. Incorrect.
   c. Incorrect.
   d. Incorrect.

7. a. *Correct.* ($300,000 – $250,000) / $300,000
   b. Incorrect.
   c. Incorrect.
   d. Incorrect.

8. a. Incorrect.
   b. Incorrect.
   c. *Correct.* $200,000 / $40,000
   d. Incorrect.

9. a. Incorrect.
   b. Incorrect.
   c. Incorrect. Variable costs change in total with changes in the activity level.
   d. *Correct.* Variable costs per unit remain unchanged with changes in the activity level.

10. a. Incorrect.
    b. *Correct.* ($12 – $8) / $12
    c. Incorrect.
    d. Incorrect.

11. a. Incorrect.
    b. Incorrect.
    c. *Correct.* $120,000 / ($30 – $18)
    d. Incorrect.

12. a. Incorrect.
    b. Incorrect.
    c. Incorrect.
    d. *Correct.*

TRUE/FALSE

1. T
2. F Mixed costs have both fixed and variable cost elements, in no particular proportion.
3. T
4. F Fixed costs will remain the same at the high and low levels of activity.
5. T
6. T
7. F Decreases in unit selling price will increase the unit break-even point.
8. F Decreases in fixed cost will reduce the unit break-even point.
9. F The operating leverage is determined by dividing the contribution margin by the income from operations.
10. T

EXERCISE 20-1

(1) Difference in total costs: $300,000 ($550,000 – $250,000)

Difference in total units of production: 30,000 units (50,000 units – 20,000 units)

(2) Variable cost per unit: $10 ($300,000 / 30,000 units)

Fixed cost estimated at highest level of production:
    Total Cost = Total Variable Cost + Fixed Cost
    $550,000 = ($10 × 50,000 units) + Fixed Cost
    $550,000 = $500,000 + Fixed Cost
    Fixed Cost = $50,000

or

Fixed cost estimated at lowest level of production:
    Total Cost = Total Variable Cost + Fixed Cost
    $250,000 = ($10 × 20,000 units) + Fixed Cost
    $250,000 = $200,000 + Fixed Cost
    Fixed Cost = $50,000

(3) Total Cost = Total Variable Cost + Fixed Cost
    Total Cost = ($10 × 80,000 units) + $50,000
    Total Cost = $800,000 + $50,000
    Total Cost = $850,000

EXERCISE 20-2

Chart: Cost-Volume-Profit Chart

(a) fixed costs
(b) break-even point
(c) operating profit area
(d) total sales
(e) operating loss area
(f) total costs

EXERCISE 20-3

(1) ($2,000,000 – $1,700,000) / $2,000,000 = 15%
(2) ($150,000 – $100,000) / $150,000 = 33%
(3) $300,000 / $175,000 = 1.71

(4)

Sales	$700,000
Variable costs	300,000
Contribution margin	$400,000

$400,000 / $200,000 = 2

PROBLEM 20-1

(1) $700,000 / $50 = 14,000 units

(2) $710,000 / $50 = 14,200 units

(3) $700,000 / $49 = 14,286 units

(4) $700,000 / $52 = 13,462 units

(5)   ($700,000 + $300,000) / $50 = 20,000 units

PROBLEM 20-2

(1)   ($180 × .80) + ($280 × .20) = $200 unit selling price of E
($140 × .80) + ($190 × .20) = $150 unit variable cost of E
($40 × .80) + ($90 × .20) = $50 unit contribution margin of E
Break-even point (units): $400,000 / $50 = 8,000 units
Sales necessary in dollars: 8,000 × $200 = $1,600,000

(2)

	Product A	Product B	Total
Sales:			
6,400 units × $180	$1,152,000		$1,152,000
1,600 units × $280		$448,000	448,000
Total sales	$1,152,000	$448,000	$1,600,000
Variable costs:			
6,400 units × $140	896,000		896,000
1,600 units × $190		304,000	304,000
Total variable costs	$ 896,000	$304,000	$1,200,000
Contribution margin			$ 400,000
Fixed costs			400,000
Operating profit			$ 0

CHAPTER 21

MATCHING

1.	J	**4.**	A	**6.**	C	**8.**	K	**10.**	H	**12.**	L
2.	E	**5.**	G	**7.**	F	**9.**	N	**11.**	D	**13.**	B
3.	O										

FILL IN THE BLANK—PART A

1. budget
2. planning
3. responsibility centers
4. control
5. slack
6. goal conflict
7. fiscal year
8. Accounting
9. static
10. relevant activity levels
11. master budget
12. quantity of estimated sales
13. expected unit selling price
14. 164,000
15. production
16. balance sheet budgets
17. cash
18. capital expenditures
19. 84,000
20. $1,500,000

FILL IN THE BLANK—PART B

1. directing
2. feedback
3. tightly
4. budgetary slack
5. goal conflict
6. continuous budgeting
7. zero-based
8. static budget
9. flexible budget
10. computerized
11. sales
12. factory overhead cost
13. cost of goods sold
14. capital expenditures
15. past sales volumes
16. production
17. direct labor cost
18. budgeted income statement
19. $56,000
20. $18,500

MULTIPLE CHOICE

1. a. Incorrect. The direct materials purchases budget is not related to the direct labor cost budget.
   b. Incorrect. Part of the cash budget is influenced by the direct labor cost budget.
   c. **Correct.** The production budget is the starting point for the direct labor cost budget.
   d. Incorrect. The cost of goods sold budget is partially prepared from the direct labor cost budget.

2. a. **Correct.** The direct materials purchases budget provides data on the quantities of direct materials purchases necessary to meet production needs.
   b. Incorrect. The sales budget provides data on the quantity of estimated sales and expected unit selling price.
   c. Incorrect. The production budget is a budget of estimated production.
   d. Incorrect. The direct labor cost budget estimates the cost of labor involved in converting raw materials into finished product.

3. a. Incorrect. The budgeted balance sheet provides an estimate of all balance sheet items, not just plant and equipment.
   b. Incorrect. The production budget is a budget of estimated production.
   c. Incorrect. The cash budget estimates the expected receipts (inflows) and payments (outflows, including acquisition of plant and equipment) of cash for a period of time.
   d. **Correct.** The capital expenditures budget summarizes future plans for the acquisition of plant facilities and equipment.

4. a. Incorrect. Variable budget is not a business term.
   b. Incorrect. A continuous budget is a method of budgeting that provides for maintaining a continuous twelve-month projection into the future, month by month.
   c. **Correct.** A flexible budget is a budget that adjusts with levels of activity and is often used in production cost centers.
   d. Incorrect. A zero-based budget is used to critically evaluate all expenditures by estimating budget data as if there had been no previous activities in the unit.

5. a. Incorrect. This is not a business term.
   b. Incorrect. A zero-based budget is used to critically evaluate all expenditures by estimating budget data as if there had been no previous activities in the unit.
   c. **Correct.** A static budget is typically used in administrative functions.
   d. Incorrect. A flexible budget is a budget that adjusts with levels of activity and is often used in production cost centers.

6. a. Incorrect.
   b. **Correct.** (80% × $860,000) + (20% × $640,000)
   c. Incorrect.
   d. Incorrect.

7. a. **Correct.** Zero-based budgets are used to critically evaluate all expenditures by estimating budget data as if there had been no previous activities in the unit.
   b. Incorrect. Master budgeting is not a business term, although a master budget is a comprehensive budget plan encompassing all the individual budgets related to sales, cost of goods sold, operating expenses, capital expenses, and cash.

c. Incorrect. Flexible budgets are budgets that adjust with levels of activity and are often used in production cost centers.

d. Incorrect. Continuous budgeting is a method of budgeting that provides for maintaining a continuous twelve-month projection into the future, month by month.

8. a. Incorrect. Annual budgeting is not a term defined in the text.
   b. **Correct.** Continuous budgeting is a method of budgeting that provides for maintaining a continuous twelve-month projection into the future, month by month.
   c. Incorrect. This is not a business term.
   d. Incorrect. This is not a business term.

9. a. Incorrect. This is not a business term.
   b. Incorrect. This is only one type of center wherein a manager has authority and responsibility for the unit's performance. It is not a general term for this definition.
   c. Incorrect. This term is not defined in the text.
   d. **Correct.** A responsibility center is one wherein a manager has authority and responsibility for the unit's performance.

10. a. **Correct.** 280,000 − 25,000 + 35,000
    b. Incorrect.
    c. Incorrect.
    d. Incorrect.

11. a. Incorrect.
    b. **Correct.** ($1,200,000 + $45,000 − $40,000) + $650,000 + $900,000 + ($80,000 − $95,000)
    c. Incorrect.
    d. Incorrect.

12. a. Incorrect.
    b. Incorrect.
    c. **Correct.** ($330,000 × 40%) + ($420,000 × 60%)
    d. Incorrect.

TRUE/FALSE

1. F A series of budgets for varying rates of activity is a flexible budget.
2. T
3. F Computers are widely used in most accounting functions, including budgeting.
4. T
5. T
6. F The expenditures for plant and equipment will vary from year to year, depending upon economic conditions, business conditions, and capital availability.
7. T
8. F The budgeted balance sheet brings together budgeted cash, capital acquisitions, financing, and other investing activities. Profit-making activities are reflected on the budgeted income statement.
9. F The first budget prepared is usually the sales budget. The cash budget is usually determined from budgets that result in receipts and expenditures, such as sales and production budgets.
10. T

EXERCISE 21-1

Texier Inc.
Sales Budget
For the Month of May, 20--

Product and Area	Unit Sales Volume	Unit Selling Price	Total Sales
Product C:			
East area	60,000	$15	$ 900,000
West area	80,000	20	1,600,000
Total	140,000		$2,500,000
Product Q:			
East area	75,000	$ 8	$ 600,000
West area	50,000	10	500,000
Total	125,000		$1,100,000
Total revenue from sales			$3,600,000

Texier Inc.
Production Budget
For the Month of May, 20--

	Units	
	Product C	Product Q
Sales	140,000	125,000
Plus desired inventory, May 31	28,000	25,000
Total	168,000	150,000
Less estimated inventory, May 1	8,000	21,000
Total production	160,000	129,000

EXERCISE 21-2

Nathalie Inc.
Factory Overhead Cost Budget
For the Month of January, 20--

Units of product	30,000	60,000	90,000
Variable cost:			
Indirect factory wages	$ 24,000	$ 48,000	$ 72,000
Indirect materials	13,500	27,000	40,500
Electric power	18,000	36,000	54,000
Total variable cost	$ 55,500	$111,000	$166,500
Fixed cost:			
Supervisory salaries	$ 30,000	$ 30,000	$ 30,000
Depreciation of plant and equipment	18,000	18,000	18,000
Property taxes	12,000	12,000	12,000
Insurance	7,500	7,500	7,500
Electric power	4,500	4,500	4,500
Total fixed cost	$ 72,000	$ 72,000	$ 72,000
Total factory overhead cost	$127,500	$183,000	$238,500

EXERCISE 21-3

(1)

Gyro Company
Production Budget

	Product A
Sales	500,000
Plus desired ending inventory	10,000
Total	510,000
Less estimated beginning inventory	12,000
Total production	498,000

(2)

Gyro Company
Direct Materials Purchases Budget

	Material XX	Material ZZ
Pounds required for production	249,000*	597,600**
Plus desired ending inventory	14,000	25,000
Total	263,000	622,600
Less estimated beginning inventory	8,000	20,000
Total pounds to be purchased	255,000	602,600
Unit price per pound	× $4	× $6
Total direct materials purchases	$1,020,000	$3,615,600

*498,000 × 0.5 lbs. = 249,000 pounds   **498,000 × 1.2 lbs. = 597,600

(3)   498,000 units × 0.25 hours × $12 per hour = $1,494,000

PROBLEM 21-1

Amant Inc.
Cash Budget
For Two Months Ending April 30, 20--

	March	April
Estimated cash receipts from:		
Cash sales	$ 96,000	$ 80,000
Collections of accounts receivable	160,200	124,800
Total cash receipts	$256,200	$204,800
Estimated cash disbursements for:		
Merchandise costs	$130,000	$140,000
Operating expenses	34,000	28,000
Capital expenditures	—	125,000
Property taxes	5,000	—
Total cash disbursements	$169,000	$293,000
Cash increase or (decrease)	$ 87,200	$ (88,200)
Cash balance at beginning of month	24,000	111,200
Cash balance at end of month	$111,200	$ 23,000
Minimum cash balance	50,000	50,000
Excess or (deficiency)	$ 61,200	$ (27,000)

PROBLEM 21-2

(1)

Fernandez Furniture Company
Production Budget

	Product A	Product B
Sales	168,000	324,000
Plus desired ending inventory	8,000	36,000
Less estimated beginning inventory	(12,000)	(24,000)
Total production	164,000	336,000

(2)

Fernandez Furniture Company
Direct Materials Purchases Budget

	Material X	Material Y	Material Z	Total
Pounds required for production:				
Product A	98,400		196,800	
Product B	604,800	1,142,400		
Plus desired ending inventory	14,500	8,700	9,800	
Total	717,700	1,151,100	206,600	
Less estimated beginning inventory	(16,000)	(5,600)	(12,400)	
Total pounds to be purchased	701,700	1,145,500	194,200	
Price per pound	× $0.40	× $0.50	× $0.60	
Total direct materials purchases	$280,680	$ 572,750	$116,520	$969,950

(3)

Fernandez Furniture Company
Direct Labor Cost Budget

	Department 1	Department 2	Total
Product A hours	32,800	24,600	
Product B hours	16,800	33,600	
Total hours	49,600	58,200	
Hourly departmental rate	× $14.00	× $18.00	
Total direct labor cost	$694,400	$1,047,600	$1,742,000

CHAPTER 22

MATCHING

1. D	**4.** I	**7.** F	**9.** G	**11.** E
2. H	**5.** K	**8.** B	**10.** C	**12.** L
3. A	**6.** M			

FILL IN THE BLANK—PART A

1. standard cost systems
2. principle of exceptions
3. ideal
4. currently attainable (or normal)
5. quantity
6. purchasing
7. cost variance
8. total manufacturing
9. direct materials quantity variance
10. $700 favorable
11. direct labor time variance
12. $1,900 unfavorable
13. controllable
14. $3,000 favorable
15. volume variance
16. total factory overhead cost
17. factory overhead cost variance report
18. Direct Materials Quantity Variance
19. cost of goods sold
20. nonfinancial performance
21. input, output

FILL IN THE BLANK—PART B

1. standard cost system
2. engineers
3. ideal standards
4. currently attainable (or normal)
5. budgetary performance evaluation
6. budget performance
7. unfavorable
8. direct materials price variance
9. unfavorable materials quantity variance
10. purchasing department
11. $320 unfavorable
12. direct labor rate variance
13. $1,100 favorable
14. production supervisors
15. flexible
16. controllable variance
17. controllable variance
18. $1,000 favorable
19. Direct Materials Price Variance
20. nonfinancial
21. linked

MULTIPLE CHOICE

1. a. **Correct.** Standard costs are a method for measuring efficiency.
   b. Incorrect. Standard costs are a financial measure of performance.
   c. Incorrect. Standard costs can be used to measure volume variances, but they are not used to measure "volume."
   d. Incorrect. Standard costs can be used to measure direct material quantity variances, but not just "quantity."

2. a. Incorrect.
   b. Incorrect.
   c. **Correct.** [4,800 − (6,000 × 0.75 hours)] × $10 per standard labor hour; the variance is unfavorable because the standard hours allowed is less than the actual hours required.
   d. Incorrect.

3. a. Incorrect.
   b. **Correct.** (5,100 pounds − 5,000 pounds) × $2 per pound; the variance is unfavorable because the standard pounds are less than the actual pounds used.
   c. Incorrect.
   d. Incorrect.

4. a. Incorrect.
   b. Incorrect.
   c. Incorrect.
   d. **Correct.** 700 hours × $2

5. a. Incorrect.
   b. **Correct.** $18,900 − [(5,000 × 0.25) × $12]
   c. Incorrect.
   d. Incorrect.

6. a. **Correct.** The difference between the actual and the standard quantity of direct materials, multiplied by the standard price, is the direct materials quantity variance.
   b. Incorrect. The direct materials price variance measures the difference between the actual price and the standard price, multiplied by the actual quantity used.
   c. Incorrect. Direct materials volume variance is not a business term.
   d. Incorrect. Controllable materials variance is not a business term.

7. a. Incorrect. Direct labor quantity variance is not a business term.
   b. Incorrect. Direct labor volume variance is not a business term.
   c. Incorrect. The direct labor rate variance measures the difference between the actual labor rate and the standard labor rate, multiplied by the actual hours worked.
   d. **Correct.** The direct labor time variance is the difference between the actual and the standard labor hours, multiplied by the standard labor rate.

8. a. Incorrect. Efficiency variance is not a term defined in this text.
   b. Incorrect. The controllable variance is the difference between the actual variable overhead incurred and the budgeted variable overhead for actual production.
   c. *Correct.* The volume variance is the difference between the budgeted fixed overhead at 100% of normal capacity and the standard fixed overhead for the actual production achieved during the period.
   d. Incorrect. The total overhead variance is the difference between the standard factory overhead applied to production and the actual factory overhead.

9. a. Incorrect.
   b. Incorrect.
   c. Incorrect.
   d. *Correct.*

10. a. *Correct.* Number of customer complaints is a nonfinancial performance measure.
   b. Incorrect. Direct labor time variance is a financial performance measure.
   c. Incorrect. Controllable (variable) overhead variance is a financial performance measure.
   d. Incorrect.

11. a. Incorrect. Accounts Payable would be credited for $5,400.
   b. *Correct.* Direct Materials Price Variance would be debited because it is unfavorable.
   c. Incorrect.
   d. Incorrect. Materials would be debited for $4,800.

12. a. Incorrect.
   b. *Correct.* $32,000 − (2,500 units × 2 hours per unit × $6 per hour)
   c. Incorrect.
   d. Incorrect.

TRUE/FALSE

1. T
2. F This would be a price variance.
3. T
4. F This is the factory overhead cost variance.
5. T
6. F Variances are usually transferred to the cost of goods sold account.
7. F An ideal standard assumes perfect operating conditions; "reasonable effort" would be a normal standard.
8. T
9. F Standards can also be applied in selling, administrative, and service settings in some cases.
10. T

EXERCISE 22-1

(1) Price variance:

Actual price	$1.82	per lb.
Standard price	1.80	per lb.
Variance—unfavorable	$ .02	per lb. × actual qty., 77,000 lbs.	$1,540

Quantity variance:

Actual quantity	77,000	lbs.
Standard quantity	75,000	lbs.
Variance—unfavorable	2,000	lbs. × standard price, $1.80	3,600

Total direct materials cost variance—unfavorable $5,140

(2) Rate variance:

Actual rate	$19.75	per hr.
Standard rate	20.00	per hr.
Variance—favorable	$ (.25) per hr. × actual time, 42,500 hrs.	$(10,625)

Time variance:

Actual time	42,500	hrs..
Standard time	42,000	hrs.
Variance—unfavorable	500 hrs. × standard rate, $20.00	10,000

Total direct labor cost variance—favorable .... $ (625)

EXERCISE 22-2

Volume variance:

100% of normal capacity	40,000 hours
Standard for amount produced	30,000 hours
Productive capacity not used	10,000 hours
Standard fixed factory overhead rate	× $3
Variance—unfavorable	$30,000

Controllable variance:

Actual variable factory overhead	$153,500
Budgeted variable factory overhead for 30,000 hours	150,000
Variance—unfavorable	3,500

Total factory overhead cost variance—unfavorable $33,500

EXERCISE 22-3

Nathalie Inc.
Budget Performance Report—Factory Overhead Cost
For Month Ended January 31, 20--

	Budget	Actual	Unfavorable	Favorable
Variable cost:				
Indirect factory wages	$ 48,000	$ 50,500	$2,500	
Indirect materials	27,000	27,600	600	
Electric power	36,000	35,000		$1,000
Total variable cost	$111,000	$113,100		
Fixed cost:				
Supervisory salaries	$ 30,000	$ 30,000		
Depr. of plant and equipment	18,000	18,000		
Property taxes	12,000	12,000		
Insurance	7,500	7,500		
Electric power	4,500	4,500		
Total fixed cost	72,000	72,000		
Total factory overhead cost	$183,000	$185,100	$3,100	$1,000

EXERCISE 22-4

(1)

30	employees
× 40	hours per week
1,200	total hours worked
× $16	labor rate per hour
$19,200	IRS labor cost

(2) Flexible budget:

No. of traditional paper returns processed .... 1,300 × 45 min. = 58,500 min.
No. of electronic returns processed .... 225 × 8 min. =   1,800 min.
                                                                      60,300 min.

60,300 / 60 = 1,005 hours flexible budget

(3) Time variance:

Actual time .... 1,200 hours
Standard time .... 1,005 hours
     Variance—unfavorable .... 195 hours × $16 rate = $3,120

PROBLEM 22-1

(1)   Direct Materials Cost Variances

		Variance
Price variance:		
Actual price	$6.20 per lb.	
Standard price	6.00 per lb.	
Variance	$ .20 per lb. × actual qty., 250,000 lbs.	$50,000 U
Quantity variance:		
Actual quantity	250,000 lbs.	
Standard quantity	255,000 lbs.	
Variance	(5,000) lbs. × standard price, $6	30,000 F
Total direct materials cost variance		$20,000 U

(2)   Direct Labor Cost Variances

		Variance
Rate variance:		
Actual rate	$14.60 per hr.	
Standard rate	15.00 per hr.	
Variance	$ (.40) per hr. × actual time, 77,400 hrs.	$30,960 F
Time variance:		
Actual time	77,400 hrs.	
Standard time	76,500 hrs.	
Variance	900 hrs. × standard rate, $15	13,500 U
Total direct labor cost variance		$17,460 F

(3)   Factory Overhead Cost Variances

		Variance
Controllable variance:		
Actual variable factory overhead cost incurred	$160,000	
Budgeted variable factory overhead for actual product produced	153,000	
Variance		$ 7,000 U
Volume variance:		
Budgeted hours at 100% of normal capacity	90,000 hrs.	
Standard hours for amount produced	76,500 hrs.	
Productive capacity not used	13,500 hrs.	
Standard fixed factory overhead cost rate	× $1.50	
Variance		20,250 U
Total factory overhead cost variance		$27,250 U

PROBLEM 22-2

Piazza Company, Inc.
Income Statement
For the Month Ended January 31, 20--

Sales		$995,000
Cost of goods sold—at standard		812,000
Gross profit—at standard		$183,000

	Favorable	Unfavorable	
Less variances from standard cost:			
Direct materials price		$ 500	
Direct materials quantity		1,500	
Direct labor rate		1,200	
Direct labor time	$3,000		
Factory overhead controllable	4,000		
Factory overhead volume		10,000	6,200
Gross profit			$176,800
Operating expenses:			
Selling expenses		$68,000	
Administrative expenses		42,000	110,000
Income before income tax			$ 66,800

CHAPTER 23

MATCHING

1. O	4. R	7. B	10. S	13. M	16. C
2. K	5. D	8. L	11. E	14. F	17. J
3. H	6. I	9. N	12. P	15. Q	18. A

FILL IN THE BLANK—PART A

1. centralized
2. responsibility centers
3. responsibility accounting
4. cost center
5. more
6. revenues
7. controllable
8. service department charges
9. activity base
10. $48,000
11. $53,000
12. investment center
13. rate of return on investment (or on assets)
14. profit margin
15. 8%
16. 3.125
17. 25%
18. DuPont formula
19. residual income
20. market price
21. negotiated price
22. balanced scorecard

FILL IN THE BLANK—PART B

1. decentralization
2. responsibility center
3. investment centers
4. costs
5. more
6. profit center
7. controllable
8. service department charges
9. indirect
10. $38,400
11. $68,000
12. residual income
13. invested assets
14. investment turnover
15. 8%
16. 2.5
17. 20%
18. nonfinancial performance measures
19. transfer price
20. market price
21. customer, financial, internal process

MULTIPLE CHOICE

1. a. *Correct.*
   b. Incorrect. A profit center has authority over revenue.
   c. Incorrect. An investment center has authority over revenues and assets.
   d. Incorrect.

2. a. Incorrect. Market price is an appropriate transfer price when the selling division has no excess capacity.
   b. **Correct.**
   c. Incorrect.
   d. Incorrect.

3. a. Incorrect. This term is the return on investment.
   b. Incorrect. This term is the investment turnover.
   c. **Correct.**
   d. Incorrect.

4. a. Incorrect. A cost center manager has authority over only costs.
   b. Incorrect. A profit center manager has authority over costs and revenues.
   c. Incorrect. A data center is a function department, not a type of responsibility center.
   d. **Correct.** An investment center manager has authority over costs, revenues, and assets.

5. a. Incorrect.
   b. Incorrect.
   c. Incorrect.
   d. **Correct.** ($750,000 – $450,000 – $228,000) / $300,000

6. a. Incorrect.
   b. **Correct.** $750,000 / $300,000
   c. Incorrect.
   d. Incorrect.

7. a. Incorrect.
   b. Incorrect.
   c. **Correct.** 15% × 1.2
   d. Incorrect.

8. a. **Correct.**
   b. Incorrect. Some bad decisions will not positively affect overall profitability.
   c. Incorrect. This is a possible disadvantage of decentralization.
   d. Incorrect.

9. a. Incorrect.
   b. Incorrect.
   c. Incorrect.
   d. **Correct.** All of these departments provide internal services to other departments.

10. a. Incorrect. This is a financial measure.
   b. Incorrect. This is a financial measure.
   c. **Correct.**
   d. Incorrect. This is a financial measure.

11. a. Incorrect.
   b. **Correct.** [$130,000 / (100 × 52)] × 30 employees × 4 weeks
   c. Incorrect.
   d. Incorrect.

12. a. Incorrect.
   b. **Correct.** [$180,000 / (10,000 × 12 months)] × 4,000 invoices; the invoices represented in the accounts receivable balance are part of the monthly invoices, so they should not be counted twice.
   c. Incorrect.
   d. Incorrect.

TRUE/FALSE

1. T
2. T
3. F   The amount of budget detail will be greater in responsibility centers at the lowest level of the organization.
4. F   A cost center would not be responsible for revenues, which are included in an income statement.
5. T
6. T
7. F   Sales divided by invested assets is the investment turnover.
8. F   The profit margin is 18% / 3 = 6%
9. T
10. F   The negotiated price (greater than variable cost, but less that market price) is a more appropriate transfer price for a selling division that has excess capacity.

EXERCISE 23-1

(1)   (a) $280,000   (c) $520,000
      (b) $120,000   (d) $135,000

(2)   Division M: 16% ($120,000 / $750,000)
      Division N: 22% ($110,000 / $500,000)

(3)   Division M

(4)   Division N

EXERCISE 23-2

(1)   Division M:

Income from operations	$120,000
Minimum income ($750,000 × 12%)	90,000
Residual income	$ 30,000

Division N:

Income from operations	$110,000
Minimum income ($500,000 × 12%)	60,000
Residual income	$ 50,000

(2)   Division N

EXERCISE 23-3

(a)   1.6
(b)   12.5%
(c)   18.9%
(d)   18%
(e)   1.5

PROBLEM 23-1

Budget Performance Report—Supervisor, Department F, Plant 7
For Month Ended July 31, 20--

	Budget	Actual	Over	Under
Factory wages	$ 65,000	$ 73,600	$8,600	
Materials	39,500	37,700		$1,800
Supervisory salaries	15,000	15,000		
Power and light	8,900	9,600	700	
Depr. of plant and equipment	7,500	7,500		
Maintenance	4,300	3,900		400
Insurance and property taxes	2,000	2,000		
	$142,200	$149,300	$9,300	$2,200

PROBLEM 23-2

Firefly Co.
Income Statement—Divisions J and K
For the Year Ended May 31, 20--

	Division J	Division K	Total
Net sales	$280,000	$420,000	$700,000
Cost of goods sold	122,500	227,500	350,000
Gross profit	$157,500	$192,500	$350,000
Operating expenses	48,000	72,000	120,000
Income from operations before service department charges	$109,500	$120,500	$230,000
Less service department charges:			
Payroll accounting	$ 24,000	$ 36,000	$ 60,000
Purchasing	48,400	39,600	88,000
Brochure advertising	31,250	18,750	50,000
Total service department charges	$103,650	$ 94,350	$198,000
Income from operations	$ 5,850	$ 26,150	$ 32,000

Supporting Schedules:

	Number of Payroll Checks	Number of Requisitions	Number of Brochure Pages
Division J	400	2,200	500
Division K	600	1,800	300
Total	1,000	4,000	800
Relative percentages:			
Division J	40.00%	55.00%	62.50%
Division K	60.00%	45.00%	37.50%
Service department costs	$60,000	$88,000	$50,000
Percentages multiplied by service department costs:			
Division J	24,000	48,400	31,250
Division K	36,000	39,600	18,750

PROBLEM 23-3

(1) (a) no effect
     (b) no effect

(2) **(a)** increase by $30,000
     (b) increase by $50,000

(3) **(a)** increase by $100,000
     (b) decrease by $20,000

CHAPTER 24

MATCHING

1. G   **4.** I   **6.** M   **8.** A   **10.** K   **12.** J
2. B   **5.** C   **7.** E   **9.** D   **11.** H   **13.** F
3. L

FILL IN THE BLANK—PART A

1. differential revenue
2. differential cost
3. sunk cost
4. income tax differential
5. $68,000
6. $5
7. opportunity cost
8. further processing
9. variable
10. variable costs
11. demand-based
12. competition-based
13. total costs
14. total fixed costs
15. 10%
16. 65%
17. 83.3%
18. drift
19. activity-based costing
20. production bottle-neck (or constraint)
21. theory of constraints

FILL IN THE BLANK—PART B

1. differential analysis
2. sunk costs
3. differential income (or loss)
4. differential revenues
5. $79,000
6. capacity
7. opportunity cost
8. $0.30
9. Robinson-Patman Act
10. total cost
11. product cost
12. variable cost
13. total cost
14. total cost
15. total manufacturing costs
16. 12.5%
17. 80%
18. 50%
19. target costing
20. production bottle-neck (or constraint)

MULTIPLE CHOICE

1. a. Incorrect. Although not defined in the text, gross profit analysis would be a type of vertical analysis of gross profit as a percent of sales compared with other companies in an industry.
   b. Incorrect. Capital investment analysis is the process by which management evaluates capital projects (as explained in the next chapter).
   c. ***Correct.***
   d. Incorrect. CVP analysis is an analysis used to determine the break-even point.

2. a. ***Correct.*** ($18 – $16 variable cost) × 10,000 units
   b. Incorrect.
   c. Incorrect.
   d. Incorrect.

3. a. Incorrect. A sunk cost is incurred in the past and is not relevant to a decision impacting a future course of action.
   b. ***Correct.***
   c. Incorrect. A differential cost is the amount of increase or decrease in cost that is expected from a course of action as compared with an alternative.
   d. Incorrect. This is not a term defined in this text, nor is it commonly used in business.

4. a. Incorrect. Under the total cost concept, only the desired profit is allowed for determining the markup.
   b. ***Correct.***
   c. Incorrect. Under the variable cost concept, the desired profit and total fixed costs are allowed for determining the markup.
   d. Incorrect.

5. a. Incorrect.
   b. Incorrect.
   c. Incorrect.
   d. **Correct.**   (5,000 gallons × 2 batches × 90% × $5 per gallon) – (2 batches × $7,800) – (5,000 gallons × 2 batches × $3 per gallon)

6. a. Incorrect.   Product cost is used for cost-plus pricing.
   b. Incorrect.   Total cost is used for cost-plus pricing.
   c. Incorrect.   Variable cost is used for cost-plus pricing.
   d. **Correct.**

7. a. Incorrect.   The total cost plus markup approach assumes the market will accept the cost-plus price.
   b. Incorrect.   The variable cost plus markup approach assumes the market will accept the cost-plus price.
   c. **Correct.**   The target cost approach begins with an assumed market price and works backwards to the markup.
   d. Incorrect.   The product cost plus markup approach assumes the market will accept the cost-plus price.

8. a. Incorrect.
   b. **Correct.**   The most profitable product is determined by dividing the contribution margin per unit by the process hours in the constraint resource; thus, Product B is the most profitable ($70 / 3 hours).
   c. Incorrect.
   d. Incorrect.

9. a. **Correct.**
   b. Incorrect.   Total cost-based is a cost-plus method.
   c. Incorrect.   Variable cost-based is a cost-plus method.
   d. Incorrect.   Product cost-based is a cost-plus method.

10. a. Incorrect.   This cost is relevant to this decision.
   b. Incorrect.   This cost is relevant to this decision.
   c. **Correct.**   A sunk cost is incurred in the past and is not relevant to a decision impacting a future course of action. The book value of previously purchased equipment is such a cost.
   d. Incorrect.   This cost is relevant to this decision.

11. a. **Correct.**   [($40 + $4) – ($50 – $9)] × 5,000 units = $15,000
   b. Incorrect.
   c. Incorrect.
   d. Incorrect.

12. a. **Correct.** $25,000 loss from operations + (30% × $50,000) depreciation = ($10,000) contribution margin; the small speaker line has a negative contribution margin, which could be avoided if the line were dropped.
   b. Incorrect.
   c. Incorrect.
   d. Incorrect.

13. a. Incorrect.
   b. Incorrect.
   c. **Correct.**   [$60 price – ($50 variable cost + $6 export fee)] × 1,000 units = $4,000
   d. Incorrect.

TRUE/FALSE

1. T

2. F   This is called a differential cost.

3. F   The special price may be less than all costs (including fixed costs), but greater than all variable costs and still produce differential income if accepted.

4. F Many common fixed costs will not be eliminated by discontinuing an unprofitable business segment. For example, the plant and equipment depreciation that is common to many products will not be eliminated if one product is discontinued.

5. F This is called an opportunity cost.

6. T

7. T

8. T

9. T

10. F The best way to evaluate profitability of products in production-constrained environments is to measure contribution margin per unit of bottleneck resource.

EXERCISE 24-1

Walden Transportation Inc.
Proposal to Lease or Sell Truck

Differential revenue from alternatives:		
Revenue from lease	$20,000	
Revenue from sale	18,000	
Differential revenue from lease		$2,000
Differential cost of alternatives:		
License expenses during lease	$ 1,100	
Repainting expense on sale	900	
Differential cost of leasing		200
Net differential income (loss) from lease alternative		$1,800

EXERCISE 24-2

Tran Inc.
Proposal to Manufacture Metal Blades

Purchase price of blades		$14.00
Differential cost to manufacture blades:		
Direct materials	$6.75	
Direct labor	5.10	
Variable factory overhead	.80	12.65
Cost savings (increase) from manufacturing blades		$ 1.35

EXERCISE 24-3

English Chairs Inc.
Proposal to Discontinue Rocking Chairs
December 31, 20--

Differential revenue from sales of rocking chairs:		
Revenue from sales		$350,000
Differential cost of sales of rocking chairs:		
Variable cost of goods sold	$180,000	
Variable operating expenses	75,000	255,000
Differential income (loss) from sales of rocking chairs		$ 95,000

The rocking chairs section probably should be continued.

EXERCISE 24-4

Golub Inc.
Proposal to Replace Machine
December 31, 20--

Annual variable costs—present machine	$ 65,000	
Annual variable costs—new machine	30,000	
Annual differential decrease (increase) in variable costs	$ 35,000	
Number of years applicable	× 7	
Total differential decrease (increase) in variable costs	$245,000	
Proceeds from sale of present machine	83,000	$328,000
Cost of new machine		370,000
Net differential decrease (increase) in cost, seven-year total		$ (42,000)
Annual net differential decrease (increase) in cost—new machine		$ (6,000)

PROBLEM 24-1

(1) $60,000 ($500,000 × 12%)

(2)   (a)   Total costs:

Variable ($5 × 50,000 units)	$250,000
Fixed ($35,000 + $15,000)	50,000
Total	$300,000

Cost amount per unit: $300,000 / 50,000 units = $6

(b)   Markup Percentage = Desired Profit / Total Costs
Markup Percentage = $60,000 / $300,000
Markup Percentage = 20%

(c)

Cost amount per unit	$6.00
Markup ($6 × 20%)	1.20
Selling price	$7.20

PROBLEM 24-2

(1)   Total manufacturing costs:

Variable ($4 × 50,000 units)	$200,000
Fixed factory overhead	35,000
Total	$235,000

Cost amount per unit: $235,000 / 50,000 units = $4.70

(2)   Markup Percentage = (Desired Profit + Total Selling and Administrative Expenses) / Total Manufacturing Costs
Markup Percentage = [$60,000 + $15,000 + ($1 × 50,000 units)] / $235,000
Markup Percentage = $125,000 / $235,000
Markup Percentage = 53.2%

(3)

Cost amount per unit	$4.70
Markup ($4.70 × 53.2%)	2.50
Selling price	$7.20

PROBLEM 24-3

(1) Total variable costs: $5 × 50,000 units = $250,000
Cost amount per unit: $250,000 / 50,000 units = $5

(2) Markup Percentage = Desired Profit + Total Fixed Costs / Total Variable Costs
Markup Percentage = ($60,000 + $35,000 + $15,000) / $250,000
Markup Percentage = $110,000 / $250,000
Markup Percentage = 44%

(3)
Cost amount per unit	$5.00
Markup ($5 × 44%)	2.20
Selling price	$7.20

PROBLEM 24-4

First, determine the contribution margin per bottleneck hour for each product.

	Product D	Product E	Product F
Sales price per unit	$750	$600	$400
Variable cost per unit	300	350	200
Contribution margin per unit	$450	$250	$200
Furnace hours per unit	÷ 15	÷ 10	÷ 8
Contribution margin per furnace hour (CM ÷ furnace hours)	$ 30	$ 25	$ 25

Product D is more profitable in per furnace hour terms than either Products E or F. Products E and F would need to increase prices enough to make their contribution margin per furnace hour equal to $30.

Product E: (X − $350) / 10 furnace hours = $30
X − $350 = $300
X = $650

Product F: (X − $200) / 8 furnace hours = $30
X − $200 = $240
X = $440

CHAPTER 25

MATCHING

1. H	**4.** E	**6.** I	**8.** C	**10.** J	**12.** B
2. K	**5.** M	**7.** L	**9.** G	**11.** D	**13.** F
3. A					

FILL IN THE BLANK—PART A

1. capital investment analysis (or capital budgeting)
2. internal rate of return
3. short
4. 25% [$53,500 / ($400,000 + $28,000 / 2)]
5. average rate of return
6. cash payback
7. 6 years [$300,000 / ($65,000 − $15,000)]
8. cash payback
9. annuity
10. net present value (or discounted cash flow)
11. $9,550 [($50,000 × 3.791) − $180,000]
12. index
13. net present value (or discounted cash flow)
14. annual net cash flows
15. highest
16. uncertainty
17. same
18. strategic
19. qualitative
20. minimum

FILL IN THE BLANK—PART B

1. present values
2. cash payback
3. time value
4. average rate of return
   (or accounting rate of return)
5. 25% [($270,000 ÷ 3) / ($680,000 + $40,000) ÷ 2]
6. net cash flow
7. cash payback period
8. timing
9. present value of an annuity
10. net present value

11. $12,060 [($30,000 × .893) + ($30,000 × .797) + ($30,000 × .712)] − $60,000
12. 1.44 ($72,000 / $50,000)
13. internal rate of return
    (or time-adjusted rate of return)
14. $5,200 [($10,000 × 3.170) − $26,500]
15. 4.975 ($79,600 / $16,000)
16. internal rate of return
17. leasing
18. inflation
19. rationing
20. strategic investments

MULTIPLE CHOICE

1. a. **Correct.**
   b. Incorrect. The discounted cash flow method uses present values.
   c. Incorrect. The discounted internal rate of return method uses present values.
   d. Incorrect.

2. a. Incorrect. The average rate of return method does not use present values.
   b. Incorrect. The cash payback method does not use present values.
   c. Incorrect. The discounted internal rate of return method computes the rate of return from the net cash flows expected from the proposals.
   d. **Correct.**

3. a. Incorrect. The average rate of return method does not use present values.
   b. Incorrect. The cash payback method does not use present values.
   c. **Correct.**
   d. Incorrect. The net present value method determines the total present value of cash flows expected from investment proposals and compares these values with the amounts to be invested.

4. a. Incorrect.
   b. **Correct.** $360,000 / $120,000 = 3 years
   c. Incorrect.
   d. Incorrect.

5. a. Incorrect.
   b. **Correct.** ($600,000 / 6 years) / ($800,000 / 2)
   c. Incorrect.
   d. Incorrect.

6. a. **Correct.**
   b. Incorrect. Expected net cash inflows is a quantitative factor.
   c. Incorrect. Amounts of cash to be invested is a quantitative factor.
   d. Incorrect. Timing of cash inflows is a quantitative factor.

7. a. Incorrect.
   b. Incorrect.
   c. **Correct.** ($50,000 × 3.17 annuity factor) / $145,000
   d. Incorrect.

8. a. Incorrect.
   b. Incorrect. Time-adjusted rate of return method is another term for the internal rate of return method.
   c. Incorrect. Average rate of discounted return method is a meaningless term.
   d. **Correct.**

9. a. Incorrect. This is an advantage of the cash payback method.
    b. Incorrect. The cash payback method does not emphasize accounting income.
    c. ***Correct.***
    d. Incorrect. The cash payback method can be used when cash flows are not equal.

10. a. Incorrect.
    b. Incorrect.
    c. Incorrect.
    d. ***Correct.***

11. a. ***Correct.*** [($70,000 + $20,000) × 3.605 present value factor] – $320,000
    b. Incorrect.
    c. Incorrect.
    d. Incorrect.

12. a. Incorrect.
    b. Incorrect.
    c. ***Correct.*** $83,200 / $20,000 = 4.16, which is the present value of an annuity factor from Exhibit 2 that is for seven periods at 15%.
    d. Incorrect.

13. a. Incorrect.
    b. Incorrect.
    c. ***Correct.*** [($15,000 × 2.991) + ($8,000 × .402)] – $45,000
    d. Incorrect.

TRUE/FALSE

1. T

2. T

3. F This time period is called the cash payback period.

4. F Longer investment horizons should take into account the time value of money.

5. F The net present value method determines the total present value of cash flows expected from investment proposals and compares these values with the amounts to be invested.

6. F The present value index is computed by dividing the total present value of net cash flows by the amount to be invested.

7. T

8. T

9. T

10. F This is an advantage of the cash payback period.

EXERCISE 25-1

(1) $48,000 / $310,000 = 15.48%

(2) $620,000 / $200,000 = 3.1 years

(3) Yes. The proposal meets the minimum rate of return desired.

(4) No. The proposal does not meet the minimum cash payback period desired.

EXERCISE 25-2

Proposal 1: $250,000 / $60,000 = 4.17 years

Proposal 2:

Year	Net Cash Flow	Cumulative Net Cash Flow
1	$100,000	$100,000
2	80,000	180,000
3	70,000	250,000
4	45,000	295,000
5	45,000	340,000
6	20,000	360,000

The cumulative net cash flow at the end of three years equals the amount of the investment, $250,000, so the payback period is three years.

EXERCISE 25-3

Proposal 1: The factor for the present value of an annuity for 6 years at 10%: 4.355

$60,000 × 4.355	$261,300
Less amount invested	250,000
Net present value	$ 11,300

Proposal 2:

Year	Present Value of 1 at 10%	Net Cash Flow	Present Value of Net Cash Flow
1	0.909	$100,000	$ 90,900
2	0.826	80,000	66,080
3	0.751	70,000	52,570
4	0.683	45,000	30,735
5	0.621	45,000	27,945
6	0.564	20,000	11,280
Total		$360,000	$279,510
Amount to be invested in equipment			250,000
Excess of present value over amount to be invested			$ 29,510

EXERCISE 25-4

(1)   Present Value Factor for an Annuity of $1 = Amount to be Invested / Annual Net Cash Flow
Present Value Factor for an Annuity of $1 = $358,900 / $120,000
Present Value Factor for an Annuity of $1 = 2.991

(2)   20%

PROBLEM 25-1

(1)

Year	Present Value of 1 at 12%	Net Cash Flow	Present Value of Net Cash Flow
1	0.893	$ 80,000	$ 71,440
2	0.797	60,000	47,820
3	0.712	60,000	42,720
4	0.636	60,000	38,160
5	0.567	60,000	34,020
Total		$320,000	$234,160
Amount to be invested in equipment			180,000
Excess of present value over amount to be invested			$ 54,160

(2) 1.30 ($234,160 / $180,000)

(3) yes

PROBLEM 25-2

(1) Project 1:

Year	Present Value of 1 at 10%	Net Cash Flow	Present Value of Net Cash Flow
1	0.909	$ 55,000	$ 49,995
2	0.826	50,000	41,300
3	0.751	45,000	33,795
4	0.683	40,000	27,320
5	0.621	40,000	24,840
6	0.564	30,000	16,920
7	0.513	15,000	7,695
Total		$275,000	$201,865
Amount to be invested			180,000
Net present value			$ 21,865

Project 2:

Year	Present Value of 1 at 10%	Net Cash Flow	Present Value of Net Cash Flow
1	0.909	$ 55,000	$ 49,995
2	0.826	55,000	45,430
3	0.751	55,000	41,305
4	0.683	55,000	37,565
5	0.621	55,000	34,155
Total		$275,000	$208,450
Amount to be invested			180,000
Net present value			$ 28,450

(2) Project 1:

Year	Present Value of 1 at 10%	Net Cash Flow	Present Value of Net Cash Flow
1	0.909	$ 55,000	$ 49,995
2	0.826	50,000	41,300
3	0.751	45,000	33,795
4	0.683	40,000	27,320
5	0.621	40,000	24,840
5 Res. value	0.621	60,000	37,260
Total		$290,000	$214,510
Amount to be invested			180,000
Net present value			$ 34,510

(3) Using a 5-year analysis, Project 1's net present value, $34,510, is greater than Project 2's, $28,450; thus Project 1 is more attractive.